"This book offers a rich trove of empirical data and theoretical arguments from around the world that will help understand further multiple communication and political aspects of the pandemic. I am particularly struck by the sophistication of the analysis and the impressive efforts to analyze the effective and botched responses to the pandemic as shaped by communicative processes, choices and styles by governments. Peter Van Aelst and the late great Jay Blumler have assembled a formidable collection that yields novel insights into classic political communication questions—polarization, government communication, elite cues, leadership, and public trust."

—*Silvio Waisbord, Director of the School of Media and Public Affairs at The George Washington University*

POLITICAL COMMUNICATION IN THE TIME OF CORONAVIRUS

This book examines how the COVID-19 pandemic impacted the flows of communication between politicians, journalists, and citizens.

Distinguished contributors grapple with how the pandemic, as a global unexpected event, disrupted the communication process and changed the relationships between politics, media, and publics, the three central players of political communication. Using different methodologies, they scrutinize changes in government communication, (new) media coverage, and public opinion during this crisis. The book moves beyond the USA and Western Europe to include cases from Eastern Europe, Latin America, and Asia, taking into account how variations in the political context, the media system, and personal leadership can influence how the COVID-19 pandemic challenged the political communication process.

It is an ideal text for advanced students and scholars of political communication, political science, and media studies.

Peter Van Aelst is Professor of Political Communication at the Department of Political Science of the University of Antwerp, Belgium.

Jay G. Blumler was an Emeritus Professor of Public Communication at the University of Leeds, UK and Emeritus Professor of Journalism at the University of Maryland, USA.

POLITICAL COMMUNICATION IN THE TIME OF CORONAVIRUS

Edited by
Peter Van Aelst and Jay G. Blumler

NEW YORK AND LONDON

First published 2022
by Routledge
605 Third Avenue, New York, NY 10158

and by Routledge
2 Park Square, Milton Park, Abingdon, Oxon, OX14 4RN

Routledge is an imprint of the Taylor & Francis Group, an informa business

© 2022 selection and editorial matter, Peter Van Aelst and Jay G. Blumler; individual chapters, the contributors

The right of Peter Van Aelst and Jay G. Blumler to be identified as the authors of the editorial material, and of the authors for their individual chapters, has been asserted in accordance with sections 77 and 78 of the Copyright, Designs and Patents Act 1988.

With the exception of Chapter 13, no part of this book may be reprinted or reproduced or utilised in any form or by any electronic, mechanical, or other means, now known or hereafter invented, including photocopying and recording, or in any information storage or retrieval system, without permission in writing from the publishers.

Chapter 13 of this book is available for free in PDF format as Open Access from the individual product page at www.routledge.com. It has been made available under a Creative Commons Attribution-Non Commercial-No Derivatives 4.0 license.

Trademark notice: Product or corporate names may be trademarks or registered trademarks, and are used only for identification and explanation without intent to infringe.

Library of Congress Cataloging-in-Publication Data
A catalog record for this title has been requested

ISBN: 978-0-367-77157-7 (hbk)
ISBN: 978-0-367-76185-1 (pbk)
ISBN: 978-1-003-17005-1 (ebk)

DOI: 10.4324/9781003170051

Typeset in Bembo
by codeMantra

CONTENTS

List of Contributors   xi
Foreword   xix

1 COVID-19 as an Ideal Case for a Rally-around-the-Flag? How Government Communication, Media Coverage and a Polarized Public Sphere Determine Leadership Approvals in Times of Crisis   1
Peter Van Aelst

PART 1
Government Communications   **15**

2 From Consensus to Dissensus: The UK's Management of a Pandemic in a Divided Nation   17
Ruth Garland and Darren Lilleker

3 Beyond Control and Resistance: The Dual Narrative of the Coronavirus Outbreak in Digital China   33
Yuan Zeng

4 COVID-19 in Chile: A Health Crisis amidst a Political Crisis amidst a Social Crisis   48
Ingrid Bachmann, Sebastián Valenzuela, and Arturo Figueroa-Bustos

5 The Italian Prime Minister as a Captain in the Storm: The Pandemic as an Opportunity to Build Personalized Political Leadership   65
Gianpietro Mazzoleni and Roberta Bracciale

PART 2
Media Coverage   81

6 Interactive Propaganda: How Fox News and Donald Trump Co-produced False Narratives about the COVID-19 Crisis   83
Yunkang Yang and Lance Bennett

7 Stooges of the System or Holistic Observers?: A Computational Analysis of News Media's Facebook Posts on Political Actors during the Coronavirus Crisis in Germany   101
Thorsten Quandt, Svenja Boberg, Tim Schatto-Eckrodt, and Lena Frischlich

8 More than "a Little Flu": Alternative Digital Journalism and the Struggle to Re-Frame the Brazilian Government's Response to the COVID-19 Outbreak   120
Stuart Davis

9 When a Polarized Media System Meets a Pandemic: Framing the Political Discord over COVID-19 Aid Campaigns in Turkey   136
Gizem Melek and Emre İşeri

PART 3
Public Opinion   155

10 Divided We Trust?: The Role of Polarization on Rally-around-the-Flag Effects during the COVID-19 Crisis   157
Ana S. Cardenal, Laia Castro, Christian Schemer, Jesper Strömbäck, Agnieszka Stępińska, Claes de Vreese, and Peter Van Aelst

11 The Role of Political Polarization on American and
   Australian Trust and Media Use during the COVID-19
   Pandemic   174
   Andrea Carson, Shaun Ratcliff and Leah Ruppanner

12 "I Don't Vote Because I Don't Want to Get Infected":
   Pandemic, Polarization, and Public Trust during the 2020
   Presidential Election in Poland   192
   Damian Guzek, Sabina Mihelj, and Václav Štětka

13 The Swedish Way: How Ideology and Media Use
   Influenced the Formation, Maintenance and Change of
   Beliefs about the Coronavirus   209
   Adam Shehata, Isabella Glogger and Kim Andersen

Index   *225*

CONTRIBUTORS

Kim Andersen is Associate Professor at the Centre for Journalism, University of Southern Denmark, and Affiliated Researcher at the Department of Journalism, Media and Communication, University of Gothenburg. His research focuses on people's news media consumption and its influence on their political knowledge, beliefs, and engagement.

Ingrid Bachmann is Associate Professor in the School of Communications at Pontificia Universidad Católica de Chile, where she chairs the Journalism Department. A former reporter, her research addresses the role of news media in defining meanings within the public sphere. She specializes in the intersections between news narratives, gender, and political communication.

Lance Bennett is Emeritus Ruddick C. Lawrence Professor Communication, Emeritus Professor of Political Science, and Senior Research Fellow at the Center for Journalism, Media and Democracy at the University of Washington. He has published widely on media and information systems in civic life with emphasis on press-government relations, the quality of public information, communication in social movements, transnational activism, citizenship and youth civic engagement, digital media and political participation, and problems of disinformation and democracy. His current work focuses on better aligning environment, economy and democracy to build more equitable and sustainable human systems on the planet. His publications include The Logic of Connective Action (with Alexandra Segerberg, Cambridge 2013), *The Disinformation Age* (with Steven Livingston, Cambridge 2020), and *Communicating the Future: Solutions for Environment, Economy and Democracy* (Polity 2021).

Jay G. Blumler was an Emeritus Professor of Public Communication at the University of Leeds and Emeritus Professor of Journalism at the University of Maryland. He is a fellow and former president of the International Communication Association, won the American Political Science Association lifetime achievement award, and is the founding Editor of the *European Journal of Communication*. His research focused on politics and media, and the comparative analysis of political communication systems across space and time.

Svenja Boberg is a communication scientist at the University of Muenster, who researches the dynamics of online social media debates and social media hypes. In her dissertation, she studies the articulation and spread of outrage in social media networks. Her research focuses on the employment of computational methods for analyzing user comments and attempts to influence public opinion. Her work has been published in national and international peer-reviewed journals.

Roberta Bracciale is Associate Professor of Media Sociology at the Department of Political Science and Director of the MediaLaB – Big Data in Social and Political Research Laboratory of the University of Pisa.

Ana S. Cardenal is a Professor of Political Science at the Universitat Oberta de Catalunya (UOC) and a lecturer at the Universitat Pompeu Fabra (UPF). In the field of comparative politics, she has published two books on Latin America and has worked as a consultant for the Inter-American Development Bank (IDB). Currently, her research interests focus on the political effects of digital media, the dynamics of online audiences, the processes of opinion formation in the current media environment, and the use of computational methods in social science. On these topics she has published several articles in top scientific journals.

Dr Andrea Carson is a political scientist and an Associate Professor in Journalism at La Trobe University in Melbourne, Australia. She has authored numerous articles on investigative journalism, Australian politics, election campaigns, media business models, and digital media. Her research focus is on information quality in the public sphere (fake news, media trust) and political communications. Her most recent book examines the role and state of investigative journalism in democracies: *Investigative Journalism, Democracy and the Digital Age* (Routledge 2020).

Laia Castro is Assistant Professor in the Department of Communication at Universitat Internacional de Catalunya and research associate at the Department of Communication and Media Research, University of Zurich. Her primary areas of research include political communication and public opinion with a comparative perspective. Her current or recent work has appeared in *Political Communication*, *Journal of Communication*, and the *International Journal of Public Opinion Research*, and revolves around cross-cutting exposure and the contribution of news use to opinion formation.

Stuart Davis is Assistant Professor in the Department of Communication Studies of the City University of New York, Baruch College, where she researches and teaches courses on comparative protest movements, digital media activism, and public health communication. He has roughly 20 pieces published in journals including *Communication Theory*, *International Journal of Communication*, *Digital Journalism*, and *Journalism Practice*, as well as edited collections such as *The Politics of Technology in Latin America* (2020) and *Mapping Citizen and Participatory Journalism* (2020). He is finishing a book manuscript examining the relationship between mass protests, digital media activism, and the recent rise of right-wing political movements in Brazil.

Claes de Vreese is Faculty Professor of Artificial Intelligence and Democracy and Professor of Political Communication. He is an *innovative* and *productive* scholar who has led several large-scale, *international, transformative* research projects. He is an elected fellow of the Royal Academy of Sciences. He has published more than 200 articles in peer-reviewed journals, co-authored books at publishers such as Cambridge and Oxford University Press, and generated more than 20,000 citations (H-index 78). He is the editor of *Political Communication*, the leading journal in the field, and President-Elect of the ICA.

Arturo Figueroa-Bustos is a doctoral student in the School of Communications at Pontificia Universidad Católica de Chile and an Assistant Professor in the Faculty of Humanities and Communications at the Finis Terrae University in Santiago. A former journalist, his research interests are related to journalism, politics, and cultural studies.

Lena Frischlich is the PI of the interdisciplinary research group DemoRESILdigital in the Department of Communication Studies at the University of Münster. Her research employs a variety of qualitative, experimental, and computational methods to examine the staging and effects of (extremist) online propaganda and to develop and evaluate strategies to foster resilience against digital manipulation. Her work has been published and presented in the central outlets and conferences of multiple disciplines.

Ruth Garland is an Associate Lecturer in Media at Goldsmiths University of London and also teaches at the LSE and Kings College London. She previously held frontline and leadership roles in public sector strategic communications. Her research focuses on public communication and the relationship between media and politics, encapsulated in the forthcoming work *Government Communications and the Crisis of Trust* for Palgrave Macmillan.

Isabella Glogger is a post-doctoral researcher at the Department of Journalism, Media and Communication, University of Gothenburg. In her research, she focuses on political communication and journalism, studying characteristics of media content and their effects on recipients' beliefs.

Damian Guzek is an Associate Professor in the Department of Journalism and Media Communication, and a leader of the research team on the cartography of new media and digital sphere at the University of Silesia in Katowice, Poland. His research is driven by questions related to digital media, religions, and politics, as well as media consumption. In 2020, he was collaborating on the project "The Illiberal Turn?" based at Loughborough University as a local research assistant. Between 2015 and 2019, he was conducting the Polish National Science Centre project "Media towards the idea of a secular state."

Emre İşeri is currently an affiliate of the Department of International Relations, Yaşar University, İzmir, Turkey. Prof. İşeri holds his PhD from Keele University (International Relations department). His research interests include energy policy, political communication, Eurasian politics, and Turkish foreign policy. He has published articles and chapters in numerous books and journals, including *Geopolitics, Journal of Balkan and Near East Studies, Energy Policy* (JBNES), *Turkish Studies, Security Journal, South European Society and Politics* (SESP), *European Journal of Communication* (EJC), and *International Journal of Communication* (IJC).

Darren Lilleker is Professor of Political Communication in the Faculty of Media & Communication, Bournemouth University and Convenor of the Centre for Comparative Politics & Media Research. He has led a range of research projects and published over 70 peer-reviewed articles, numerous chapters, and books including *Political Communication and Cognition* (Palgrave, 2014).

Gianpietro Mazzoleni is Professor of Political Communication at the University of Milan (Italy) and Fellow of the International Communication Association. He is internationally known for his work on the impact of media on political systems and on the communication patterns of political institutions and actors. He is serving as a member of the editorial boards of various scholarly journals and is Editor-in-Chief of *The International Encyclopedia of Political Communication* (Wiley, 2016).

Gizem Melek is an Assistant Professor in the Faculty of Communication, Yaşar University. Her main academic research areas include political communication and climate change communication. In addition to her academic work, she is an experienced journalist who worked both in Turkey and in the UK for six years. The places she worked include Izmir Life news magazine, NTV-nationwide Turkish news network, ITV-British TV network, and the British Museum's Broadcast Unit.

Sabina Mihelj is Professor of Media and Cultural Analysis in the School of Social Sciences, Loughborough University. Sabina's research focuses on the comparative study of media cultures across both traditional and new media, with a focus on nationalism, identity, memory, and Eastern and Central Europe. Her latest book is entitled *From Media Systems to Media Cultures: Understanding Socialist Television* (Cambridge University Press, 2018). Since 2019, she has been Co-Investigator on the ESRC-funded project "The Illiberal Turn?".

Thorsten Quandt is the Professor of Online Communication at the University of Münster. His research interests include online journalism, propaganda and populism, dysfunctional online use, as well as digital games and VR. Currently, he's working on changes in information flows, including forms of (dark) participation, and how this affects liberal democratic societies. Quandt has published more than 150 scientific articles and several books, including publications in leading journals in communication studies and psychology.

Dr Shaun Ratcliff is a Lecturer in political science at the United States Studies Centre of the University of Sydney, Australia. He is a quantitative political scientist whose research focuses on using novel data sources to study the issue preferences and behavior of political actors, including voters, interest groups, media, and elites. He has a PhD in political science and a Masters in communications and politics both from Monash University.

Dr Leah Ruppanner is an Associate Professor of Sociology and Co-Director of The Policy Lab at the University of Melbourne, Australia. As a quantitative survey expert, Ruppanner's work investigates how policy and gender reinforce inequalities. Her work is comparative, focusing on gender, government, family, and work to provide clear policy directions for governments and key stakeholders. She has a PhD and Masters in sociology from University of California at Irvine. She also has expansive media coverage in the *New York Times, Washington Post*, and the *Guardian*.

Tim Schatto-Eckrodt is a communication scientist who researches methods to identify attempts to influence public opinion through online propaganda at the University of Muenster. He specializes in computational social science (CSS), focusing on natural language processing. His dissertation deals with the development of a framework for online conspiracy theories from a communication science perspective. His work has been published and presented in the central outlets of the field.

Christian Schemer is a Professor for Communication at the Department of Communication of the Johannes Gutenberg University in Mainz, Germany. He is an expert on political information use, political communication and survey research in comparative perspective. He is and was involved in various large-scale research projects based on cross-cultural survey research combined with comparative content analyses (e.g., EU H2020 on attitudes toward migration).

Adam Shehata is an Associate Professor at the Department of Journalism, Media and Communication, University of Gothenburg. His research focuses on patterns of media use and opinion formation in a changing media environment.

Agnieszka Stępińska is a Professor at the Faculty of Political Science and Journalism of the Adam Mickiewicz University in Poznań, Poland. Her main area of research is political communication, including election campaigns. She has been also conducting studies on journalism and media content. She edited a book on *Populist Political Communication across Europe* (2020) and co-authored a book on *Populist Political Communication in Poland* (2020). Recently, she is participatig in the NORFACE program project "THREATPIE: The Threats and Potentials of a Changing Political Information Environment" (2020–2023).

Václav Štětka is Senior Lecturer in Communication and Media Studies at the School of Social Sciences and Humanities, Loughborough University, where he has been working since 2016. His research interests encompass political communication and the role of new media, media systems in Central and Eastern Europe, media ownership, and journalistic autonomy. Since 2016, he has been Vice-Chair of the Political Communication Section of ECREA. Currently, he is Principal Investigator of the ESRC-funded project "The Illiberal Turn? News Consumption, Polarization and Democracy in Central and Eastern Europe" (2019–2021).

Jesper Strömbäck is Professor in Journalism and Political Communication. Prof. Strömbäck is former chair of the International Communication Association's Political Communication Division and Associate Editor of Political Communication. He has published more than 20 monographs and edited books.

Sebastián Valenzuela is an Associate Professor in the School of Communications of Pontificia Universidad Católica de Chile and Associate Researcher in the Millennium Institute for Foundational Research on Data (IMFD). He specializes in digital media, political communication, and media effects.

Peter Van Aelst is Professor of Political Communication at the Department of Political Science and a founding member of the research group "Media, Movements and Politics" (www.m2p.be) at the University of Antwerp. His research focuses on the relationship between media and politics in the digital era. He has published widely on election campaigns, agenda setting, political news, and the growing influence of social media in political life. In a current collaboration with the University of Zurich, he studies disinformation in comparative perspective.

Yunkang Yang is a post-doctoral research scientist at the Institute for Data, Democracy & Politics (IDDP) in the School of Media and Public Affairs of the George Washington University. His research at IDDP, funded by John S. and James L. Knight Foundation, includes right-wing media in the USA, disinformation, social media, and social movements. He is currently working on a book project on the right-wing media ecosystem in the USA. He is also the PI for several interdisciplinary research projects that use graph embedding, machine learning, and natural language processing techniques to study the diffusion of online disinformation and coordinated content sharing behavior.

Yuan Zeng is a Lecturer at the School of Media and Communication, University of Leeds. Her research interests focus on the interplay between media and politics, mainly in the areas of journalism and political communication. She is currently working on the role of social media in China's political communication. She is the author of *Reporting China on the Rise: Habitus and Prisms of China Correspondents* (Routledge, 2019).

FOREWORD

On 12 May 2020, I received an email from Jay G. Blumler titled "An idea from Jay for your consideration". Jay's idea was to co-edit a book on the impact of the COVID-19 pandemic on the field of political communication. "The source is my impression that although we have all been exposed to communications about the coronavirus in our respective countries, there has been little if any academic analysis of them". Jay even had a title in mind for the book. "My suggested title for such a work, harking back to a famous South American novel, would be Communications in the Time of Coronavirus". It took me a while before I realized he was talking about *Love in the Time of Cholera* from Gabriel García Márquez. To be honest, I was not immediately convinced. Editing a book is time consuming and the pandemic was not making our academic lives more easy. During a follow-up Zoom talk, Jay was able to persuade me. He needed something "to get his teeth in". Initially this was what Jay did, contacting Routledge, suggesting authors, formulating central questions that needed to be addressed by the different authors. After a few months, however, Jay became less active. Time finally caught up with him, and his personal health limited him to be the brilliant and hyperactive scholar he always was. Jay was able to comment on a few chapters, but it became ever more difficult to remain active and involved. Luckily we managed to gather a great and diverse set of contributors for the book, and I was getting ever more enthusiastic about the outcome.

The insights come from chapters about the usual suspects in political communication studies such as the UK, Italy, and the USA, but are complemented by analyses from China, Turkey, and Brazil. Although the pandemic left no country unharmed, it is striking how much variation there is in how politicians, media actors, and citizens reacted to this unseen health crisis. Some of this variation is captured in the opening chapter of the book, where I show how in different countries national leaders experienced a (short) boost in popularity, while others saw their approval ratings being unchanged or in decline. The reasons for this country variation can, as scholars prove empirically, be related to government performance and real-world differences. However, I argue that also individual differences in government communications, and structural factors such as fragmentation of media landscapes and growing polarization of electorates play a role in how people perceive their leaders in times of crisis. These different factors are based on my close reading of the 12 chapters that made it into this book. I thank the authors for their hard work, the openness for feedback, and the respect for deadlines. Although these contributions do not provide a complete picture of what happened across the globe during the first year of the ongoing pandemic, it does show that this crisis impacted many aspects of the media–politics–public triangle that Jay G. Blumler studied for half a century.

Jay, I consider it as an honor that you came to me with your idea. I always admired you as a scholar and as a person. Your kindness and enthusiasm motivated me to finish this book on my own. I am confident you would have liked the result. I will miss you, but find comfort idea that you will live on in your work and as a source of inspiration for so many of us.

Peter Van Aelst
26 March 2021

1

COVID-19 AS AN IDEAL CASE FOR A RALLY-AROUND-THE-FLAG?

How Government Communication, Media Coverage and a Polarized Public Sphere Determine Leadership Approvals in Times of Crisis

Peter Van Aelst

Introduction: Political Communication in Times of Crisis

The COVID-19 virus was first identified in December 2019 in Wuhan, China. In the beginning of 2020, this obscure virus reached Europe and other parts of the world. In the beginning of March, the Italian government ordered a lockdown of parts of the country, and many other countries would follow, as it became clear that nations were experiencing a worldwide pandemic. The amount of virus-related coverage of news media across the globe increased exponentially as concerned publics seemed eager to know more about this imminent threat. The health crisis profoundly affected almost all aspects of social, economic and political life for people across the globe. This book deals with the meaning of this unseen crisis for the interactions between politicians, journalists and citizens. Did the crisis suddenly change how political leaders communicate with the public? Did journalists report more or less critically about government policy? What was the balance between traditional media and social media in these insecure times for becoming informed about the virus? These and other questions ask for a deeper investigation in how the COVID-19 pandemic has changed, challenged or confirmed the traditional rules of the political communication game.

The increasing importance of communication processes in the world of politics has contributed to the growing importance of the study of political communication, which has become an established subfield in both communication science and political science in countries across the globe. The theoretical origins of political communication not only come from these two disciplines, but

DOI: 10.4324/9781003170051-1

also insights from sociology, psychology and economics "have helped illuminate the role of communication in shaping the conduct of politics" (Bennett & Iyengar, 2008: 712). The interdisciplinary nature of the field makes it not easy to clearly define what it is, and what its main object of study is. Although the field of political communication is wide and fluid, there is fairly broad consensus that it deals with the interactions between three central players: political actors, citizens and journalists (e.g. McNair, 2003). Often depicted as a triangle between media, public and politics, with arrows of influence going in all directions. However, the exact composition and role of these three actors are not a given. In particular as the field seems to study an object that continually evolves—including the growing disconnection between citizens and political institutions, major developments in communication technologies, structural changes in media environments and the rise of online disinformation (Bennett & Pfetsch, 2018; Blumler, 2015; Van Aelst et al., 2017). For instance, social media platforms are difficult to conceptualize in the politics-media-public triangle as they are a tool and a platform that are used by all three actors, but also operate as an actor on their own (Klinger & Svensson, 2015). Therefore, we define 'media' not narrowly as traditional journalism, but broadly including alternative digital outlets and platforms that often take a much more activist role in (mis)informing the public.

This book seeks to explore how a crisis like the COVID-19 pandemic confirms or rather questions some of the classical ways policymakers, citizens and different types of media practitioners interact. Several scholars have shown that in times of crisis the rules of the game can change. For instance, in the case of an unexpected event such as a terrorist attack or an environmental disaster, journalists and politicians alike are less prepared. This means that media coverage is less driven by traditional news routines, and politicians need to think out of their 'strategic communication box'. Based on the work of Lawrence (2000) on police violence, we know that dramatic events have the ability to change how an issue is discussed and defined in the press, and offer the possibility for outsiders to challenge the traditional dominance of elite actors in the news. We also know that in times of crisis the public might feel a higher need for information and orientation. Althaus (2002) showed, for example, that in the week after the 9/11 terrorist attacks the television network audience doubled. Multiple other studies, on a range of dramatic events, confirm that people turn to the news in times of fear and uncertainty (e.g. Boomgaarden & de Vreese, 2007; Casero-Ripollés, 2020; Westlund & Ghersetti, 2015). Previous studies have suggested that during a crisis uncertainty can trigger anxiety which people try to reduce by seeking more information (e.g. Lachlan et al., 2016). Finally, we also expect politicians to change their policy and communication strategy in reaction to an exogenous shock. Scholars in political science and public administration have, for instance, documented how leaders addressed and communicated differently about the economic crisis of 2008 (e.g. König, 2016; t Hart & Tindall, 2009). However, a major health crisis might be an even bigger challenge. "Nothing tests a government leader like a deadly pandemic" (Kahn, 2020: ix). Kahn, an expert on leadership in times of health crisis, argues that a pandemic is a multidimensional crisis and that a leaders' response impacts all aspects of social and political life.

So there is little doubt that a pandemic is not simply a dramatic event, but perhaps more comparable with war time, when people are dying, fear for their lives or cannot perform their job anymore. In this context of military conflict and anxiety, the support for leaders is often stronger than ever. Political scientists have documented this positive side effect that became known as the 'rally-around-the-flag' theory. This concept of a rally-around-the-flag will be used as a way to organize the different contributions to this book. We do so for mainly two reasons. First, while a rally effect might be expected during such a profound crisis (see further), it is really more complicated than that. Because of national differences in leadership and communication, fragmentation in media ecologies, and growing polarization of electorates and media landscapes, there can be a huge variation in the presence and duration of a rally effect. The different chapters in this book provide the necessary national context or comparative insights to understand this variation in leadership approval. Second, the rally-around-the-flag effect basically involves the three central players in political communication. Although most scholars have focused on the reaction of the national leader, the interaction with and between media actors and ordinary citizens plays a crucial role. Therefore, we will first discuss the rally-around-the-flag from this broader political communication perspective.

Rally-around-the-Flag from a Political Communication Perspective

The rally-around-the-flag theory basically claims that in times of crisis the popularity of and trust in the political leader of the country increases. Confronted with a sudden attack or threat to a country, the public is expected to form ranks behind its leader and the flag (Brody & Shapiro, 1991). Research shows that an important pre-condition for a rally effect is that the opposition (temporarily) refrains from critiquing the government (Hetherington & Nelson, 2003). Mueller was the first to systematically study this effect in the context of US foreign policy. He argued that rally effects occurred when the president of the USA was involved in international events with a specific and dramatic focus. Mueller mainly referred to military interventions and ongoing wars, but also included important diplomatic events and major summits (Baker & Oneal, 2001; Mueller, 1973). Later on the theory was mainly applied in the context of violent conflicts, and on terrorist attacks in particular (Chowanietz, 2011). In the aftermath of the terrorist attacks of 9/11, President Bush enjoyed a boost in his popularity that was stronger (+35 percent points) and lasted longer (more than a year) than in any other case in history (Hetherington & Nelson, 2003).

During the last two decennia, the theory has been applied also in a broader range of contexts and types of crises. Most recently, scholars are using the theory to study the effect of the COVID-19 pandemic on the popularity and trust in governments (e.g. Bol, Giani, Blais, & Loewen, 2020; Shino & Binder, 2020), thereby extending the focus on mainly military events to an unprecedented international health crisis. In line with these studies, the pandemic in many ways is an ideal case to test a rally effect. In addition, we argue that the rally-around-the-flag effect basically involves the three central players of political communication. Since the theory has been mainly used by scholars in international politics and public opinion, the focus has been on government leaders and the public, leaving the role of the media largely out of sight. Only a few studies have explicitly included the important intermediary role of media coverage into their design. In their study of military interstate conflict, Baker and Oneal (2001) found that the amount of coverage by the *New York Times* played a significant role in the presence or absence of a rally effect. The work of Baum and colleagues has elaborated more on the specific role of the media in connecting political leaders and the public in times of crisis (Baum & Potter, 2008; Groeling & Baum, 2008). They argue that an increase in popularity of the government and its leader is less determined by the objective characteristics of the crisis, but more by how governments communicate about it, to what extend the government's handling of the crisis is criticized by the opposition and how this political debate is reported in the news. Groeling and Baum (2008) state that journalists seldom simply parrot statements of the political elites, but play an active role by selecting and ignoring certain actors and messages. Only in very unique dramatic incidents (like the 9/11 attacks), both the opposition and the media lower their normal critical voices, and a positive rally effect around the flag and the leader becomes possible.

This raises the question whether the ongoing COVID-19 pandemic is a similar 'exceptional' event that could have a similar effect on the public's perception of its leader(s). Recent studies show that as a consequence of the coronavirus a clear rally effect happened in many countries across the globe, but not in all and in many cases the effect was short-lived (e.g. Bol et al., 2020; Herrera, Ordoñez, Konradt, & Trebesch, 2020). This suggests that the rally-around-the-flag effect is contingent on different factors related to the interactions between political actors, media players and citizens. Before elaborating on these conditions, we focus on some concrete cases that clearly show the variation in rally effects across countries.

Different Countries, Different Effects

Did COVID-19 lead to a rally-around-the-flag across the globe? Looking at the leadership approval numbers of five head of states across the globe in Figure 1.1 the easy answer is: mostly, but not always. We focus on these cases because of

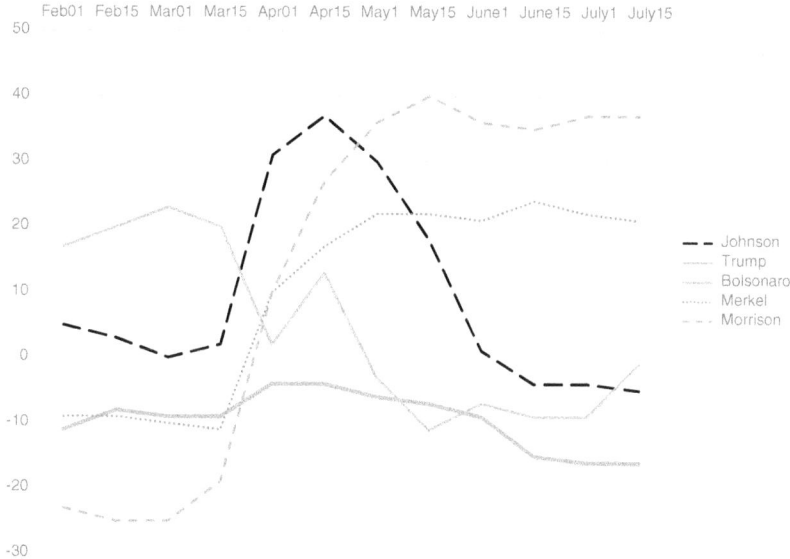

FIGURE 1.1 Leadership approval for five countries (February–July 2020).

data availability, and because specific aspects of all of them are further discussed in different chapters in this book. But most importantly, the five politicians represent different types of public responses to the pandemic.

We can witness two types of rally-around-the-flag effects, a short-term effect and a long-term effect. The German Chancellor Angela Merkel and Australian Prime Minister Scott Morrison both represent the latter. Their approval rating increased quite spectacularly after mid-March when the governments of both countries decided to implement harsh measures and basically ordered a lockdown. Their popularity increase continued until the beginning of May and remained quite stable at this high level. The popularity of both leaders remained high even through a second wave of the virus and new restrictions of the economic and social lives in their countries. In this respect, both leaders seem to 'enjoy' a similar rally effect as President Bush after 9/11. Boris Johnson represents a second, shorter and more classic version of the rally effect. His approval rating increased firmly after March 15, but after a month gradually goes down, and after two months his popularity is lower than it was before the crisis. President Trump presents a third type, mainly characterized by stability and lack of a substantial effect. The small increase in approval rating in the initial weeks of the crisis is hardly significant compared to the changes in the public perception of other leaders. The fourth and rather exceptional case is represented by Jair Bolsonaro, the president of Brazil, for whom this pandemic implied a clear decrease of popular support.

How can we explain this large variation, knowing that all countries were hit by the same virus and experienced a similar threat to public health? Without claiming to offer an empirical or extensive explanation, we provide several possible reasons that will be further developed and supported within several chapters of this book. We will structure these potential explanations in three sections that largely parallel the structure of this book: government performance and communication, media coverage and criticism, and the level of polarization among the public (and the media).

1   Government policy and communication strategy

A life-threatening event can lead to strong emotional reactions, such as anxiety, and bring people closer to their leaders. The political leader personifies the unified nation under attack, and people expect him or her to protect them against the external threat. This can explain why in some countries public support of the head of government increased without taking into account how the leader addressed the crisis. In an intriguing study, De Vries, Bakker, Hobolt and Arceneaux (2020) showed that government support increased in several European countries after the lockdown in Italy, but before these governments implemented their own measures. The authors consider the Italian lockdown as a 'crisis warning' that boosted incumbent support unrelated to actual government policy.

However, after such an initial emotional response we can expect citizens to take into account how their leaders reacted to the crisis. Probably the most obvious reason why political leaders are rewarded with public support has to do with the actual outcomes of their policy. If unemployment or crime rates go down, chances are high that the popularity of the government leader goes up. In the case of the coronavirus crisis, this would primarily mean that (relatively) few people get infected. A comparative analysis of public opinion and public health data in 35 countries by Herrera and colleagues shows that leadership approval is clearly (negatively) correlated with the increase in COVID-19 cases, "especially when unaccompanied by efforts to curb them with stringent policies, even at the expense of economic activity" (Herrera et al., 2020: 20). Put differently, political leaders do well when they manage to keep the public 'healthy', or at least try everything in their power to do so. This general explanation also applies when trying to clarify the steep increase in approval rating of Scott Morrison and Angela Merkel as it turns out that both leaders have reacted swiftly and firmly, prioritizing public health above economic and other concerns. They also showed flexibility in adjusting their policy to new scientific insights and realities as the virus spread around the world. As a result, the number of COVID-19 infections remained relatively low throughout 2020 compared to neighboring or similar countries.

In addition, to government policy, we notice that Morrison and Merkel share similarities in the way they communicated about the crisis and their response to it. They personally communicated regularly about the crisis, strengthening their visibility and leadership. However, at the same time they clearly aligned themselves with scientists and experts who were also given a prominent position in their communication strategy to inform the public (see also Chapters 7 and 11). Second, both leaders did not downplay the impact of the virus or its devastating consequences. This difference in content and style of communication can also partly explain why other leaders were much less successful in terms of public support.

The UK prime minister initially enjoyed a similar rally effect, although he waited longer before implementing a lockdown of his country (March 23). In the first weeks, Boris Johnson gave several prime time press conferences addressing the nation live on television attracting a large audience (Newman, Fletcher, Schulz, Andi, & Nielsen, 2020). Furthermore, Johnson himself was hospitalized with COVID-19 leading initially to feelings of solidarity among the British public with the leader. However, as Garland and Lilleker show (see Chapter 2), the clarity of the initial policy was replaced by a somewhat confused plan for easing the lockdown and also accompanied by a less consistent communication strategy in which the leader was often absent. This lack of consistency in both policy and communication decisions toward the handling of the crisis drew harsh critique from the opposition, and can be seen as partly responsible for the gradual decline in leadership approval.

Furthermore, as the devastating impact of the crisis became clear in the following months, the critique of political leaders, such as Johnson, that initially downplayed the crisis also became louder. This is probably even more the case for Donald Trump. Images and quotes of the US president telling the public that the coronavirus would magically 'disappear' were repeated endlessly in the majority of mainstream media coverage and in campaign ads of his political opponent, Joe Biden, during the elections of November 2020. Trump found it difficult to take a clear position in addressing the pandemic, as he feared the economic consequences and the skepticism of his loyal supporters toward measures that limited their personal freedom (see Chapter 6). One of the few leaders who went even further in denying the threat and consequences of COVID-19 was the Brazilian president (Friedman, 2020; Jennings, 2020). As Davis shows (see Chapter 8), Bolsonaro not only publicly minimalized the severity of the virus's impact on individuals but also hardly addressed the causes and consequences of the crisis on citizen's everyday life, strengthening the deep social divisions in his country. The lack of policy and a communication strategy focused on denial, misinformation and minimizing the crisis became more problematic and at odds with reality, as the number of cases and reported casualties in Brazil rose. In sum, it seems that political leaders who firmly and consistently addressed the crisis, including harsh measures supported by experts, and communicated about it openly and regularly, had most chance of seeing their approval ratings go (and stay) up.

2   Media coverage and (lack of) criticism

When turning to the role of the media, it is clear that news media across the globe focused heavily on the COVID-19 pandemic—at least in countries where journalists were not censored. Besley and Dray (2020) show that overall countries with free media are more truthful in counting COVID-19 deaths and implementing more efficient and responsive lockdowns. They argue that press freedom not only allows citizens to be better informed about the pandemic but also makes governments more accountable. That media in democratic countries focused heavily on the crisis is not surprising as there was a high need for information among a growing number of concerned citizens. Previous studies have indicated that in times of crisis people rely on media such as television and radio that can provide 'immediate' news updates, and more recently also online news sources (Westlund & Ghersetti, 2015). Newman et al. (2020) suggest that in particular the 'live' aspect of television news played a role during the COVID-19 crisis, as political leaders opted to directly address the nation or opted for daily press conferences. For instance, the press conference of British Prime Minister Johnson on 23 March 2020, in which he asked the nation to stay home, was one of the most-watched broadcasts in UK television history (Newman et al. 2020). In short, the media's agenda narrowed and focused almost exclusively on one issue, and the spotlights shined brightly on the political leaders who were expected to address that issue.

However, for a rally effect to take place it is important that media coverage should be extensive but it also needs to be less negative or critical about the government's' handling of the crisis. To a large extent, the media reflect the political debate, meaning that media criticism is closely related to the presence or absence of opposition voices (Baum & Potter, 2008). However, journalists can downplay or strengthen opposition voices and influence the level of polarization in the political debate. For instance, a recent study has shown that in the USA the first three months of newspaper and television coverage on COVID-19 was at least as politicized and polarized as recent news coverage of global climate change (Hart, Chinn, & Soroka, 2020). Put differently, the crisis was not covered in terms of a crisis that requested a 'unified' response, but rather as a classical partisan struggle. While some media focused on the president's mishandling of the pandemic, even mocking his unscientific responses to combat the crisis, other more partisan media opted to vividly support him. Yang and Bennett argue that media outlets like Fox News even 'co-produced' Trump's response to the pandemic, by spreading misinformation and promoting unproven cures that needed to show that the president had this crisis under control (see Chapter 6). The widely diverging media coverage of the president and his government's policy and communication not only contributed to a further deepening of the partisan perception of issue, but also further intensified the battle between Trump and the majority of journalists covering him. Although Trump initially liked the daily press briefings on the pandemic (as the viewer ratings were high), he quickly started to complain that the "press is very dishonest—they are siding with China, they are doing things they shouldn't be doing" (Manuel Roig-Franzia & Ellison, 2020).

This type of coverage and struggle between politicians and the press is very different from those countries where a rally effect was taking place. This is of course closely related to the fact that some countries performed better in terms of infections and casualties, but also more specifically attached to the performance of the political leader. In Germany, for instance, there was a rather broad consensus that Angela Merkel, as a former scientist, was the right person, in the right place. Or as a journalist of the newsmagazine Der Spiegel (Kurbjuweit, 2020) formulated it: "When it comes to insight, to understanding, she was the right person to have in the Chancellery". The media analyses of Quandt and colleagues (Chapter 7) confirm how Merkel remained the central actor in the network throughout the pandemic. More generally, Cardenal and colleagues (Chapter 10) show in their comparative study of European countries that the degree of polarization of the media landscape has a significant influence on the presence and size of the rally-around-the-flag effect. In countries where online news consumption is more polarized, meaning there is more partisan selective exposure, there clearly were less positive changes in trust in government because of the COVID-19 pandemic. This is also reflected in the analysis of the media coverage in the Turkish case where pro-government media and pro-opposition media have a very different way of portraying how the Turkish President Erdogan dealt with the health crisis (see Chapter 9).

3   Public opinion and the level of polarization

Next to the government-opposition dynamic, and the role of the media, several studies have stressed that a rally effect is contingent on individual attitudes and the degree of partisanship among the public (Baker & Oneal, 2001; Groeling & Baum, 2008). It is hardly surprising that the more negative people's views are of the political leader the less likely they are to reevaluate their perception in times of crisis. At the aggregate level, this implies that countries with a higher level of polarization are less likely to witness a rally effect. In those cases, the public perception of the government and political leadership is too much 'frozen' along partisan lines that even a dramatic external event fails to have an impact on how people perceive their leaders in government.

Although the discussion of the US case seems to suggest that polarization (among others) hindered a rally effect, it is hard to determine whether a different approach to the pandemic by the Trump administration could have impacted the leadership perception of democratic voters. Carson and colleagues (Chapter 11) find greater political and media polarization and partisan distrust of experts in the USA compared to Australia. The authors conclude that polarization has serious real-world consequences for governments' capacities to protect public health in this time of crisis. Studying a larger number of countries, Cardenal and colleagues (Chapter 10) conclude that political polarization at the country level has fairly limited impact on a rally effect, and was dependent on the reaction of the political opposition. A more in-depth analysis by Mihelj and colleagues (Chapter 12) of Poland, a highly polarized country, shows that initially the Polish public was rather united in their rejection of the politicization of the pandemic, but the government's handling of the upcoming election brought back the classical partisan divide. Also the example of Chile proves that existing political polarization can temper a strong rally-around-the-flag effect (see Chapter 4). Furthermore, Bachmann and colleagues show that this overall rally effect, however, masked an important polarization in attitudes toward government. While more affluent citizens, the traditional base of support for the Piñera government, became more confident in government during the pandemic, those who already protested against the government before became significantly disaffected. In this regard, the Chilean case shows how government policy and communication is contingent upon existing political and social conditions. The authors conclude that "In a divided and unequal country, the pandemic further stressed the inequalities and further alienated citizens".

Structure of the Book

In this book, a diverse set of scholars in political communication examine how the pandemic and its consequences have affected the relationships between politicians, journalists and citizens. The book is divided into three parts where each part focuses on one of the three central actors of political communication. The chapters of Part 1 focus on the political world, and government communication in particular. The chapters of Part 2 are mainly devoted to the role of the news media: both traditional mainstream outlets and new social or alternative media. Finally, Part 3 puts citizens central and deals mainly with how the pandemic influenced trust in political and media institutions. This division in three parts is of course somewhat artificial as each chapter deals with the interactions and relationships between politics-media-public, but mainly indicates which actor is central in the story.

Several chapters use survey data or content analysis, while others have a more descriptive case study approach. All contributions, however, share an analytical focus comparing through space or time. For instance, Chapters 10 and 11 use recent public opinion data to compare between countries, while Shehata and colleagues (Chapter 13) focus on Sweden and use panel data to show how Swedes were fairly consistent in perceiving the crisis and the reaction of their government over time. Several other chapters also focus on one country to provide in-depth analyses of the government communication strategy, providing strong cases of structurally different reactions in terms of style and level of personalization. For instance, in Chapter 5 Mazzoleni and Bracciale show how the Italian Prime Minister Giuseppe Conte seized the opportunity to build a highly personalized leadership, using skilled communication strategies to manage the emergency as a captain in the storm. This is in sharp contrast with the Chilean case (Chapter 4) where rather than the president, several ministers and undersecretaries made the official communications regarding the pandemic. In a similar way, Chapter 2 shows how in the UK Boris Johnson often remained absent in the public communication about the coronavirus, while Scottish first minister Nicola Sturgeon remained visible throughout the crisis and positioned herself as an alternative national leader within Scotland. This clearly reflects the different leadership styles in response to a pandemic that previous studies have indicated (Kahn, 2020; Lilleker, Coman, Gregor, & Novelli, 2021).

In discussing how political and media institutions have reacted to and been impacted by the corona crisis, this book goes beyond the traditional focus on the USA and Western Europa (UK, Germany, Sweden, Italy), including cases from Latin America (Chile, Brazil), Asia (Turkey, China) and Eastern Europe (Poland). In doing so, we take into account how variation in the political context, the media system and personal leadership can influence the many ways this pandemic has challenged the political communication process. In particular, the chapters on a semi- or competitive authoritarian regime (Turkey) and an absolute authoritarian regime (China) show that this pandemic gave some oxygen to opposition voices using both traditional and new media. However, as Zeng (Chapter 3) describes in the Chinese case, as soon as the authority has the crisis under control, the situation returns to 'normal', meaning with a public sphere dominated by government propaganda. Also Quandt and colleagues (Chapter 7) observe in their study a 'normalization' of the media coverage over time, turning COVID-19 into a prominent, but not fully dominant topic. This idea of things returning back to normal applies probably to many contexts described in this book. A crisis of more than a year is no longer an event, but rather a new normal. As this pandemic is ongoing, we hope this book inspires the many political communication studies that will examine its impact on the triangle between media, public and politics.

Acknowledgments

I would like to thank Jesper Strömbäck, Lance Bennett and Darren Lilleker for their constructive feedback on an earlier version of this chapter.

References

Althaus, S. L. (2002). "American News Consumption during Times of National Crisis." *PS: Political Science and Politics, 35*(3), 517–521. doi:10.1017/S104909650200077X

Baker, W. D., & Oneal, J. R. (2001). "Patriotism or Opinion Leadership? The Nature and Origins of the 'Rally Round the Flag' Effect." *Journal of Conflict Resolution, 45*(5), 661–687. doi:10.1177/0022002701045005006

Baum, M., & Potter, P. (2008). "The Relationship between Mass Media, Public Opinion, and Foreign Policy." *Annual Review of Political Science, 11*, 39–65.

Bennett, L., & Iyengar, S. (2008). "A New Era of Minimal Effects? The Changing Foundations of Political Communication." *Journal of Communication, 58*, 707–731.

Bennett, W. L., & Pfetsch, B. (2018). "Rethinking Political Communication in a Time of Disrupted Public Spheres." *Journal of Communication, 68*(2), 243–253. doi:10.1093/joc/jqx017

Besley, T., & Dray, S. (2020). *The Political Economy of Lockdown: Does Free Media Make a Difference?* Retrieved from https://www.economicsobservatory.com/ongoing-research/the-political-economy-of-lockdown-does-free-media-make-a-difference

Blumler, J. G. (2015). "Core Theories of Political Communication: Foundational and Freshly Minted." *Communication Theory, 25*(4), 426–438. doi:10.1111/comt.12077

Bol, D., Giani, M., Blais, A., & Loewen, P. J. (2020). "The Effect of COVID-19 Lockdowns on Political Support: Some Good News for Democracy?" *European Journal of Political Research.* doi:10.1111/1475-6765.12401

Boomgaarden, H. G., & de Vreese, C. H. (2007). "Dramatic Real-world Events and Public Opinion Dynamics: Media Coverage and Its Impact on Public Reactions to an Assassination." *International Journal of Public Opinion Research, 19*(3), 354–366. doi:10.1093/ijpor/edm012

Brody, R. A., & Shapiro, C. R. (1991). "The Rally Phenomenon in Public Opinion." In R. A. Brody (Ed.), *Assessing the President: The Media, Elite Opinion, and Public Support*. Stanford: Stanford University Press.

Casero-Ripollés, A. (2020). "Impact of COVID-19 on the Media System. Communicative and Democratic Consequences of News Consumption during the Outbreak." *El profesional de la información, 29*(2), e290223. https://ssrn.com/abstract=3594133

Chowanietz, C. (2011). "Rallying around the Flag or Railing against the Government? Political Parties' Reactions to Terrorist Acts." *Party Politics, 17*(5), 673–698. doi:10.1177/1354068809346073

De Vries, C. E., Bakker, B. N., Hobolt, S., & Arceneaux, K. (2020). "Crisis Signaling: How Italy's Coronavirus Lockdown Affected Incumbent Support in Other European Countries." Retrieved from https://papers.ssrn.com/sol3/papers.cfm?abstract_id=3606149

Friedman, U. (2020, March 27). "The Coronavirus-Denial Movement Now Has a Leader." *The Atlantic.* Retrieved from https://www.theatlantic.com/politics/archive/2020/03/bolsonaro-coronavirus-denial-brazil-trump/608926/

Groeling, T., & Baum, M. A. (2008). "Crossing the Water's Edge: Elite Rhetoric, Media Coverage, and the Rally-Round-the-Flag Phenomenon." *The Journal of Politics, 70*(4), 1065–1085. doi:10.1017/s0022381608081061

Hart, P. S., Chinn, S., & Soroka, S. (2020). "Politicization and Polarization in COVID-19 News Coverage." *Science Communication, 42*(5), 679–697. doi:10.1177/1075547020950735

Herrera, H., Ordoñez, G., Konradt, M., & Trebesch, C. (2020). *Corona Politics: The Cost of Mismanaging Pandemics.*
Hetherington, M. J., & Nelson, M. (2003). "Anatomy of a Rally Effect: George W. Bush and the War on Terrorism." *PS: Political Science and Politics, 36*(1), 37–42.
Jennings, W. (2020, March 30). "COVID-19 and the 'Rally-Round-the-Flag-Effect.'" *UK in a Changing Europe.* Retrieved from https://ukandeu.ac.uk/covid-19-and-the-rally-round-the-flag-effect/
Kahn, L. H. (2020). *Who's in charge? Leadership during epidemics, bioterror attacks, and other public health crises.* Santa Barbara: Praeger Security International
Klinger, U., & Svensson, J. (2015). "The Emergence of Network Media Logic in Political Communication: A Theoretical Approach." *New Media & Society, 17*(8), 1241–1257. doi:10.1177/1461444814522952
König, P. D. (2016). "Communicating Austerity Measures during Times of Crisis: A Comparative Empirical Analysis of Four Heads of Government." *The British Journal of Politics and International Relations, 18*(3), 538–558. doi:10.1177/1369148115625380
Kurbjuweit, D. (2020, December 18). "Germany's Chancellor Hits the Wall." *Der Spiegel* Retrieved from https://www.spiegel.de/international/germany/angela-merkel-in-the-corona-crisis-germany-s-chancellor-hits-the-wall-a-48674d4e-ef28-4cfe-8f7a-65a5b14025a9.
Lachlan, K. A., Spence, P.R., Lin, X., Najarian, K., & Del Greco, M. (2016). "Social Media and Crisis Management: CERC, Search Strategies, and Twitter Content." *Computers in Human Behavior, 54*, 647–652. doi:10.1016/j.chb.2015.05.027.
Lawrence, R. G. (2000). *The Politics of Force: Media and the Construction of Police Brutality.* Berkeley: University of California Press.
Lilleker, D., Coman, I. A., Gregor, M., & Novelli, E. (2021). *Political Communication and COVID-19: Governance and Rhetoric in Times of Crisis.* London and NewYork: Routledge.
Manuel Roig-Franzia, M., & Ellison, S. (2020, March 29). "A History of the Trump War on Media—The Obsession Not Even Coronavirus Could Stop." *The Washington Post.* Retrieved from https://www.washingtonpost.com/lifestyle/media/a-history-of-the-trump-war-on-media--the-obsession-not-even-coronavirus-could-stop/2020/03/28/71bb21d0-f433-11e9-8cf0-4cc99f74d127_story.html
McNair, B. (2003). *Introduction to Political Communication.* London: Routledge.
Mueller, J. E. (1973). *War, Presidents, and Public Opinion.* New York: Wiley.
Newman, N., Fletcher, R., Schulz, A., Andi, S., & Nielsen, R. K. (2020). *Reuters Institute Digital News Report 2020.* Oxford: Reuters Institute for the Study of Journalism.
Shino, E., & Binder, M. (2020). "Defying the Rally during COVID-19 Pandemic: A Regression Discontinuity Approach." *Social Science Quarterly, 101*(5), 1979–1994. doi:10.1111/ssqu.12844
t Hart, P., & Tindall, K. (2009). *Framing the Global Economic downturn: Crisis Rhetoric and the Politics of Recessions.* Canberra: ANU Press.
Van Aelst, P., Strömbäck, J., Aalberg, T., Esser, F., de Vreese, C., Matthes, J., … Stanyer, J. (2017). "Political communication in a high-choice media environment: a challenge for democracy?" *Annals of the International Communication Association, 41*(1), 3 27. doi:10.1080/23808985.2017.1288551
Westlund, O., & Ghersetti, M. (2015). "Modelling News Media Use: Positing and Applying the GC/MC Model to the Analysis of Media Use in Everyday Life and Crisis Situations." *Journalism studies, 16*(2), 133–151.

PART 1
Government Communications

2
FROM CONSENSUS TO DISSENSUS

The UK's Management of a Pandemic in a Divided Nation

Ruth Garland and Darren Lilleker

Introduction

The UK government ran 92 live coronavirus media briefings from 16 March until 23 June 2020, devoting an hour each evening to unseen questions from journalists and later members of the public. The sessions formed the centrepiece of the government's communication campaign and fed directly into advertising and partner communication through outdoor sites, mainstream media and social media. The three devolved governments of Scotland, Wales and Northern Ireland ran parallel sessions, while their respective Chief Medical Officers collaborated through UK government committees such as COBRA,[1] the emergency planning meeting usually chaired by the Prime Minister and the scientific advisory group, SAGE.

This commitment to UK-wide public communication was unprecedented and substantial, involving 12 cabinet ministers, including the Prime Minister. It also exposed the public to daily interventions by scientists and clinicians, some of whom became household names. Beyond the briefings, the wider scientific community joined the debate in a display of pluralism rarely seen in contemporary public communication. This was a *volte face* by a government led by a colourful rogue who eschewed factual detail, which had previously avoided scrutiny, questioned the role of experts, threatened the BBC and challenged the access rights of the Westminster press corps (Shipman, 2020; Mayhew, 2020). Johnson was one of the least trusted leaders in recent history, including among his own parliamentary party (Curtis, 2019). Like previous post-1997

---

1 COBRA is a Whitehall acronym referring to the room where the meetings take place – Cabinet Office Briefing Room A.

governments Johnson's showed a preference for anonymous, partisan briefing of favoured sources rather than open and transparent public communication (Garland, 2016). However, he had three sources of political capital: a manifesto commitment to equality, known as "levelling up"; an 80-seat parliamentary majority; and a clear manifesto commitment to increasing investment in one of the UK's most cherished institutions, the NHS.

While the UK appeared at first to "rally around the flag" the absence of the Prime Minister due to him catching coronavirus and being hospitalized between 27 March and 27 April was not the only threat to the notion of one nation, one leader. Disagreements with the three devolved nations threatened consensus. Scottish Nationalist (SNP) First Minister Nicola Sturgeon in particular positioned herself in opposition to Johnson, with a different approach to handling the pandemic. On the back of her opposition to Brexit in EU-supporting Scotland, Sturgeon used daily coronavirus media briefings to demonstrate a contrasting style of leadership, and an increasingly oppositional national narrative. Unlike Johnson, who fronted just 16 (17%), and terminated them on 23 June, Sturgeon chaired all but two of the 107 briefings to the end of August (98%), and kept them running throughout 2020, thus controlling the public messaging.

The course of the epidemic was similar in Scotland to that in the wider UK, albeit running a few weeks behind, but support for Sturgeon's handling of the crisis contrasted with plummeting poll ratings for Johnson and the governing party. An approval rating of 72% in late March for the UK government's handling of the coronavirus when the first lockdown was implemented fell to 47% when these measures were eased in mid-May and continued to decline to 32% by October (YouGov, 2020c). Johnson enjoyed similar high support in March and April but public approval in his performance as Prime Minister tracked government approval ratings for the rest of the year. Hence, the handling of the pandemic is the story of an initial spike in support followed by a significant decline in public confidence in government and Johnson as the crisis unfolded (see Figure 2.1). From September 2020, in particular, Johnson faced rebellion and unrest on Conservative benches following a series of high-profile U-turns, blunders and contradictory public health messages (Garland & Lilleker, 2021). Sturgeon was significantly ahead of Johnson in public approval for her handling of the coronavirus pandemic (YouGov, 2020a), and the SNP was predicted to make gains in the 2021 Scottish parliamentary elections, although they only gained one seat, that could challenge Johnson's resistance to a second independence referendum. Johnson also faced a more forensic political opposition after April 2020 when former lawyer and Director of Public Prosecutions Sir Keir Starmer was elected Labour leader. Starmer initially supported Johnson's call for all political leaders to work together to tackle the crisis but as government competence came into question Starmer went on the attack, citing public interest as justification.

This chapter conducts a thematic content analysis of the 92 daily Westminster media briefings and 107 Edinburgh briefings to the end of August to ask

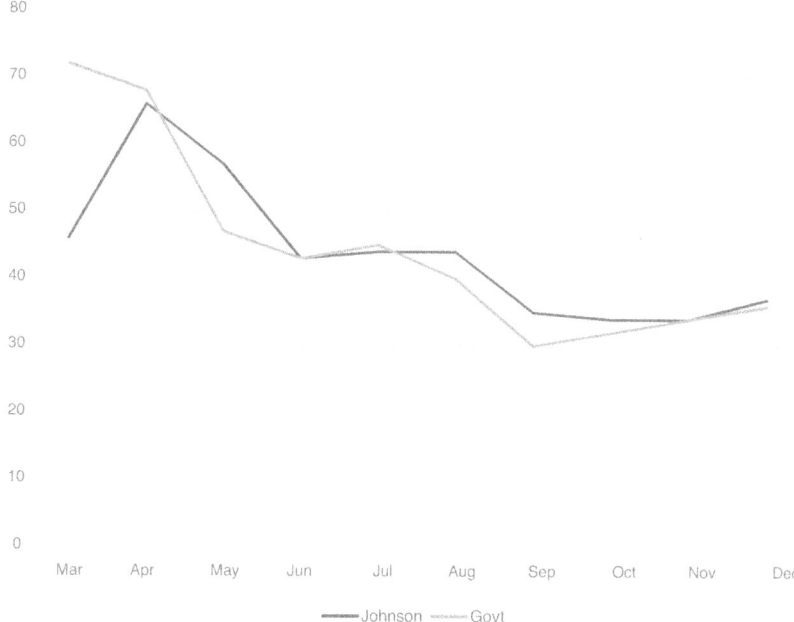

FIGURE 2.1 Johnson's approval ratings and confidence in government.

what visions of national leadership and national identity were presented during the briefings. Evident are the contrasting backgrounds, personalities and rhetorical styles of the two leaders. Like Starmer, Sturgeon is a former lawyer from a relatively humble background who employs a precise and reserved style of presentation. Johnson, an expensively educated former newspaper columnist and Mayor of London, has long practised a flamboyant schoolboy style of address, coining phrases like "moonshot" for mass testing, describing himself as "fit as a butcher's dog" and "bursting with antibodies" when questioned about his health.

Three distinct phases of communication during the pandemic are identified:

1 2 to 27 March – Johnson announcing the lockdown: from partisanship to consensus.
2 27 March to 26 April – Johnson's absence with coronavirus: the political vacuum and the election of Starmer as opposition leader.
3 27April to date – Johnson's attempted "bounce back": the return of partisan politics and Sturgeon's growing oppositional rhetoric.

This chapter argues that just as the daily media briefings presented a faltering image of Johnson's leadership and the UK government's efficacy in controlling the epidemic and public messaging around it, they enhanced Sturgeon's legitimacy as a national leader, offering a challenge to the continuation of the Union after Brexit. This was exacerbated by further divergences from a national approach taken in Wales and Northern Ireland, and calls within England for more regional devolution of decision-making. Sturgeon arguably used the coronavirus briefings to portray herself as the leader-in-waiting of a modern Scottish nation, in turn acting as a fillip to other regional and opposition leaders. This led Johnson to appear isolated and on the wrong course, loosely governing England, while deploying grandiose and outdated UK rhetoric.

The Crisis in Public Communication

Aeron Davis' (2018) critique of the British political elite casts them as precarious, rootless and self-serving. Challenged by systemic changes within the global economy, society and the communication environment, their strategy has narrowed to the management of perceptions and the retention of power. In common with Blumler, Davis' critique develops a current of thought which highlights a crisis in public communication (Blumler, 2018). Responding to structural change, the political sphere has witnessed increased personalization of power, attempts at control of media and political messaging, and a shift towards permanent campaigning (Foley, 2000). These trends are only restrained by the size of parliamentary majorities and the levels of control prime ministers can exert over their cabinets, as well as their relationship with media owners, and their standing in public opinion (Langer & Sagarzazu, 2018). Modern leadership in the UK thus involves attempting to maintain the support of the public and media and retain political control with minimal scrutiny or critique.

The drift towards a more presidential style and the extraordinary statutory law-making abilities bestowed on the executive in order to deal with the COVID-19 pandemic combine theoretically to award Johnson significant control over public communication. However, crisis leadership is also reliant on performance. Performance encompasses framing the national understanding of the crisis, taking ownership of critical decisions, facilitating horizontal and vertical communication between key actors and agencies, being accountable, building resilience and demonstrating learning and interaction (Boin et al., 2013). To achieve this, leaders must create the perception they are trustworthy, competent, decisive, empathic and courageous (James & Wooten, 2005). Johnson's colourful rogue with little care for detail needed to be sidelined, replaced with a more serious demeanour suited to the gravity of the situation and the decisions being taken.

Johnson's style proved sufficiently successful to win victory at the 2019 general election securing a significant 80 seat parliamentary majority from 42.4% of the votes, but only 2.4% more than secured by Labour (Cutts et al., 2020). Unlike elections, however, crises require a unifying leader, which is problematic for one who polarizes opinion and does not enjoy the trust of a majority of the electorate (Marland, 2016). A health pandemic requires a shared sense of national identity around the "we" concept (Jetten et al., 2020). The people need to trust their leader and believe they are being "shepherded by a paternalistic government" (Jetten et al., 2020, p. 6). Leaders must therefore perform the roles of "representing us", "doing it for us" and crafting and embedding a sense of "us" in all communication (Jetten et al., 2020, pp. 25–30). Embedded within this is an emphasis on the character and values of a nation. Johnson has been known for his optimistic and nationalist rhetoric relating to Brexit, invoking Churchillian rhetoric to sell his vision (Yates, 2018); however, what may be appropriate for campaigning does not necessarily translate into a one nation policy given the post-Brexit polarization within and between the nations of the UK.

Bækgaard et al. (2020) highlight how people tend to rally around the flag and their leader in times of crisis with reference to the lockdown in Denmark, a phenomenon evident across a range of nations (Lilleker et al., 2021). However, prolonged crisis can lead to a collapse in public support if the leader fails to show competence and get results, all of which are key for maintaining community resilience (Jetten et al., 2020). A clear sense of the values of a nation, built around inclusivity, strength in the face of threats, with a history of working together, is important to foster within such crisis conditions (Pamment & Cassinger, 2018). For Johnson, this required transitioning his rhetorical style to one that brings all UK inhabitants together around a common focus bound by a sense of identity. For this leader, in a post-Brexit context, there are significant challenges in terms of his character and style. The extent COVID-19 demonstrated Johnson's capacity to be a unifying leader in the face of existential challenges to the health and unity of the nation and growing opposition from emergent alternative models of leadership is the core question for our analysis.

Public Communication in Practice: An Analysis of the UK and Scottish Coronavirus Media Briefings

After an initially slow response to the coronavirus, the UK government instituted daily coronavirus media briefings from Number 10 Downing Street ("No. 10") on 16 March, and a UK-wide lockdown began on 23 March. A national campaign *Stay at Home, Protect the NHS, Save Lives* ran until 10 May when it was superseded by a new slogan, *Stay Alert, Control the Virus, Save Lives*, that marked a phased lifting of restrictions. The *Stay at Home* campaign was judged by advertisers to be "one of the most effective messages in the history of government communications", achieving awareness levels of 92% (Lee & Spanier, 2020), and enjoyed high public support. The Scottish government began daily media briefings on 20 March, until 10 May deploying broadly similar messages to the UK government. The sessions were broadcast live by the BBC and BBC Scotland respectively, and archived by the broadcaster on the relevant government websites.

A provisional coding exercise identified key themes informed by these four key public communication norms (Blumler & Gurevitch, 1995; Blumler, 2018) and developed in previous similar research (Garland, 2016):

1. coherent, factual and unified messaging for all citizens,
2. transparency and accountability in public communication,
3. a commitment to serving the public interest,
4. maintaining the dividing line between partisan and impartial communications.

The analysis provides an opportunity to juxtapose different styles of leadership and visions of nation and contrasting degrees of commitment to public accountability. The analysis reveals a perhaps unintended outcome – the honing of a distinctive governing style in Scotland that undermined the constitutional relevance of the UK itself. The crisis also provided an opportunity for Labour. At his first party conference on 22 September 2020 Starmer berated the government for "losing control" of the virus and promised to "act in the public interest", noting "the challenges we now face mean that even the questions of 2019 already seem like ancient history" (Starmer, 2020). This analysis will first examine the media briefings overall, and then turn to a more detailed examination of two key themes: leadership and national identity. As the findings show, the disparity between the two narratives reveals a fragmented and confused picture of national identity.

Assessing the "Look" of the Daily Briefings

The staging of the daily briefings in Westminster and Edinburgh was similar, consisting of three lecterns with the chair of the panel at the centre, slogans on the lecterns, and, at the Scottish briefings, also projected onto a screen behind the speakers. The Westminster No. 10 briefings took place in a traditional wood-panelled room with the central lectern flanked by two large Union Jack flags and one or two senior advisers. Each 60- to 90-minute briefing started with a short update by the chair, followed by thankyous, acknowledgements and announcements. The senior adviser provided a statistical update using a series of slides. This was followed by two questions from members of the public (from 27 April), then questions from journalists, always starting with the BBC.

The Edinburgh briefings took place in a modern-looking, black painted and carpeted room in St Andrews House, the office of the First Minister and the Scottish Government, with three white lecterns placed on a podium. The screen projection initially read "Scottish government" in English and Gaelic with an image of the Scottish blue and white saltire on the right although the set carried no flags. The sessions were rarely shorter than 60 minutes and began with Sturgeon's summary of daily statistics, although there were no slides.

Other panellists did not always speak, and questions for journalists lasted up to 45 minutes with as many as 20 questions answered, usually starting with the BBC. Unlike the UK media briefings, no follow-up questions were allowed.

Given Sturgeon's prominence, it is not surprising the gender balance between the briefings varied. The 26-strong UK cabinet at the time included seven women (27%), two occupied roles relevant to the coronavirus crisis. The Prime Minister chaired 16 of the 92 daily media briefings (17%), sharing the role with ten male cabinet colleagues and one female, the Home Secretary Priti Patel who appeared three times. The Health Secretary Matt Hancock made the most appearances at 24 (26%). Scientific, medical and other advisers appeared 123 times, and of these one third were women, a fifth of the experts were scientific advisers. Sturgeon's 12-strong Scottish cabinet included seven women (58%) and five men. Women accounted for 87% of appearances by politicians. Nine officials and experts made a total of 110 appearances, the most frequent being the Chief Medical Officer with 51% of appearances, the National Clinical Director 26% and the Chief Nursing Officer at 18 (16%).

Thus, while political representation on the UK panels was overwhelmingly male, the opposite was true in Scotland. The dominant expertise was medical, especially in Scotland, with scant representation for nursing, social work, social care, general practice or public health, although Scotland's chief nurse made nine times as many appearances as her UK counterpart. Behavioural specialists did not attend either briefing, a strange omission given the centrality of behavioural science in informing public health campaigns (Lawton, 2020). The public were exposed to unprecedented levels of scientific discourse and statistical analysis that helped to counter misinformation, while the experts drawn upon reinforced traditional images of public health this mirrored an approach taken in many countries, a major comparative study found 21 of the 27 countries included placed scientific experts at the forefront of the communication strategy.

Visions of National Leadership: Boris Johnson

Johnson's decisive general election victory in December 2019 is argued to owe much to his optimism and bumptious style of campaigning and his disavowal of his own party's ten-year austerity programme (Flinders, 2020). His initial approach to communication tried to marginalize established journalistic institutions, relying instead on direct communication through social media and interviews with favoured media outlets. As the pandemic gathered pace in China and parts of Europe in early 2020, Johnson played down its seriousness, failing to attend five COBRA meetings and spending ten days at his country home. On 3 March at a televized briefing with the Chief Scientific Adviser, Johnson launched an action plan to tackle the outbreak, yet cheerfully admitted to shaking hands with coronavirus patients. Consistent with his extravagant rhetorical style he praised the UK's "world leading scientists", claiming that the country was "extremely well prepared". Such claims later left him exposed to widespread media criticism once it became clear the government had acted late and demonstrated incompetence and indecisiveness over a range of issues.

The tone and style changed after the media briefing of 12 March when Johnson said "I must level with the British public. Many more families are going to lose loved ones before their time". On 16 March, he chaired the first daily briefing, urging everyone to work from home and avoid pubs and restaurants. Schools closed on 20 March and a full lockdown began on 23 March. Until his absence through illness, Johnson chaired seven of the ten daily briefings, setting the tone for decisive, science-led yet positive communication that sought and largely achieved massive compliance, and high levels of media and political co-operation (Schofield, 2020). Consensus and compliance remained high during the Prime Minister's absence (Opinium, 2020). The science-led approach was a remarkable pivot for a politician who, as leader of the Leave campaign during the 2016 EU referendum, had been accused by the country's chief statistician of "a clear mis-use of official statistics" (Norgrove, 2017).

The second pivot came in May following Johnson's return from illness. Consensus and clarity gave way to what turned out to be a confused "bounce back" plan for easing the lockdown and opening up the economy. A series of unattributable briefings to preferred newspapers prefigured a much-criticized TV broadcast on Sunday, 10 May where Johnson launched the new slogan *Stay Alert, Control the Virus, Save Lives*, and sketched out a "roadmap" actively encouraging people to go to work. Schools would begin a phased return from 1 June. By 9 June, after failed attempts to shame teachers back into the classroom, the Education Secretary admitted schools would not open to most pupils before the summer holidays. Devolved governments claimed they found out about the "roadmap" changes through the media and messaging began to diverge immediately. Sturgeon opened up new lines of attack that would position Scotland in opposition to the UK by adopting a cautious approach. She hinted that unlike Johnson she was not prepared to "risk unnecessary deaths by acting rashly or prematurely" (11 May).

The image of leadership projected by Johnson was of a leader who made sporadic appearances, lacked consistency, did not take time to understand the detail, and veered between misplaced optimism and sudden and ill-explained centralized diktats. He chaired just nine (17%) of the 54 remaining broadcasts, two of which were mainly concerned with the defence of his chief political adviser Dominic Cummings for breaking lockdown rules. Sturgeon had faced a similar dilemma when Scotland's Chief Medical Officer, Dr Catherine Calderwood, was found to have broken lockdown by travelling twice to her second home. Sturgeon immediately stated that this was wrong and against the rules but that she needed Calderwood in post to help her "steer the country through this crisis". Calderwood resigned later that day as it became clear that her presence was undermining the Scottish government's messages. Sturgeon faced a day of negative headlines compared to the five days of media frenzy endured by the Johnson government as Cummings remained in post despite calls from within the party and public for his resignation. In a distinct change of tone that emerged after the Cummings controversy, Keir Starmer's demonstrated a knack for creating headlines. On 3 June he accused the government of "winging it" in its handling of the pandemic, telling the PM to "get a grip" (Mason, 2020). Numerous polls demonstrated this proved a turning point in public confidence in Johnson and the UK government's capacity to handle the pandemic (Cartwright, 2020; Smith, 2020).

Government competence was called into question by the media and Starmer over a series of damaging U-turns on the return of schools (9 June), the provision of free school meals over the summer holidays (16 June), the launch of an NHS contact tracing app (18 June), the publication of exam results based on algorithms (11 and 17 August) and working from home (22 September) (Devlin, 2020). Johnson's reputation hit a new low on 29 September, when, as nearly a third of the UK population faced various degrees of local lockdown, he had to apologize for having "mis-spoke" when asked about COVID rules in the North East (*BBC News*, 2020). Footage of him fumbling and failing to answer journalists' questions was widely circulated. On 13 October, as cases rose steeply, it emerged SAGE had recommended a short "'circuit breaker lockdown" of a few weeks at their 21 September meeting. On 14 October, Starmer held a press conference urging the government to implement this advice, warning the country could "sleep walk into a long and bleak winter" (*Sky News*, 2020). In parliament the same day Starmer warned "we're at a tipping point; time is running out". This stance was supported by the devolved governments of Wales and Northern Ireland which implemented national lockdowns in October. Despite dismissing this proposal as a "disaster", Johnson later implemented a four-week lockdown in England, starting on 5 November.

Visions of National Leadership: Nicola Sturgeon

Sturgeon's immaculate presentation and her dominance of the daily panels contrasted with Johnson's dishevelled appearance and vagueness with the facts. The daily briefings showed her on top of her brief, precise in her language, in command of the machinery of government, and as protector of the health and welfare of the Scottish people, often positioning herself in opposition to the UK government. Operational issues such as PPE, testing and the crisis in care homes were dealt with by her co-panellists, leaving her free to focus on the statistics and broader strategy and tactics.

Her messaging was consistent, with regular recourse to keywords such as "clarity", "transparency", "calm", "control", "cautious optimism" and "proper scrutiny". Her mastery of data and how this fed into behavioural recommendations were demonstrated daily; at times she spent as long as 12 minutes explaining the statistics. She showed decisiveness, for example in relation to the Scottish school exams fiasco of 10 August, where she acknowledged that "we did not get this right and I'm sorry", adding in a veiled contrast with Johnson "when we do make a mistake we are big enough to say so". Several times she remarked "this is not a popularity contest"; she would take the right decision, however unpopular. From the launch of the Scottish government's "route map" to ease the lockdown on 21 May, she consistently reiterated that the reopening of schools on 11 August was a priority – an ambition that informed much of the decision-making from then on.

Visions of National Identity: Britain as One Nation

The crisis exposed the fact that key public services such as policing, justice, education and public health had already been devolved to the Scottish government. The Coronavirus Act 2020 devolved further powers, and the Scottish government introduced an additional Coronavirus (Scotland) Act that improved tenant protection, and relaxed planning and licensing rules (Institute for Government, 2020). The UK government glossed over the complexities of an increasingly fragmented country in its daily media briefings, presenting the UK, Britain and England, or England and Wales, as largely synonymous. Scotland, Wales and Northern Ireland were either not mentioned or subsumed within "a united national effort". "Britain" or "the British" was referred to regularly. Johnson particularly invoked the idea of "Britishness", for example, praising "fantastic British workers" and "freedom loving Britons" (20 March). On 5 May, he praised the resilience of the UK economy adding "we're an ingenious bunch, the Brits".

Despite evidence of deficiencies, the UK's approach to coronavirus was presented uncritically. On 28 March, the Business Secretary claimed, "Britain is meeting the challenge". Two days later, the Communities Secretary praised Britain as the world's leading country for vaccine research. It was claimed that "we" have the strongest supply chains and PPE guidelines in the world (31 March). As UK coronavirus deaths passed 20,000, among the worst death tolls in Europe, and shortcomings in infection control emerged, media consensus became increasingly tempered by criticism, most notably on 19 April with an in-depth *Sunday Times* investigation into the 38 days before lockdown when "Britain sleepwalked into disaster" (Calvert et al., 2020). The contrasts between the effusive language of the government and contrary evidence as represented through media weakened Johnson's image as leader of the whole nation.

In a ministerial address on his return to work on 27 April, Johnson invoked the nation, praising our "collective national resolve", and "all the effort and sacrifice of the British people". He committed himself to leading a national consensus across party lines, promising that "the UK will emerge stronger than ever before". On 30 April, he repeated the pledge on political consensus but by 10 May this was falling away following the botched launch of the roadmap, as the devolved nations, especially Scotland, took every opportunity to criticize Johnson's government for easing lockdown too quickly. When Johnson visited Scotland on 23 July to mark one year of his premiership, he chose to praise the work of two UK-wide institutions, the British Army and HM Treasury, for showing "what we can achieve when we stand together as one United Kingdom" (Honeycombe-Foster, 2020). Given the sentiment in Scotland, he would have done well to praise some Scottish Institutions. By October, a poll showed just 19% of Scots were satisfied with Johnson's leadership, compared with 72% for Sturgeon and 44% for Starmer (IpsosMORI, 2020).

Visions of National Identity: Independent Scotland

An obvious contrast was the absence of the concept of "Britain" at the Edinburgh briefings. The UK government was referenced mainly as a constraining or reckless force that should be resisted. As Scottish and English policy diverged, the border between Scotland and England assumed greater significance and the cultural, historical and social links represented by "Britain" were rendered invisible. Sturgeon denied making party political points at the daily briefings but her strategy to differentiate Scotland from the UK served a nationalist purpose. Her regular exhortations for people to holiday "at home" rather than travel abroad and risk quarantine referred solely to Scotland. By doing this, she stated, we could prevent the virus from "coming in from outside", including across the border with England (30 June). On 28 July as quarantine was reimposed on travellers from Spain, Sturgeon stated that the safest holiday was "here in Scotland", and that if she had time for a holiday she'd choose "to spend it here".

Scotland was the central brand throughout the briefings. In one early session, Scotland was mentioned 17 times in under 30 minutes (25 March). Comparisons were rarely made with England or the UK, but with other European countries such as Germany and France, as if to emphasize parity with large sovereign nations. When presented with criticisms or proposals from the Conservative or Labour opposition she invariably pointed out that although they had a right to oppose, we "hope at times like this that people would rise above it" (11 June). Her job was to focus on the "here and now" by "getting the country through the pandemic" (21 August). Nomenclature was used to distinguish between Scottish and UK-wide responses to the pandemic, sometimes churlishly. The slogan "Stay at Home", for example, did not appear on lecterns or the backdrop until 11 May, the day after it was dropped by the Westminster government. The plan to ease lockdown was referred to as Scotland's "route map" to differentiate it from Johnson's "roadmap". While the UK government referred to NHS Test and Trace, Scotland's was branded "Test and Protect".

At times the localization of brands appeared parochial, as with the reference to celebrations "across Scotland" on 5 July to mark "the 72nd anniversary of our National Health Service". The NHS was set up in 1948 on the same day across all four nations of the UK.

Sturgeon's approach changed in line with the three phases referred to earlier. Initially, Scotland was presented as observing the same lockdown as the rest of the UK. Sympathy was expressed for Johnson in his illness and his return was welcomed as viewers were assured "we are working with the UK government and the other devolved administrations". She and Johnson were "at one in wanting to see the virus beaten". Her response to criticism that the UK had not locked down soon enough was the same – the situation was unprecedented, we took the right decisions informed by the best evidence at the time (28 April). The tone started to change in the lead up to Johnson's announcement of 10 May. As media stories claimed the PM would announce an easing of lockdown, Sturgeon insisted she would "not be pressured into lifting restrictions prematurely" and dropping the "Stay at Home" advice "could be a catastrophic mistake". On 10 May she broke from consensus, telling viewers she had "not seen the detail of this plan… let me emphasize at the outset that the lockdown remains in place". She added: "we should not be reading of each other's plans for the first time in the newspapers and decisions that are being taken for one nation only … should not be presented as if they apply UK wide". She repeated the message the next day, insisting Johnson's announcements "do not apply here".

Stiffer criticism of the UK government emerged after 29 June, when exemptions for quarantine after arriving from certain countries were announced from London "unfortunately without any prior consultation at all with the Scottish government". The next day, when Johnson announced a UK-wide fiscal stimulus package claiming it was comparable to Roosevelt's "New Deal" Sturgeon was "extremely underwhelmed … it's no New Deal". Three days later she referred to the "shifting sands of the UK government's position" and its "shambolic decision-making process". On 8 July, she insisted "we are not a rubber stamp for decisions taken by another government". She intensified the Scottish government's "strong representations" to the UK government to increase Scotland's borrowing powers, extend support for those losing pay and boost the UK's fiscal stimulus closer to Germany's. It is clear that while initially Sturgeon sought to appeal to all Scots, including Unionists, by maintaining a tolerant approach to the UK government, she was later able to exploit its weaknesses and inject an increasingly nationalistic tone.

This deterioration in regional and political consensus signalled a return to more adversarial media reporting as journalists struggled to report each twist and turn in UK government policy. By September, as scientists warned of a likely second wave and SAGE called for more draconian measures, regional mayors in the North of England and Midlands, where cases were rising quickest, mostly Labour and echoing Starmer's calls, joined the First Ministers in a rising chorus of opposition. Johnson's attempt to reassert control and inject hope by announcing plans to implement possible new vaccines was sabotaged by a growing crisis at No. 10 that dominated the news headlines in mid-November, culminating in the dismissal of Cummings. At this point each of the four nations of the UK had divergent strategies with Johnson appearing increasingly isolated and his government lacking a strategy for emerging from the second lockdown.

Conclusion

Between 2 and 27 March, Boris Johnson attempted to develop a public-oriented brand to reflect the four dimensions of public accountability referred to earlier: factual and unified messaging, transparency in public communication, a commitment to the public interest and maintaining the dividing line between partisan and impartial communications. Johnson initially demonstrated a commitment to the briefings, attempting to unite a fragmented nation around a Churchillian style of "Britishness" which largely drove both rallying around the flag and for a wartime community spirit to emerge. This continued during his illness and there was generally strong support for his authenticity in thanking those who had cared from him (Johnson, 2020). A commitment to accountability was mirrored in the Edinburgh briefings but with recourse to "Scottishness". This diverged after 10 May when Johnson launched what was seen as a premature and confused roadmap for lifting the lockdown. He rarely appeared thereafter and ended the briefings on 23 July while Sturgeon continued. U-turns, as well as his retention of Cummings, undermined his credibility. Sturgeon meanwhile maintained a consistent message and reflected the national consensus over lockdown. She also demonstrated a greater work ethic but her shift to an oppositional narrative could be interpreted as opportunistic, using the pandemic, and her handling of it juxtaposed with that of Johnson, to strengthen her argument for independence. The sympathy Johnson earned through his hospitalization was squandered following the Cummings debacle and failure to manage the easing of restrictions (Johnson, 2020). There has been a dramatic fall in his personal approval ratings since May 2020, while Sturgeon's popularity has been consistently high in Scotland and Starmer's has largely been positive in comparison to Johnson (YouGov, 2020a, 2020b) a situation that was only reversed as the vaccine rollout proved successful from January 2021. The data thus indicate a failure in Johnson's performance of leadership, actual and rhetorical, as well perhaps as a rejection of Westminster rule among Scots.

The pandemic accentuated three extant challenges. Johnson's bumptious style is appropriate for campaigns but less during a crisis, when alternative foci of leadership appear to have a clearer vision and mastery of the detail. The settlement between the regions of the UK with different powers devolved to

Northern Irish, Scottish and Welsh parliaments as well as elected mayors for regions or cities of the UK means there are multiple layers of governance. When regions are led by politicians from opposition parties, there is always an opportunity for conflict and the pandemic exacerbated these in the UK as well as in other nations such as France and Italy (Lilleker et al., 2021). But UK regional differences were already strained by Brexit. With England being most strongly in favour, Scotland against and Northern Ireland's stability and economy threatened by the possibility of a border either within the island of Ireland or in the Irish Sea, regional leaders took an oppositional stance to Johnson as the champion of Brexit. During the early stages, the logic was to follow the science and the Westminster approach. As cracks appeared in the credibility of the government, alternative power bases used the crisis to exert their authority. Hence the pandemic has exposed inconsistencies in the UK constitutional settlement, exacerbated rifts between parties and regions, and laid bare the deficiencies of the Johnson administration. The crisis of public communication, especially where national peculiarities accentuate tensions, creates an environment where adopting a one-nation, inclusive strategy for crisis management can prove impossible. As unity and credibility falter, oppositional forces muster arms to exacerbate the fissures.

References

Bækgaard, M., Christensen, J., Madsen, J. K., & Mikkelsen, K. S. (2020). Rallying around the flag in times of Covid-19: Societal lockdown and trust in democratic institutions. *Journal of Behavioral Public Administration*, 3(2). doi:10.30636/jbpa.32.172

BBC News. (2020). Boris Johnson 'misspoke' over North East Covid restrictions. 29 September 2020. https://www.bbc.co.uk/news/uk-54342688

Blumler, J. G., & Gurevitch, M. (1995) 'The Crisis of Public Communication'. New York: Routledge.

Blumler, J. G. (2018) The crisis of public communication, 1995–2017. *Javnost – The Public*, 25(1–2), 83–92. doi:10.1080/13183222.2018.1418799

Boin, A., Kuipers, S., & Overdijk, W. (2013). Leadership in times of crisis: A framework for assessment. *International Review of Public Administration*, 18(1), 79–91.

Calvert, J, Arbuthnot, G., & Leake, J. (2020, April 19). 38 days when Britain sleepwalked into disaster. *Sunday Times*. https://www.thetimes.co.uk/article/coronavirus-38-days-when-britain-sleepwalked-into-disaster-hq3b9tlgh

Cartwright, E. (2020, June 3). We asked people if they were breaking lockdown rules before and after the Dominic Cummings scandal – here's what they told us. *The Conversation*. https://theconversation.com/we-asked-people-if-they-were-breaking-lockdown-rules-before-and-after-the-dominic-cummings-scandal-heres-what-they-told-us-139994

Curtis, C. (2019, July 23). Everything we know about what the public think of Boris Johnson. https://yougov.co.uk/topics/politics/articles-reports/2019/07/23/everything-we-know-about-what-public-think-boris-j (accessed 26 July)

Cutts, D., Goodwin, M., Heath, O., & Surridge, P. (2020). Brexit, the 2019 General Election and the realignment of British politics. *The Political Quarterly*, 91(1), 7–23.

Davis, A. (2018). *Reckless opportunists: Elites at the end of the establishment*. Manchester: Manchester University Press.

Devlin, K. (2020, August 26). Boris Johnson's coronavirus U-turns: A timeline of government indecision during the pandemic. https://www.independent.co.uk/news/uk/politics/boris-johnson-school-meals-prime-minister-u-turns-brexit-a9568956.htm

Flinders, M. (2020). Not a Brexit election? Pessimism, promises and populism 'UK-style'. *Parliamentary Affairs*, 73(Suppl 1), 225–242.

Foley, M. (2000). *The British Presidency*. Manchester: Manchester University Press.

Garland, R. (2016). Between media and politics: Can government press officers hold the line in the age of 'political spin'? PhD Thesis. London School of Economics. http://etheses.lse.ac.uk/3463/

Garland, R., & Lilleker, D. (2021). From consensus to confusion: The UK. In Lilleker, D., Coman, I., Gregor, M., & Novelli, E. (Eds.) *Political communication and COVID-19: Governance and rhetoric in times of crisis* (pp. 165–176). London: Routledge.

Honeycombe-Foster, M. (2020, July 23). Boris Johnson hails 'sheer might of our union' in Covid-19 fight as he heads to Scotland to mark first year as Prime Minister. *PoliticsHome*. https://www.politicshome.com/news/article/boris-johnson-hails-sheer-might-of-our-union-in-covid19-fight-as-he-heads-to-scotland-to-mark-first-year-as-pm

IpsosMORI. (2020). Satisfaction with leaders and oppositions. *Scottish Political Monitor*. https://www.ipsos.com/sites/default/files/ct/news/documents/2020-10/scotland-spom-october-2020-charts.pdf

Institute for Government. (2020). Legislation to manage the coronavirus pandemic. https://www.instituteforgovernment.org.uk

James, E. H., & Wooten, L. P. (2005). Leadership as (un) usual: How to display competence in times of crisis. *Organizational Dynamics*, 34(2), 141–152.

Jetten, J., Reicher, S. D., Haslam, S. A., & Cruwys, T. (Eds.). (2020). *Together apart: The psychology of COVID-19*. London: Sage.

Johnson, J. (2020). 2020 was the year Boris Johnson threw away public trust. *The Guardian*. https://www.theguardian.com/commentisfree/2020/dec/30/2020-boris-johnson-public-trust-goodwill-barnard-castle?

Langer, A. I., & Sagarzazu, I. (2018). Bring back the party: Personalisation, the media and coalition politics. *West European Politics*, 41(2), 472–495.

Lawton, G. (2020, May 6). Can nudge theory really stop covid-19 by changing our behaviour? *New Scientist*. https://www.newscientist.com/article/mg24632811-400-can-nudge-theory-really-stop-covid-19-by-changing-our-behaviour/#ixzz6MDPXaYLO

Lee, J., & Spanier, G. (2020, May 11). 'Single-minded and unavoidable': How the government honed 'Stay Home' message. *Campaign*. https://www.campaignlive.co.uk/article/single-minded-unavoidable-government-honed-stay-home-message/1682448

Lilleker, D., Coman, I., Gregor, M., & Novelli, E. (2021). Political communication and COVID-19: Governance and rhetoric in global comparative perspective. In Lilleker, D., Coman, I., Gregor, M., & Novelli, E. (Eds.) *Political communication and COVID-19: Governance and rhetoric in times of crisis* (pp. 333–350). London: Routledge.

Marland, A. (2016). *Brand command: Canadian politics and democracy in the age of message control*. Vancouver: UBC Press.

Mason, R. (2020, June 3). Keir Starmer warns PM: get a grip or risk second coronavirus wave. *The Guardian*. https://www.theguardian.com/politics/2020/jun/02/keir-starmer-warns-pm-get-a-grip-or-risk-second-wave-of-coronavirus

Mayhew, F. (2020, February 3). Lobby journalists in walkout over 'selective' government briefings barring some titles. *Press Gazette*. https://pressgazette.co.uk/lobby-journalists-walkout-selective-government-briefings-barred-titles/

Opinium. (2020, April 27). *The political report: From the opinium/observer polling series*. Opinium Research. https://www.opinium.co.uk/wp-content/uploads/2020/05/Opinium-Political-Report-27th-April.pdf

Norgrove, D. (2017, September 17). Letter to Boris Johnson, Foreign Secretary. London: UK Statistics Authority. https://www.statisticsauthority.gov.uk/wp-content/uploads/2017/09/Letter-from-Sir-David-Norgrove-to-Foreign-Secretary.pdf

Pamment, J., & Cassinger, C. (2018). Nation branding and the social imaginary of participation: An exploratory study of the Swedish Number campaign. *European Journal of Cultural Studies*, 21(5), 561–574.

Schofield, K. (2020, May 28). Public support for government's handling of coronavirus continues to grow. *PoliticsHome*. https://www.politicshome.com/news/article/public-support-for-governments-handling-of-coronavirus-outbreak-continues-to-grow

Shipman, T. (2020, February 16). No 10 tells BBC licence fee will be scrapped. *The Times*. https://www.thetimes.co.uk/article/no-10-tells-bbc-licence-fee-will-be-scrapped-hzwb9bzsx (accessed 10 March 2020).

Sky News. (2020, October 14). Coronavirus: Labour leader demands two to three week circuit breaker lockdown over half term. https://news.sky.com/story/coronavirus-labour-leader-demands-two-to-three-week-circuit-breaker-lockdown-12103329

Smith, M. (2020, September 17). Approval of Government handling of COVID-19 hits new low. *YouGov*. https://yougov.co.uk/topics/politics/articles-reports/2020/09/17/approval-government-handling-coronavirus-sinks-low

Starmer, K. (2020, September 22). Speech at labour connected. https://labour.org.uk/press/full-text-of-keir-starmers-speech-at-labour-connected/

Yates, C. (2018). On the psychodynamics of Boris Johnson and Brexit. *New Associations*, 25, 4–5.

YouGov. (2020a, July 27). Which country do you think has handled the coronavirus outbreak better between England and Scotland? https://yougov.co.uk/topics/politics/survey-results/daily/2020/07/23/29884/2

YouGov. (2020b). Boris Johnson approval rating. https://yougov.co.uk/topics/politics/trackers/boris-johnson-approval-rating

YouGov. (2020c). COVID-19: Government handling and confidence in health authorities. https://yougov.co.uk/topics/international/articles-reports/2020/03/17/perception-government-handling-covid-19

3

BEYOND CONTROL AND RESISTANCE

The Dual Narrative of the Coronavirus Outbreak in Digital China

Yuan Zeng

Introduction

Political communication in China is known to be opaque and self-serving, characterized by the party-state's rigorous and sophisticated propaganda apparatus. In the most recent decade, the authoritarian state has further tightened its grip over the media so as to make sure political discourse is unequivocally controlled and framed in the party-state's favor. Yet the massive propaganda apparatus is never monolithic. Non-state actors, including citizens, journalists, and dissidents, are constantly contesting the official narrative in various ways. It is especially true given the affordances of social media in today's state-capitalist China, which boasts the world's largest online population and leading internet companies. Social media (predominantly Weibo and WeChat) has emerged as the main battleground for both political and ideological contestations, prompting some rosy views on the prospect of a democratic alternative in China. Yet China's increasingly authoritarian governance promises tenacious and more sophisticated state control over cyberspace. The 'New Era' governance under President Xi Jinping features a vision for 'digital China' to promote the use of digital technologies to advance the party-state's ideology control (Creemers, 2017), displaying what some scholars call 'authoritarianism 2.0' or 'networked authoritarianism' (MacKinnon, 2011). The process of narrative contestation between the state and non-state actors in most cases therefore is not an antagonistic struggle, but more a coevolution (wittingly or unwittingly) among various actors. Hence, as previous scholars rightly noted, to better understand the fluid and complex dynamics of contestations in Chinese digital spaces, one should adopt a more nuanced lens, rather than the oversimplified democratization-versus-authoritarianism dichotomy (DeLisle, Goldstein & Yang, 2016; Lee, 1994; Schneider, 2018; Yang, 2014).

Such dynamics are especially interesting to observe during times of critical events, or 'radical discontinuities' that focus public attention, when it is more likely for intense competition between different actors over meaning-making (Kraus et al., 1975; Pride, 1995; Staggenborg, 1993). The current global crisis—the coronavirus pandemic which originated in the Chinese city of Wuhan—manifests in full swing how these fluid and complex dynamics play out during critical events in digital China. Keen to promote 'stability and positivity' in public discourse as a key means to maintain regime stability, the party-state has been unequivocally framing an indoctrinating and monotonous narrative, playing down the severity of the outbreak and emphasizing the heroic and victorious efforts of the state in containing the outbreak. Social media provides a window for alternative narrative which dares question the government's initial delays and cover-ups, although such contesting narrative is often short-lived, disrupted by the country's sophisticated censorship. As we will see, the party-state, seeing the regime stability and legitimacy being challenged by the epidemic and the contesting narrative, acted swiftly to take full advantage of its paramount control over the country's digital infrastructure and the participatory nature of social media, flooding the cyberspace with official narrative and co-opting non-state actors to drown alternative narrative into 'digital exodus' and abeyance. Through a case study on the most prominent example of such citizen-generated alternative narrative, 'Fang Fang Diary', this chapter examines the extent and dynamics of narrative contestation during critical public crisis in digital China.

Political Communication in Digital China: Beyond Control and Resistance

China today is not just an authoritarian, but a digital authoritarian. In the country's most recent five-year plan laid out by President Xi Jinping, 'digital China' is highlighted as a key goal in strengthening the regime's grip in cyberspace (China Daily, 2020). As of June 2019, internet users in China have reached 854 million (CNNIC, 2019), the largest online population in the world. One of the biggest social media platforms, WeChat, reports more than 1.6 billion monthly active users in 2019. Although the country's internet penetration rate at 61% is still far behind developed countries, the sheer size of internet users and the leading mammoth social media platform providers (Alibaba, Tencent, Bytedance, Baidu) has risen as an enormous social force which the authoritarian regime has been trying to incorporate into its overall social control. With what is popularly dubbed as the 'Great Firewall' effectively in place since early noughties, Chinese cyberspace posits itself as an alternative model to the idea of an open internet (Griffiths, 2019). In this 'Chinese internet' (Yang, 2012), most large international players are excluded and content is strictly censored. State media are all over social media platforms, reaching millions of viewers. Commercial social media platforms are co-opted into the party-state's sophisticated ideology control. The country's cyberspace regulator Cyberspace Administration of China (CAC) in 2019 issued new regulation asking social media platforms, websites, and apps that use algorithms to 'build recommendation systems that promote mainstream values'. Large social media platforms such as Weibo are quick to follow the guidance, having modified their algorithm to prioritize topics promoting 'positive energy' (Gan, 2019). Such apt control over online discourse embodies an ever-nuanced propaganda that combines both direct indoctrination and manipulation in the digital age that is becoming growingly reliant on platforms and algorithms (Liu, 2019).

Where there is control, there is resistance. China's political narrative control, albeit one of the most sophisticated in the world, presents a multidirectional contestation involving multiple actors including the Party, government agencies, internet firms, and citizens, among others (Yang, 2009, 2014). Social media provides an outlet, though constantly disrupted, for alternative voices. But in a country with a huge digital divide and totalitarian tradition, the resistance is fluid and fragmented, vulnerable to co-option by the party-state. In democracies, political communication scholars have for decades found consistent patterns that citizens care little about politics (Kreiss, 2018). The political apathy is only worse in authoritarian China, where under strict state control and indoctrination, citizens have long been discouraged, if not forbidden, from public deliberation of social issues. Even with prolific (but mundane) online activities in the digital age, the younger generation in China are found to be shunning discussing politics and social issues (Mou, Atkin, & Fu, 2011). Collective and overt expression of resistance is rare, only seen during critical events where the public (usually of higher socioeconomic status) feel their well-being being threatened, such as in the event of food safety (Rauchfleisch & Schäfer, 2015; Yang, 2013). The collective resistance, if any, is soon diffused by state censorship, with discontented citizens either returning to apathy or persuaded into participating in the state propaganda. The party-state conducts massive astroturfing to hire cheerleading '50 cents army'[1] to fabricate public opinion on social media (King, Pan & Roberts, 2017). Others, bolstered by nationalistic sentiment, may voluntarily troll to flood the communication platforms with pro-government and pro-Party content, and/or attack critical opinions (Han, 2018). Repnikova and Fang (2018) call such increasingly participatory nature of the regime's narrative control 'authoritarian participatory persuasion 2.0'. It is a digital co-production of narrative, though official in nature.

---

1 State backed online commentators, said to be paid 50 cents for every post.

The intricate dynamics ranging from control, resistance, and anywhere in between as seen in the public narrative contestation and co-construction in digital China are best illustrated during the coronavirus outbreak in Wuhan, the largest global crisis of our generation. This chapter draws upon data collected through what Yang (2003) calls 'guerrilla ethnography'. Starting from 31 December 2019, when social media posts about the unknown virus first emerged in China, the author has been following Chinese media coverage and online discussion on coronavirus and Fang Fang Diary on two of the largest Chinese social media sites Weibo and WeChat. Although a less systematic method, guerrilla ethnography is considered suitable in studying the fluid and complex narrative contestations in Chinese cyberspace. The flexibility of such method is particularly helpful in capturing the dynamics of public discourse online when censors are constantly on the move, making retrospective data collection difficult.

The Absent Mainstream Media and the Digital Samizdat

The coronavirus outbreak was first picked up by alerted medics in the Chinese city of Wuhan in December 2019. A copy of local CDC (Centre for Disease Control and Prevention)'s internal notice was leaked to the public via WeChat and Weibo on 30 December, forcing local authorities to confirm the outbreak on the next day, but only to try to tone down the severity of the outbreak (Xu, 2019). State media including *People's Daily* and CCTV also resorted to their influential social media accounts to reassure the public that the virus was 'controllable' and urge the public that here was 'no need to panic'. Meanwhile, citizens including medics discussing the outbreak were swiftly censored on Weibo and WeChat. At least eight medics, after sharing information on the 'SARS-like virus'[2] via WeChat, were reprimanded by local authorities for 'mongering rumors'. The reprimand was made public by local authorities on both social media and local newspapers, and picked up by state broadcaster CCTV, in an apparent effort to stifle any unsettling information about the outbreak, so to not disrupt 'stability maintenance' (*weiwen*), the routinized mode of governance in China (Yuen, 2014). One of the eight reprimanded medics, ophthalmologist Doctor Li Wenliang, would later die from contracting the virus, just one month after the punishment.

In the space of three weeks until 20 January 2020, there was hardly any media coverage on the outbreak except for some sanitized officially sanctioned information reassuring the public that the outbreak was 'controllable and preventable', 'not transmissible between humans'. Local authorities report 'no new

---

2 In reference to its resemblance to Severe Acute Respiratory Syndrome, an earlier deadly coronavirus outbreak that originated in China and killed hundreds in 2002–2003.

cases' for 12 consecutive days. *Chutian Metropolis Daily*, the largest local tabloid in Wuhan, was extensively reporting Chinese New Year festivities and the annual provincial political meetings. Most Chinese public remained utterly unaware of the outbreak until 20 January 2020, when the virus was rampaging out of control in Wuhan and President Xi ordered to 'make efforts to curb the virus'. Only then state media finally sounded the alarm and announced the virus is indeed transmissible between humans (Xinhua, 2020a).

Just two days later, in the early hours of 23 January, Wuhan, a megacity with 11 million residents, was put under unprecedentedly strict city-wide lockdown, with little preparation, little communication to the public. State media coverage on coronavirus grew full-blown overnight but only to tone down the severity and highlight positive sides: central government mobilizing medical resources from all over the country to assist Wuhan, generous donations flooding in from businesses and citizens, people recovering from coronavirus and optimistic about the future of the city, and, most importantly, the party-state's heroic effort to safeguard the people. A week into Wuhan's lockdown, the state news agency Xinhua reassured the whole country in an uplifting report asserting that with arduous efforts mobilized into the city, 'in Wuhan, life goes on'. Except that life hardly went on as normal, with death tolls soaring, patients struggling to get a bed in the overwhelmed hospitals, residents looked on in shock and panic. Yet anything that might cast doubt over the government's insufficient response or that zooms in on individuals' sufferings found no place in official narrative. Newsrooms were receiving directives banning independent reports on the outbreak (Yang & Men, 2020). A *New York Times* investigation reveals that directives are as specific as asking online news headlines to 'steer clear of the words "incurable" and "fatal"', "to avoid causing societal panic"'. 'When covering restrictions on movement and travel', the directives read, 'the word "lockdown" should not be used' (Zhong et al., 2020).

But anxious citizens desperate for vital information were left discontented. They turned to social media. The digital infrastructure China boasts today has made it possible for the public to join the guerrilla fights against the censors online. With hospitals gravely overwhelmed, desperate families of critical coronavirus patients posted on Weibo cries for medical help (Cao & Feng, 2020). Ill-equipped frontline medical workers went to WeChat pleading for help with acute PPE shortages (Li, 2020). Ordinary Wuhan residents took it to various social media platforms to record their lockdown life, their stress and anger for lives being upended overnight while not knowing how long this ill-prepared lockdown might last (Kuo, 2020). Scholars call it 'the first major disaster in China to be "televised"—via smartphones by the participants themselves' (Repnikova, 2020). These grassroots voices collectively tell a harrowing story in stark contrast to the official narrative, inevitably subject to censorship. From January to mid-February, WeChat has censored content critical of the government, including references to Dr. Li Wenliang, the ophthalmologist reprimanded for sounding the alarm about the virus (Ruan, Knockel, & Crete-Nishihata, 2020). Even neutral health information such as patients seeking medical help was sometimes censored. Yet internet users, not new to being censored, improvised creative methods to relentlessly pass on 'sensitive' information in a relay race, in effect creating a wave of 'digital samizdat'.

The most prominent example of such digital samizdat is 'Fang Fang Diary', a Wuhan-based fiction writer Fang Fang's personal account of the outbreak, posted online daily from 25 January to 24 March, chronicling the crisis and the lockdown life in Wuhan. The 60 entries of Fang's diary include forthright criticism of the government's mishandling of the outbreak, the agony over people dying after being refused hospitalization due to overcapacity, and the desperation over Doctor Li Wenliang's death, which the state made huge effort to play down. In criticizing local officials' incompetence, Fang Fang wrote: '"Not Contagious Between People; It's Controllable and Preventable"—those eight words have transformed Wuhan into a city of blood and tears filled with endless misery' (Fang & Berry, 2020).

The grief and trauma recorded in Fang Fang Diary is no more special than other coronavirus samizdat during the time. But her established status as a prominent writer helps with its wide circulation and huge popularity, also posing a conundrum for the censors who would have to think twice before deleting her posts. Fang Fang Diary has hence stood out as a symbolic unofficial outlet in China's cyberspace during the coronavirus outbreak. The panicking public flocked in to get a glimpse of uncomfortable truth and seek solace in Fang Fang's writing, which was synchronized on four platforms: the two largest social media platforms Weibo and WeChat; Caixin, a revered business magazine; and Toutiao, a popular news-aggregation app. On Weibo alone, each entry has been viewed millions of times by the time of the writing. Fang Fang usually posted her diary around midnight on Weibo and WeChat, and many readers would stay up late just for her latest record of the day. 'I just cannot go to bed without reading Fang Fang Diary', a reader commented under one of the WeChat posts. 'Arrogant power always tries to cover things up, but Fang Fang's diary removes those covers. Clear, simple, gentle speaking, yet it has the power to move one's heart and soul', wrote another (Su, 2020).

As Fang Fang's telling of uncomfortable truth contested the official 'truth' and asked to hold the authorities to account, despite of her prominent status, it did not take censors long to act. Posts and reposts of Fang Fang Diary series were deleted from WeChat and Weibo. Her Weibo account was suspended after the tenth entry. On WeChat, Fang Fang had a friend post her diary, whose own WeChat accounts have been suspended repeatedly for publishing her diary. Social media users have been sharing and reposting Fang Fang's diary via creative ways such as taking screenshots and sharing pictures instead of text to circumvent automated keyword deletion. Fellow citizens were also inspired to post their own account of the outbreak and how their life is affected, rather than passively accept the official narrative. After Fang Fang Diary was discontinued, some social media users took on a 'diary relay' to produce another 60 entries of their personal account of the darkest lockdown.

'Traitor!'—Crashing Down the Virus and the Contesting Narrative

During the early stage of the outbreak, despite the omnipresent censorship, alternative narrative from citizens like Fang Fang and some independent news outlets could find certain compromised ways to co-exist, albeit narrowly, with official narrative in the public space. But the brief window was shut down since early February, when President Xi unequivocally demanded to tighten control over both online and offline information and streamline China's coronavirus narrative into the government's 'stirring achievements of epidemic prevention' and 'the heartwarming stories of frontline workers' (Xinhua, 2020b). The popular, but largely underground, alternative narrative of Fang Fang Diary posed as an inconvenient thorn for the party-state.

In the following months, while the virus dashed on to engulf the rest of the world, China's strong measures have largely brought the outbreak under control in the country. On 8 April, Wuhan's 76-day-long total lockdown was officially lifted. For the party-state mired in both the epidemic and public criticism, this grand victory in containing the coronavirus in the country served as a prime opportunity to steer the narrative. The mammoth propaganda apparatus geared up to mobilize traditional media, social media, opinion leaders, and ordinary citizens, in an all-front narrative battle to frame a positive story unswervingly focusing on the victorious achievements, where no cover-up or missteps have ever happened, where China, led by President Xi, has responded swiftly and decisively, showcasing the greatness of CCP in China, and probably China's superiority to the failing West.

In June, China published a meticulously worded lengthy White Paper framing the country's response to coronavirus as

> in an open, transparent, and responsible manner and in accordance with the law, China gave timely notification to the international community of the onset of a new coronavirus, and shared without reserve its experience in containing the spread of the virus and treating the infected… China has protected its people's lives, safety and health, and made a significant contribution to safeguarding regional and global public health.
> *(Xinhua, 2020d)*

The White Paper, with no mention of any government's missteps or public grievance, was extensively promoted across all state media and platforms, epitomizing the party-state's full-spectrum propaganda campaign to shape the narrative.

The sheer volume of the official narrative echoes what Roberts (2018) identifies as flooding the public discourse with coordinated official narrative to compete with information that the government wants to hide, to distract, confuse the public. This includes traditional online propaganda and astroturfing. On social media, millions of online astroturf commentators (*wang ping yuan*) are recruited to flood the cyberspace with officially sanctioned narratives. When Xinhua published the official White Paper on WeChat, comments were unanimously supportive and patriotic. 'I'm proud to be a Chinese. I feel blessed living in today's China!' read one comment. 'This is the advantage of Chinese system: put people first', read another.

In such a narrative, the origin of the outbreak was wiped out, only the state's heroic and victorious efforts were repeated tirelessly. State media also encouraged the public to participate in the 'flooding' with positive news on social media. Led by state broadcaster CCTV, the construction of two makeshift hospitals in Wuhan was livestreamed for days on multiple platforms, inviting millions of viewers to participate as 'online overseers' of the construction, which was completed within ten days and hailed as a 'China speed' miracle. On Weibo alone the livestreaming was viewed 130 million times, making it a patriotic spectacle. Nationalism has hence been further stoked to mobilize ordinary citizens to rally around the flag.

When positive stories are the only allowed narrative, anything else is delegitimized as 'smearing China'. Apart from attacking Fang Fang Diary as 'hearsay' that hyped biased 'doomsday scenarios' (*Global Times*, 2020b), state media relentlessly warned Chinese public to stay on high alert for critical voices, as critical views, according to official narrative, might be colluding with the West, which are the evil forces always trying to sabotage *our* hard earned victory. As Han (2018) observes, through imagining 'online enemies of the Chinese nation', a large number of the public have been persuaded into seeing critics as 'saboteurs of the nation'.

This tactic became convenient when in late April Fang Fang Diary was reported to be translated into English and German and published overseas. Against the backdrop of the ever-heated US-China tensions and the increasing international pressure on investigating the origin of the coronavirus and the initial negligent response in China, a tsunami of nationalistic anger has been stirred up in Chinese cyberspace. Fang Fang was accused of smearing the country by exposing its dark corners to the 'malicious West'. State media have largely avoided direct reference to Fang Fang Diary all together, but jingoistic tabloid *Global Times* did not refrain from discrediting the author as a 'liar and traitor' who 'fell from grace', and that she 'might have become just another handy tool for the West to sabotage Chinese people's efforts to fight the COVID-19 outbreak' (Cao, 2020a). The tabloid's editor-in-chief, Hu Xijin, an influential public figure with 24 million followers on Weibo, also weighed in to call Fang Fang an 'opportunist' and warned that 'the Chinese people, including those who have supported Fang Fang, will pay for her fame in the West' (Cao, 2020b). Interestingly, just a month earlier, when the window for alternative narrative was not completely shut, the same Mr. Hu commented in a different tone: 'When Wuhan faced its greatest difficulties, "Fang Fang Diary" prodded at the sore spot of our collective psych... it is one dimension in the palette of the grand national narrative' (Hu, 2020). This is just a glimpse of how China's nuanced, porous state propaganda apparatus works differently at different stages of the outbreak, to aptly legitimize the regime.

Intelligentsia polarized over the debate. Academics and literati who voiced support for Fang Fang found themselves the collateral casualties of public castigation, being singled out one by one and attacked by nationalists on social media as 'traitorous intellectuals' (*mai guo gong zhi*). Several nationalistic opinion leaders, enabled by the state propaganda apparatus, were leading the public castigation. Zhang Boli, a traditional Chinese medicine (TCM) expert who has made fame for advocating for TCM use in treating coronavirus patients, bashed Fang Fang and intellectuals sympathetic with Fang as 'a handful of Chinese intellectuals' with 'distorted values and twisted souls' (Global Times, 2020a). Zhang's comments were soon picked up and amplified by the state tabloid *Global Times* and major social media platforms, where millions of viewers were 'recommended' the content via ideologically modified algorithms. The public's comments under the posts were selectively moderated, leaving only homogenous voices hailing Zhang as the 'national hero' whereas Fang Fang and her supporters denounced as the 'traitors'. Such astroturfing, following opinion leaders endorsed by state media, echoes Repnikova and Fang's notion of 'authoritarian participatory persuasion 2.0' where the public are not forced to become propagandists, but are 'carefully cajoled into the official orbit' (Repnikova & Fang, 2018). Once again, led by the state propaganda machine, in a witting or unwitting collaboration between state and non-state actors, Fang Fang and other critical voices are collectively defined as the common enemy of patriotic Chinese people.

Dust Settled? Advancing Narrative Dominance and Digital Exodus

Five months on since Wuhan was lifted out of lockdown in April 2020, with hardly any new coronavirus cases reported and life heading back to normal in China, public attention on Fang Fang Diary seems to be waning. The party-state has regained the dominance over the coronavirus narrative, which is now full of heroic stories and patriotic pride, leaving no room for grieving. But the dust is far from settled. Still faced with the increasing international criticism over China's initial cover-ups and the country's persistent reluctance on the international call for independent investigation into the virus origin, the Chinese state propaganda machine has been trying to further this victory, attempting to rewrite the narrative about the pandemic's origins, by touting a thin theory that the virus originated outside China. Via cherry-picking isolated scientific studies and foreign media reports on unfounded speculations, state media have been finger-pointing countries including Italy (CCTV, 2020), Spain (Xinhua, 2020c), and India as the more likely origins of the virus (Hernández, 2020), and blaming imported frozen food as the potential culprit for China's outbreak (Zhao, Cao, & Fan, 2020). China hence posits itself as a glorious victim and heroic fighter, who has first alerted the world about the unknown virus and since championed in the global fight against the epidemic, showcasing the advantages of 'China model' over its crumpling Western rivals, namely, liberal democracy. The coronavirus narrative in the country has been so streamlined that the latest YouGov poll shows only half of the Chinese public believe that coronavirus was first detected in China (Wintour & Thomas, 2020).

But the party-state's seemingly victorious narrative control is by no means secure. The transnationality of political communication in today's networked world and the tech-savvy Chinese internet users make it possible to preserve sources and resources for counter-narrative which is momentarily silenced or forced into what I call 'digital exodus', where domestic contesting narrative is expelled to alternative platforms. Young activists launched digital archive projects hosted on GitHub, an open-source programming platform which is spared from Chinese censorship, to document news articles and social media posts deleted by censors in Chinese cyberspace, including Fang Fang Diary. Outside China, Fang Fang Diary was translated into English, German, and French and published as a book; mainstream English-language publications including the *New York Times*, BBC, *Financial Times*, and *Washington Post* extensively reported China's openly contentious debate over Fang Fang Diary. *Washington Post* rates the book among the '10 books to read in November', along with Barack Obama's memoir (Patrick, 2020). These alternative platforms provide sanctuaries for critical voices expelled, further complicating the political communication in digital China, preserving sources and resources for civic actions.

Similar sanctuaries also exist within the country's cyberspace, where alternative narrative is now pushed into abeyance or hibernation, instead of demise. Doctor Li Wenliang, the ophthalmologist who was reprimanded for sounding the alarm on social media and later died from contracting the virus, pleaded for more openness and transparency before his death. 'A healthy society shouldn't have just one voice' is his legacy left for his fellow compatriots. The plea, deemed dangerous by the authorities, was wiped out from public narrative in China; yet on social media, citizens have been paying tribute to Li on his Weibo page, effectively making his Weibo page a 'digital wailing wall'. On the day of his death, his Weibo page was flooded with thousands of messages in a rare outcry demanding freedom of speech, which were deleted by censors hours later. One year on, people are still posting messages—more subtle ones—on the 'digital wailing wall'. By the time of the writing, the number of messages under Doctor Li Wenliang's final Weibo post before his death has passed 1 million. Some are questioning the 'reprimand'; some are simply reposting the doctor's final plea for openness and transparency. In a discreet way, a collective memory different from the officially sanctioned version is being preserved in some sanctuaries in Chinese cyberspace.

Discussion: Framing Critical Events in Digital Age—Analytical Implications of the Chinese Case

By examining how 'Fang Fang Diary' contested with the official narrative and became part of the public discourse in China, this chapter combs through the rarely seen open narrative contestation between state and non-state actors and the intricate dynamics between various actors in digital China. Different from what Entman (2003) calls the continuum of frame contestation in democracies, where narrative contests fall somewhere between complete frame dominance and frame parity, in authoritarian China, with the party-state holding firm grip over resources and tactics necessary for discursively defining public issues, official frame dominance has long been the norm. But in times of critical events such as the coronavirus outbreak, norms are disrupted; non-state actors, galvanized by a collective sense of urgency, resort to social media to fill the information vacuum, creating a contesting narrative that alarms the party-state. Yet the latter, adjusting tactics in light of the radical disruption, further mobilizing political and symbolic resources on a large scale, soon regain narrative dominance. Criticism of the government is hence diluted, forced into digital exodus or abeyance.

This Chinese case of narrative contestation over the coronavirus outbreak illustrates what political communication scholars call 'the power of critical events' (Lee & Chan, 2010; Schudson, 1992). Critical events as radical disruptions have the power to engage the public in intensive communication activities, where strong emotions are usually aroused, triggering 'an interactive dynamics' and 'discursive contests of how the meanings of the event should be deciphered' (Lee & Chan, 2010, p. 10). At the start of the coronavirus outbreak, out of fear, misery, and anxiety, the usually politically apathetic Chinese public have overnight fixated to this public crisis. The usual censorship is also disrupted, leaving a window (albeit fleeting) for less censored information about the outbreak, critical voices questioning the government, and even rare calls for speech freedom. Recognizing the gravity of the redefining power of such a critical event, the party-state didn't wait long to shut down the window for non-official narrative. With nationalistic sentiment mobilized and grief downplayed in the propaganda campaign, the public, still fixated on the outbreak which is now spiraling into a pandemic, are persuaded into co-constructing the official narrative of the coronavirus outbreak. The public crisis of the coronavirus outbreak is hence framed as a triumphant victory of Xi's leadership, the highlight moment for China's authoritarian model.

In framing the coronavirus narrative as such, apart from the usual tactics of selection and salience, the party-state resorts to all resources to flood both traditional media and cyberspace with favorable rhetoric; the public are also mobilized to participate in large volume to cement the official narrative and drown out contesting narrative. The key to this mass participation is to fuel nationalism: by framing boundaries to clearly separate 'us' from 'them', 'patriots' from 'traitors', the party-state persuades the public into forming a patriotic alignment while alienating others. As Pan and Kosicki (2001) note, through boundary framing, 'cultural categories are reproduced and enriched and the sociological boundaries of these physical units are also reinforced and remapped' (Pan & Kosicki, 2001, p. 44). The spectrum of diverse voices over the mess of an unknown lethal virus is remapped into the opposing dichotomy of 'us' versus 'them'. The contesting narrative—Fang Fang and her supporters—thereby becomes the 'traitor', and is made into part of the symbolic resources the party-state mobilizes into framing the nationalistic narrative which serves to legitimize and reinforce the party rule amidst the public crisis.

Finally, this case study shows the complex role social media plays in narrative contestation in authoritarian China. Social media is neither a democratic panacea nor an authoritarian game changer. It is true that with paramount control over media and the digital infrastructure, the party-state is cementing its narrative dominance in public discourse. However, no control is total. Resistance, though fluid and fragmented, is resilient especially during times of disruptive critical events, when the anxious public resort to social media as an alternative public arena, leading to some salient narrative contestation. Yet the decentralized and participatory nature of social media works both ways. Thanks to the party-state's proactive co-option of social media platforms, official narrative takes the upper hand overnight, and further nurtures a nationalistic momentum which goads the public to participate in the meaning-making in favor of the party-state.

The complex dynamics of narrative contestation as shown in this case study echoes what Jiang (2016) calls the 'coevolution' of civil space, uncivil space (exemplified here by nationalism emboldened online) and authoritarian control in digital China. The transnationality of political communication and digital affordances of this new global power add a further facet of the intricate dynamics, where domestic alternative narrative is found in digital exodus rather than dying out, potentially incubating tactical repertoire for future contestation. All these factors are promising a nuanced and complex narrative contestation in digital China far beyond the oversimplified control-versus-resistance, or democratization-versus-authoritarianism dichotomy.

References

Cao, S. (2020a, April 8). Chinese vigilant on deifying writer Fang Fang amid publication of Wuhan diary in English. *Global Times*. Retrieved from https://www.globaltimes.cn/content/1185055.shtml

Cao, S. (2020b, April 23). 'Wuhan diary' writer escalates online spat, wears out dwindling fans. *Global Times*. Retrieved from https://www.globaltimes.cn/content/1186483.shtml

Cao, Y., & Feng, Y. (2020, February 28). Coronavirus patients seeking help on Weibo. *Southern Weekly*. Retrieved from https://www.infzm.com/contents/178003

China Daily. (2020). Course set for long-term development. Retrieved from http://epaper.chinadaily.com.cn/a/202010/30/WS5f9b49fea31099a2343515ca.html

CCTV. (2020, November 19). New study reveals coronavirus may have already existed in Italy since September 2019. Retrieved from http://m.news.cctv.com/2020/11/19/ARTIlNgkPWsSsBzhXsb97ouJ201119.shtml

CNNIC. (2019). Statistical report on internet development in China. Retrieved from http://cnnic.com.cn/IDR/ReportDownloads/201911/P020191112539794960687.pdf

Creemers, R. (2017). Cyber China: Upgrading propaganda, public opinion work and social management for the twenty-first century. *Journal of Contemporary China*, 26(103), 85–100.

DeLisle, J., Goldstein, A., & Yang, G. (2016). The internet, social media, and a changing China. In DeLisle, J., Goldstein, A., & Yang, G. (Eds.). *The internet, social media, and a changing China*. Philadelphia: University of Pennsylvania Press, pp. 1–27.

Entman, R. M. (2003). Cascading activation: Contesting the White House's frame after 9/11. *Political Communication*, 20(4), 415–432.

Fang, F., & Berry, M. (2020). *Wuhan diary: Dispatches from a quarantined city*. New York: HarperCollins.

Gan, N. (2019, September 11). China's internet regulator orders online AI algorithms to promote 'mainstream values'. *South China Morning Post*. Retrieved from https://www.scmp.com/news/china/politics/article/3026784/chinas-internet-regulator-orders-online-ai-algorithms-promote

Global Times. (2020a, May 14). Some Chinese intellectuals hold distorted values, represented by Fang Fang: Academician Zhang Boli. Retrieved from https://www.globaltimes.cn/content/1188347.shtml

Global Times. (2020b, May 15). Fang Fang and her followers criticized for weaponizing netizen's post to create biased narrative. Retrieved from https://www.globaltimes.cn/content/1188474.shtml

Griffiths, J. (2019). *The great firewall of China: How to build and control an alternative version of the internet*. Zed Books Ltd.

Han, R. (2018). *Contesting cyberspace in China: Online expression and authoritarian resilience*. New York: Columbia University Press.

Hernández, J. (2020, December 6). China peddles falsehoods to obscure origin of Covid pandemic. *The New York Times*. Retrieved from https://www.nytimes.com/2020/12/06/world/asia/china-covid-origin-falsehoods.html

Hu, X. (2020). Hu Xijin on Fang Fang Diary Phenomenon. Retrieved from https://news.sina.com.cn/c/2020-03-19/doc-iimxxsth0267775.shtml

Hui, M. & Li, J. (2020). China's coronavirus outbreak is unfolding in a new age of information—And surveillance. *Quartz*. Retrieved from https://qz.com/1790719/china-coronavirus-outbreak-unfolds-in-a-new-age-of-information/

Jiang, M. (2016). The co-evolution of the internet, (un) civil society & authoritarianism in China. In DeLisle, J., Goldstein, A., & Yang, G. (Eds.), *The internet, social media, and a changing China*. Philadelphia, PA: University of Pennsylvania Press, pp. 28–48.

King, G., Pan, J., & Roberts, M. E. (2017). How the Chinese government fabricates social media posts for strategic distraction, not engaged argument. *American Political Science Review, 111*(3), 484–501.

Kraus, S., Davis, D., Lang, G. E., & Lang, K. (1975). Critical events analysis. In S.H. Chaffee (Ed.), *Political communication: Issues and strategies for research*. Beverly Hills, CA and London: SAGE, pp. 196–216.

Kreiss, D. (2018). The media are about identity, not information. In Boczkowski, P. J., & Papacharissi, Z. (Eds.), *Trump and the media*. Cambridge, MA: MIT Press, pp. 93–99.

Kuo, L. (2020, March 15). Write a diary, take action: Hubei residents on fighting coronavirus anxiety. *The Guardian*. Retrieved from https://www.theguardian.com/world/2020/mar/15/write-a-diary-take-action-hubei-residents-on-fighting-coronavirus-anxiety

Lee, C. C. (1994). Ambiguities and contradiction: Issues in China's changing political communication. *Gazette* (Leiden, Netherlands), *53*(1–2), 7–21.

Lee, F. L., & Chan, J. M. (2010). *Media, social mobilisation and mass protests in post-colonial Hong Kong: The power of a critical event*. London and New York: Routledge.

Li, C. (2020, January 31). Protective Supplies in Shortage at Xiehe Hospital. *Yicai*. retrieved from https://www.yicai.com/news/100484329.html

Liu, H. (2019). *Propaganda: Ideas, discourses and its legitimization*. London and New York: Routledge.

MacKinnon, R. (2011). Liberation technology: China's "networked authoritarianism". *Journal of Democracy, 22*(2), 32–46.

Mou, Y., Atkin, D., & Fu, H. (2011). Predicting political discussion in a censored virtual environment. *Political Communication, 28*(3), 341–356.

Pan, Z., & Kosicki, G. M. (2001). Framing as a strategic action in public deliberation. In Reese, S. D., Gandy, O. H. Jr., & Grant, A. E. (Eds.), *Framing public life: Perspectives on media and our understanding of the social world*. Mahwah, NJ: Lawrence Erlbaum Associates, pp. 35–65.

Patrick, B. (2020, November 1). 10 books to read in November. *The Washington Post*. Retrieved from https://www.washingtonpost.com/entertainment/books/2020-books-november/2020/10/31/51da2450-1ae4-11eb-aeec-b93bcc29a01b_story.html

Pride, R. A. (1995). How activists and media frame social problems: Critical events versus performance trends for schools. *Political Communication, 12*(1), 5–26.

Repnikova, M. (2020). The subtle muckrakers of the coronavirus epidemic. *The New York Times*. Retrieved from https://www.nytimes.com/2020/02/05/opinion/coronavirus-china-news-journalism.html

Repnikova, M., & Fang, K. (2018). Authoritarian participatory persuasion 2.0: netizens as thought work collaborators in China. *Journal of Contemporary China, 27*(113), 763–779.

Roberts, M. E. (2018). *Censored: Distraction and diversion inside China's Great Firewall*. Princeton: Princeton University Press.

Rauchfleisch, A., & Schäfer, M. S. (2015). Multiple public spheres of Weibo: A typology of forms and potentials of online public spheres in China. *Information, Communication & Society, 18*(2), 139–155.

Ruan, L., Knockel, J., & Crete-Nishihata, M. (2020). Censored contagion: How information on the coronavirus is managed on Chinese social media. *The Citizen Lab*. Retrieved from https://citizenlab.ca/2020/03/censored-contagion-how-information-on-the-coronavirus-is-managed-on-chinese-social-media/

Schneider, F. (2018). *China's digital nationalism*. Oxford: Oxford University Press.

Schudson, M. (1992). *Watergate in American memory: How we remember, forget, and reconstruct the past*. New York: Basic Books.

Staggenborg, S. (1993). Critical events and the mobilization of the pro-choice movement. *Research in Political Sociology*, 6(1), 319–345.

Su, A. (2020, March 21). Two months into coronavirus lockdown, her online diary is a window into life and death in Wuhan. *Los Angeles Times*. Retrieved from https://www.latimes.com/world-nation/story/2020-03-21/china-wuhan-coronavirus-diary-fang-fang

Wintour, P., & Thomas, T. (2020, October 27). China loses trust internationally over coronavirus handling. *The Guardian*. Retrieved from https://www.theguardian.com/world/2020/oct/27/china-loses-trust-internationally-over-coronavirus-handling

Xinhua. (2020a, January 20). Xi orders resolute efforts to curb virus spread. Retrieved from http://www.xinhuanet.com/english/2020-01/20/c_138721535.htm

Xinhua. (2020b, February 3). Central politburo meets to discuss coronavirus containment. Retrieved from http://www.xinhuanet.com/politics/2020-02/03/c_1125527334.htm

Xinhua. (2020c). News analysis: Spain detects coronavirus from wastewater sampled in March 2019. Retrieved from http://www.xinhuanet.com/2020-06/27/c_1126165776.htm

Xinhua. (2020d, June 7). Fighting Covid-19 China in Action. Retrieved from http://www.xinhuanet.com/english/2020-06/07/c_139120424.htm

Yang, G. (2003). The Internet and the rise of a transnational Chinese cultural sphere. *Media, Culture & Society*, 25(4), 469–490.

Yang, G. (2009). *The power of the Internet in China: Citizen activism online*. New York: Columbia University Press.

Yang, G. (2012). A Chinese Internet? History, practice, and globalization. *Chinese Journal of Communication*, 5(1), 49–54.

Yang, G. (2013). Contesting food safety in the Chinese media: Between hegemony and counter-hegemony. *The China Quarterly*, 337–355.

Yang, G. (2014). Political contestation in Chinese digital spaces: Deepening the critical inquiry. *China Information*, 28(2), 135–144.

Yang, Y. & Men, Y. (2020). 疫情與輿情十七年：被瞞報的SARS與被孤立的武漢 [Plague and public sentiment in 17 years]. *The Initium*. Retrieved from https://theinitium.com/article/20200125-mainland-wuhan-sars-pneumonia-publicity/

Yuen, W. H. S. (2014). The politics of Weiwen: Stability as a source of political legitimacy in post-Tiananmen China. *European Consortium for Political Research*, 1–31.

Zhao, Y., Cao, S., & Fan, L. (2020, December 6). Could cold-chain imports have sparked Wuhan early Covid-19 outbreak? *Global Times*. retrieved from https://www.globaltimes.cn/content/1209141.shtml

Zhong, R., Mozur, P., Kao, J., & Krolik, A. (2020, December 19). No 'negative' news: How China censored the coronavirus. *The New York Times*. Retrieved from https://www.nytimes.com/2020/12/19/technology/china-coronavirus-censorship.html

4
COVID-19 IN CHILE

A Health Crisis amidst a Political Crisis amidst a Social Crisis

Ingrid Bachmann, Sebastián Valenzuela, and Arturo Figueroa-Bustos

Introduction

The COVID-19 pandemic is a crisis all-around. With its impact on social and economic life, tensions about containment measures, and polarization of public support of governmental action to mitigate the spread of the virus, it is a health crisis as much as an economic, social, and political one (Allcott et al., 2020; Lin & Meissner, 2020; Van Bavel et al., 2020). Thus, any examination of government communication about this pandemic must consider prevailing political and socioeconomic conditions in which public officials are situated when managing the emergency (e.g., Canel & Sanders, 2016; Crozier, 2007).

In this regard, Chile represents a poignant example of how government communication about the pandemic is contingent upon prevailing political conditions. As we review below, by the time COVID-19 hit the country in March 2020, the government led by Sebastián Piñera—Chile's center-right president—encountered a new public communication scenario: skeptical, mobilized citizens, new oppositional media, a stalled economy, and a polarized political scenario as not seen since the 1980s. Unlike the cholera outbreak of 1991—the last major epidemic in the country—the coronavirus found Chileans at a major sociopolitical juncture, following the massive riots of October 2019 that led to a referendum for a new constitution in October 2020. Hence, when COVID-19 spread to Chile, the political and economic upheaval triggered by the protests would hinder relationships with key stakeholders in the adoption of policies to minimize the spread of the virus.

Based on data from an original panel survey fielded in 2019–2020 and a narrative analysis of public discourse of key government interventions during the first six months of the pandemic in Chile, this chapter pays attention to

DOI: 10.4324/9781003170051-5

individuals' perceptions toward the government's handling of the coronavirus crisis, and the erratic strategy of health officials and the president himself. The administration clashed with the medical and scientific community, reporters, and politicians, and as a result the country has endured both the public health and economic consequences of the pandemic, making an exemplary case of things that have gone wrong.

The Political Context

Often regarded as a stable democracy in Latin America with sound policy-making and an overall strong free-market economy, Chile has long been experiencing increasing levels of political disaffection and a growing elite-mass cleavage. Thirty years after the end of Augusto Pinochet's civic-military dictatorship (1973–1990), Chile still functions under the neoliberal policies and constitutional system inherited from the authoritarian regime. While successful at reducing poverty levels, there is a shared perception that the "Chilean model" has perpetuated all sorts of inequalities (González & Morán, 2020; Somma et al., 2020).

It was against this background that social unrest exploded in the country on 18 October 2019, when massive protests that started in the capital city of Santiago in response to a subway fare increase turned into violent riots, clashes with the police, looting, and arson. When violence expanded to other cities, the Piñera administration decreed a state of emergency, handed control of security to the Army, and placed most of the country under curfew for the first time since 1987 (González & Morán, 2020; Somma et al., 2020). A week later, more than 1.2 million people gathered in downtown Santiago in the largest pacific demonstration since the fall of Pinochet to demand a new constitution.

Unforeseen by the country's political and social elites, the so-called *estallido social* (social outbreak) of October 2019 was long in the making. With vanishing political identities (less than one in five voters identifies with a political party) and large protests in 2006, 2011, and 2018, politics on the streets began to be conceived as an alternative to institutional politics (Bargsted & Maldonado, 2018; Donoso, 2013; Valenzuela, 2013). A succession of corruption scandals involving political and business elites, and an economic growth that stalled for most of 2010–2020, added to mounting social discontent (Bargsted et al., 2017; Cabalín, 2014: Donoso, 2013; González & Morán, 2020; Somma et al., 2020). At the core of citizens' grievances laid the unfulfilled promises of the "Chilean model," where expectations of new middle-class sectors and the strengthening of upward intergenerational social mobility clashed with vulnerability, income inequality, and increasing financial debt (Garcés, 2019; González & Morán, 2020; Luna, 2016).

While the country has a free press, most media outlets in Chile have a conservative, pro-business leaning, in contrast to an increasingly progressive public.

Concerns about the highly concentrated and homogeneous media system coexist with high levels of political parallelism, for most media owners are closely related to the political and economic elites (Araya, 2014; Bachmann & Mujica, 2019; Cabalín, 2014). Thus, as the discourse against "elite abuse" included mainstream media, the public was avid for alternative outlets (e.g., activist websites, citizen journalism), which gained steam after the 2019 riots (Grassau et al., 2019; Luna, Toro, & Valenzuela, 2021). Furthermore, Chile has been experiencing an information disorder for a while, as evidenced by the growth of misinformation on social media (Grassau et al., 2019; Valenzuela et al., 2019). Thus, when COVID-19 arrived in March 2020, it encountered a country with a weakened government, a mobilized population, and an ongoing crisis.

Public Perceptions of Government Performance

From the beginning, there were doubts that the coronavirus would result in a substantial rally-round-the-flag effect in Chile. In a polarized nation, the argument went, it would take more than a pandemic to unify citizens in the face of a threat, more so when political leadership was at record-low levels of approval and the government's ability to manage this—or any other crisis, for that matter—was heavily under question. However, overall public approval for Piñera, which was extremely low at the start of the crisis, did see a significant increase during the first months, going from 15% in March up to 24% in May 2020 (see Criteria, 2020), a boost not seen in his three years in office and, we would argue, marked by important diverging views among the public with regard to the government. The pandemic also made evident that the troubling levels of inequality that had spurred the 2019 protests also included health access and epidemiological outcomes (Lincoln, 2020), further highlighting the cleavage between the haves and the have-nots.

To shed light on public perceptions of government performance, we analyzed data from an original panel survey. Wave 1 was launched after the October 2019 protests, while Wave 2 included the peak of the first wave of the pandemic, May–June 2020.[1] At the aggregate level, trust in government (measured

---

1 We used the opt-in internet panel administered by Tren Digital, a think tank housed in the School of Communications at Pontificia Universidad Católica de Chile (see Grassau et al., 2019, 2020). Quota sampling was applied to make sure the sample matched the country's adult population in terms of age, gender, and socioeconomic status. Of the 1,639 Wave 1 participants (completion rate: 72%; fielded: 6–14 November 2019), we were able to recontact 589 participants (attrition rate: 64%). However, 71 participants were removed because they did not finish the study, finished it in less than one-third (i.e., five minutes or less) of the median time of completion (14 minutes), or were living abroad by the time of Wave 2. Hence, the final sample consisted of 518 participants. A benchmark analysis showed that this sample resembled the age ($M = 42.8$, SD = 15.2),

on a 5-point scale) increased slightly between waves, from a mean of 1.93 to 2.23, a difference that was statistically significant ($p < 0.001$). This overall rally-round-the-flag effect, however, masked an important polarization in attitudes toward government. As shown in Table 4.1, while high-income respondents (a traditional base of support for the Piñera administration) became increasingly confident in government during the pandemic, those who supported the October 2019 protests grew significantly disaffected.

Importantly, respondents who experienced a significant cost in economic terms by the pandemic were also the ones who exhibited the largest increase in trust in government. This may be explained by the massive handouts and

TABLE 4.1 Ordered Logistic Regression of Trust in Government

	Trust in Government in Wave 2	
	(1)	(2)
Sociodemographics		
Age	0.01	−0.00
	(0.01)	(0.01)
Gender (female)	0.40	0.34
	(0.33)	(0.33)
Household income	**0.30***	**0.43****
	(0.15)	**(0.16)**
Santiago resident	−0.46	−0.44
	(0.35)	(0.36)
Political Orientations		
Political interest in Wave 1	−0.15	−0.12
	(0.13)	(0.13)
Trust in government in Wave 1	**1.18****	**1.29****
	(0.19)	**(0.20)**
Left-wing ideology	−0.75	−0.55
	(0.56)	(0.53)
Center/moderate	0.26	0.35
	(0.72)	(0.74)
Right-wing ideology	0.56	0.63
	(0.46)	(0.46)
Supports protests in Wave 1	**−0.88***	**−0.92***
	(0.41)	**(0.39)**

(Continued)

gender (51.7% female), region of residence (43.9% living in the metropolitan region), and social media use (82.6% use Facebook) distributions of the target population. Still, respondents had higher levels of household income (Mdn = CLP 800,001 to 1,500,000 monthly) and access to private health insurance (39%), which suggests caution in terms of interpreting the sample as nationally representative.

	Trust in Government in Wave 2	
	(1)	(2)
News Media		
Legacy news exposure in Wave 2	0.19	0.15
	(0.13)	(0.13)
Social media news exposure in Wave 2	0.03	0.02
	(0.07)	(0.07)
Experience with COVID-19		
Economic costs		**0.38***
		(0.19)
Psychological costs		−0.32
		(0.22)
Health costs		0.01
		(0.17)
Fear of COVID-19		0.39
		(0.24)
Cutoff 1	2.17**	3.98*
	(0.84)	(1.62)
Cutoff 2	3.55***	5.42***
	(0.87)	(1.64)
Cutoff 3	5.41***	7.35***
	(0.99)	(1.69)
Cutoff 4	9.19***	11.29***
	(1.16)	(1.90)
Observations	454	454
Pseudo R^2	0.25	0.27

Standard errors in parentheses. $^*p < 0.05$, $^{**}p < 0.01$, $^{***}p < 0.001$.

economic relief package launched by the government to tackle the economic crisis in the first months of the pandemic. Other than this effect, however, respondents' experiences with the pandemic at the personal level had little role in explaining changes in the levels of trust in government.

Table 4.2 further confirms that people's response to government action related to the COVID-19 crisis was colored by political attitudes, rather than by experiences and beliefs about the coronavirus. When regressing evaluations of how the government was handling the pandemic in Chile, the most important predictors were trust in government in 2019 and support for the October 2019 protests. None of the variables about COVID-19 had a significant relationship with performance ratings.

TABLE 4.2 Linear Regression of Evaluation of Government Performance in Handling the Pandemic

	Evaluation of Government Performance in Wave 2	
	(1)	(2)
Sociodemographics		
Age	0.02*	0.02*
	(0.01)	(0.01)
Gender (female)	0.45*	0.37
	(0.20)	(0.22)
Household income	0.08	0.10
	(0.11)	(0.11)
Santiago resident	−0.21	−0.20
	(0.23)	(0.24)
Political Orientations		
Political interest in Wave 1	0.02	0.02
	(0.10)	(0.09)
Trust in government in Wave 1	0.59***	0.61***
	(0.12)	(0.12)
Left-wing ideology	−0.62*	−0.55*
	(0.27)	(0.28)
Center/moderate	−0.01	0.05
	(0.45)	(0.47)
Right-wing ideology	0.46	0.48
	(0.34)	(0.35)
Supports protests in Wave 1	−0.87***	−0.89***
	(0.22)	(0.23)
News Media		
Legacy news exposure in Wave 2	0.11	0.08
	(0.07)	(0.07)
Social media news exposure in Wave 2	−0.06	−0.07
	(0.04)	(0.04)
Experience with COVID-19		
Economic costs		0.04
		(0.11)
Psychological costs		−0.01
		(0.12)
Health costs		0.01
		(0.10)
Fear of COVID-19		0.18
		(0.15)
Constant	1.36**	0.62
	(0.46)	(0.91)
Observations	454	454
R^2	0.54	0.55

Standard errors in parentheses. *$p < 0.05$, **$p < 0.01$, ***$p < 0.001$.

The Lackluster Governmental Response to the COVID-19 Pandemic

Since the pandemic arrived in Chile, President Piñera took a secondary role in government communications, which is somewhat surprising considering the strong presidentialism of Chilean politics. Throughout the crisis, Piñera has only occasionally addressed the country or held press conferences, and he even postponed his annual message of the state of the nation to Congress. Instead, cabinet members were the main executive politicians interacting with stakeholders and engaging with the media to inform and explain about policy measures to contain the spread of the virus. Because Piñera is neither a good public speaker—indeed, he is known for his gaffes, and seldom uses social media—nor a figure with much remaining political capital, the decision to keep him out of the spotlight might have been part of a strategy to portray government decisions in the best possible light and win public support.[2]

Despite announcements of being long-prepared for managing the coronavirus pandemic, the reaction of government officials once COVID-19 reached Chile left much to be improved. The response was slow, more reactive than proactive, and unclear about its aims. Its communication was not any better. While the first confirmed COVID-19 case was reported in the first week of March 2020, it would take several weeks for the government to have an official standing about personal protection equipment, define protocols on how to prevent contagions, or adopt official guidelines to define confinement measures in different parts of the country, with government official insisting lockdowns would be exceptional. An advisory committee formed by a panel of experts was convened only in late March, well after the virus had arrived in Chile, and its members complained several times about their access to data and the willingness of the government to heed the scientific community advice (Bartlett, 2020; Fuentes & Sanders, 2020). However, by the end of March, with about 300 new daily cases, the government issued a seven-hour nightly curfew and started a lockdown in several cities, while also rolling a plan to provide massive testing and secure additional ventilators. Wearing a mask in public became mandatory, and officials regularly appeared on press conference to announce new or revised policies with regard to closures of business and schools, restrictions to public events, permits to move around areas in lockdowns, some of them *after* city councils had already decreed to close schools and shopping malls, and public gatherings of more than 20 people (e.g., Bartlett, 2020; Beaubien, 2020; Sherwood & Ramos, 2020).

---

2 Piñera's lesser role in the public eye is more surprising when considering that Chile was amidst a particular electoral context. In the wake of 2019 protests, lawmakers agreed to hold referendum on the country's dictatorship-era constitution. Originally scheduled for April 2020, the vote was postponed to October 2020 because of the pandemic. Nearly 80% of voters approved drafting a new constitution, a process taking place between 2021 and 2022 (Elliott & Bartlett, 2020).

Government officials insisted they were basing their decisions on medical and scientific guidelines, but political and economic considerations weighed heavily on policymakers. When prompted by journalists about the clinical attributes of their efforts to contain the pandemic, officials would often deflect, and insist they were doing what was necessary. In press conferences and government websites, the official messages avoided talking about scientific evidence supporting their approach, despite public cynicism about such responses (Bartlett, 2020; Sherwood & Ramos, 2020). The government's persistent failure to provide full access to relevant data also caused tensions with scientists, to the extent that in April 2020 the Millennium Institute for Foundational Research on Data (IMFD), a prominent academic center, pulled out of the Ministry of Health's COVID-19 advisory committee.

Moreover, during the first few weeks of the pandemic it became evident that the erratic communication from government officials stemmed from lack of strategy. Other than the state of emergency proclaimed early on, there were no long-term plans, neither for containing the spread of coronavirus nor for the social and economic outcomes of the pandemic (see Malinowski et al., 2020), and no clear guidelines about how to proceed. Chile's inaction was more evident in comparison to other neighboring countries. Argentina, for instance, went into lockdown early on, but Chilean health officials opted for so-called dynamic quarantines in specific neighborhoods and parts of the country, in which residents in one area were ordered to stay at home while those in bordering districts could freely circulate. In so doing, they clashed with medical experts, scientists, and political opponents alike, which ended up fostering a political climate not favorable for managing a large-scale crisis. Furthermore, it threatened to revive social unrest, especially among those suffering the economic toll of the pandemic (Bartlett, 2020; Contesse, 2020; Malinowski et al., 2020).

Confusing and misleading messages further complicated the handling of the pandemic. On 9 April 2020, then Health Minister Jaime Mañalich announced plans to issue a so-called COVID card for patients once discharged from isolation, as proof of their recovery and immunity. This contravened warnings from Chile's Medical Association about the lack of scientific evidence showing people ceased to be contagious in a short time, or the calls for caution by the World Health Organization regarding any immunity passport. Three weeks later, Mañalich ended up dismissing the original idea—immunity certification was not possible (Sherwood & Ramos, 2020). Along the same lines, numerous changes were made on the fly to the rather complicated scheme of permits that allowed citizens to move around lockdown areas (which also changed from district to district) and further confused citizens. The requirement of a unique password to enter the police website to request weekly permits to circulate was postponed on several occasions due to the problem that this represented for certain sectors of the Chilean population with low digital literacy or lack of internet access: senior citizens, inhabitants of rural areas, and low-income individuals.

It would soon become clear that the policy measures adopted by the government were not only erratic, but they were not working either. Despite early claims of success, cases spiraled and hospitals were full. Further, officials were overconfident about Chile's ability to contain the virus, and were not really expecting the rapid infection rates. In the words of Lincoln (2020, p. 395), the Chilean government's "self-flattering image could have caused its leaders to underestimate its vulnerability to the virus." In a divided and inequal country, the pandemic further stressed the inequalities and further alienated citizens. It would also alienate the main stakeholders for a successful strategy against the spread of COVID-19.

Game Changers in Political Communication

The COVID-19 crisis also changed the typical flows of political communication in Chile. Rather than the President, it was the ministers and undersecretaries who made the official communications regarding the pandemic, in particular those in charge of public health, internal affairs, the economy, labor, and education. President Piñera tried to set up a parallel agenda that had little to do with major developments of the COVID-19 crisis, consisting in brief press conferences and photo-ops during the afternoon, such as the establishment in August 2020 of two new national parks. Several opinion leaders harshly criticized Piñera's profile during the pandemic, as he mostly left the communication of the most critical matters facing the nation to his subordinates. Others stated that it was wise to delegate the more technical issues associated with the pandemic to those directly in charge, since Piñera clearly was not good at public messaging. While understandable as a strategy to shield the presidential figure, it did not work in the long run. Piñera's public evaluation saw an important boost in the first three months of the pandemic—although remaining at somewhat low levels—but by October 2020 his approval ratings had fallen again under 15% and were only slightly higher than a year before (see Criteria, 2020).

On 15 May 2020, almost two months after the first case in the country, the Greater Santiago area—the most populous of the country—was put on total lockdown. However, six weeks earlier, when Europe was registering record numbers of daily infections and deaths in the first wave, then Health Minister Jaime Mañalich insisted that the Chilean government had been prepared "since January [2020]" to deal with the pandemic, and that the country was doing much better than neighboring countries. In an interview with the national public network, he dismissed requests by citizens and experts for total lockdown as something "foolish and unnecessary," and argued that since the virus was new, spur-of-the-moment reactions were unadvisable. "What happens if [the virus] mutates and becomes a good person?" he asked. Two months later, when COVID-19 infections surged after reaching low-income communities and with hospitals on the verge of collapse, Mañalich admitted on another interview that "he was not aware of the magnitude" of the level of poverty and overcrowding in the country's large cities, a situation that complicated quarantines and favored contagions, more so among a massive off-the-books workforce that was also enduring the economic toll of the pandemic. The man leading the country's strategy to curtail COVID-19 was thus disconnected from a large part of the population, once again evidencing the divide between the elites who run the government and the rest of society.

Mañalich's early proclamations of success would prove wrong, and his self-assured character and confrontational attitude, especially with regard to journalists and the scientific community, made his tenure in office unfeasible—he resigned on 13 June 2020. Since then, he has been accused of manipulating COVID-19 data and knowingly underplaying the scope of the crisis, and by December 2020 he was under a criminal investigation. Overall, President Piñera did not comment on these situations, other than to insist that the Health Minister was doing his best and that policymakers were constantly consulting scientists.

The inconsistent and misleading messages from the government included several statements about a state of "new normalcy" and talks of "gradually and safely" going back to business, just weeks before the death toll started to increase. During daily press conferences in April, government officials insisted on a return to a less restrictive scenario, in order to reactivate the economy. The undersecretary of Health, Paula Daza, went to the extent of announcing that soon it would be possible to "go out for coffee with friends." The government also called for public sector employees to return to their workplaces for in-person tasks (which was rejected by civil servant unions and eventually dismissed by the Comptroller General office), the return of children to schools, and the reopening of shopping centers and businesses under certain operation protocols. Similarly to what happened in the United States (Pew Research Center, 2020), public opinion in general considered it was too early to lift COVID-19 restrictions, and only those strongly supporting the government would support reopening business and schools (Criteria, 2020; see also Grassau et al., 2020).

However, and despite criticism from the Medical Association, scientists, and politicians from different parties, officials started advancing by the end of April 2020 the idea of a "safe return," mimicking other slogans used in government-backed programs, such as "safe stadium" (regarding football-related violence) or "safe classroom" (to curtail violence within schools). The argument went that along with the COVID-19 pandemic, there was an "unemployment pandemic" in full swing, and that the entire country needed to resume work activities. President Piñera even claimed that since the estimated peak of infections was already being reached, cases could only go down or plateau, thus allowing for a safe return to business as usual.

Actual facts in the upcoming days would tell a different story. Apparently, people heeded the advice, went out for coffee, and abandoned self-isolation. A study commissioned by the Medical Association concluded that government messages correlated with an increase in recreational outings, even in people with COVID-19-compatible symptoms. By June 2020, Chile had the highest per capita infection rate of any major country, with 13,000 cases for every 1 million people (Beaubien, 2020; see also Fuentes & Sanders, 2020). Thus, the "safe return" was changed in July to a new strategy, the "step by step" plan, a more discreet and prudent concept that divided deconfinement into several progressive phases. This plan has been one of the hallmarks of the new Health Minister, Enrique Paris, a more measured, technical, and dialogue-prone official, who proved to be a more emphatic spokesperson for policy measures.

Taken altogether, the government's handling of the pandemic led to a paradoxical situation: while the government was enacting containment measures such as lockdowns, quarantines, and curfews, both its supporters and adversaries were critical of these measures but for very different reasons. The former thought the measures were heavy handed and exaggerated; the latter perceived they were too lax and insufficient. This paradox is well illustrated by our panel survey data. In Table 4.3 we show the results of regressing support for strict containment measures on a host of social, political, and media variables, in addition to experiences and government performance evaluation related to the coronavirus. First, right-wing respondents who support the government are rather critical of restrictive measures, whereas respondents who support the protests and are in opposition to government are rather supportive of stricter containment policies. Likewise, respondents who evaluate more positively the Piñera administration's handling of the pandemic want less restrictions. Those in the opposition, however, want more restrictions.

TABLE 4.3 Linear Regression of Support for COVID-19 Containment Measures

	Support for COVID-19 Containment Measures in Wave 2	
	(1)	*(2)*
Sociodemographics		
Age	−0.01	−0.00
	(0.00)	(0.00)
Gender (female)	0.05	0.10
	(0.09)	(0.08)
Household income	0.04	0.06
	(0.04)	(0.04)
Santiago resident	−0.06	−0.08
	(0.09)	(0.08)
Political Orientations		
Political interest in Wave 1	**−0.10★**	**−0.10★**
	(0.05)	**(0.04)**

Trust in government in Wave 1	0.03	0.10
	(0.06)	(0.05)
Left-wing ideology	0.00	−0.06
	(0.10)	(0.10)
Center/moderate	−0.12	−0.12
	(0.16)	(0.14)
Right-wing ideology	**−0.39***	**−0.33***
	(0.15)	**(0.14)**
Supports protests in Wave 1	**0.33****	**0.23***
	(0.11)	**(0.11)**
News Media		
Legacy news exposure in Wave 2	0.01	0.02
	(0.03)	(0.03)
Social media news exposure in Wave 2	−0.00	−0.01
	(0.02)	(0.02)
Experience with COVID-19		
Economic costs	−0.03	−0.03
	(0.05)	(0.05)
Psychological costs	0.09	0.09
	(0.05)	(0.05)
Health costs	0.03	0.03
	(0.05)	(0.04)
Fear of COVID-19	**0.30*****	**0.32*****
	(0.06)	**(0.06)**
Evaluation of government performance in handling the pandemic		**−0.12*****
		(0.03)
Constant	3.08***	3.15***
	(0.37)	(0.40)
Observations	454	454
R^2	0.39	0.43

Standard errors in parentheses. $^*p < 0.05$, $^{**}p < 0.01$, $^{***}p < 0.001$.

The COVID-19 crisis in Chile also opened the door to a more political and visible role for other actors from the public sphere, such as the Medical Association, city mayors, the scientific community, and several NGOs and think tanks. Most of these openly questioned official statistics and strategies to a greater extent than fact-checking initiatives in legacy media. In fact, since the arrival of a new Health Minister, these new actors had a more evident role in the daily press conferences, which changed their format: a panel with the three highest authorities from the Health Ministry and guest spokespersons who rotated according to the emphasis of the message of that day (e.g., health workers, mayors, civil society representatives). Also, the initial daily press conference was eventually changed to a thrice-a-week event.

Some city mayors successfully took advantage of the crisis to gain in media positioning, ahead of the April 2021 nationwide city council elections. Mayors' increasingly mediated public role brought them benefits: they were among the actors best evaluated by citizens in this crisis and by January 2021 three of them—two from the government coalition, one from the opposition—led presidential polls. Mayors proved to be key actors in the most restrictive moments of the lockdown, for example, organizing in May 2020 the logistics of an emergency aid program by the national government to deliver food boxes to households suffering an economic toll under lockdown. The president of the Medical Association, Izkia Siches, also achieved notable media prominence as an important critic of the government's handling of the pandemic, to the extent that her name has been mentioned in some presidential polls.

The opposition, in contrast, has played a minor role in the crisis. At best, the COVID-19 crisis has helped them further demonize the economic model of Chile and lack of access to affordable health. Opposition leaders coined a catchy phrase—"the government, again, is late and bad at it"—as a recurrent slogan to describe government response, such as a proposal to provide financial aid to people so that they could better endure confinement (e.g., Thomson, 2020). Perhaps the only successful opposition initiative during the crisis was the approval, on 23 July, of a bill allowing the withdrawal of up to 10% of individual retirement funds to help people endure the economic externalities derived from the health crisis. Polls showed that most citizens supported such bill, intensely opposed by the Piñera administration. However, the bill passed with overwhelming support in Congress, drawing votes even from members of Pinera's own coalition, which supposed a political blow to the government (Fuentes, 2020).

Along with all these developments, there were new media routines. Noteworthy is the consolidation of broadcast television morning shows—on four national networks, three private and one state-own—as platforms for political debates, a trend that burst into force after the social outbreak of 2019. These programs, which now last almost five hours, regularly have mayors and other politicians from different sectors debating what the government should do in managing the pandemic. There are figures who are invited more frequently and who have benefited from this exposure and there are others who have taken advantage of the platform to return to the public sphere, as is the case of a former presidential candidate who underwent a judicial process and had distanced from the media (Marco Enríquez-Ominami, from the left).

Lessons Learned

The coronavirus crisis found in Chile a government already weakened by a political crisis long in the making and resulting from the social unrest because of long-standing inequalities. Responding to a health crisis amidst extremely low levels of political trust proved to be quite a challenge, and the administration of Sebastián Piñera was not up to the task.

On a communicational level, one of the main errors of the Chilean government was its failure to develop a solid strategy to manage the pandemic—one that would anticipate to different scenarios, consider different outcomes, engage relevant stakeholders, and ponder different courses of actions. Instead, several blunders along the way confused citizens and made individuals further skeptical of the government's ability to effectively handle the situation. For one, there were multiple authorities in charge of communicating the ever-changing strategies and policies to contain the spread of the virus, rather than a few officials with a consistent message. The President himself took a secondary role, other than to join the salutary tone with which public health authorities claimed early on to be a world model in their handling of the emergency.

In a country with low levels of trust, the lack of transparency with regard to official statistics on the scope of the crisis was particularly problematic. It further eroded public trust and lends itself to a political climate not favorable for such a crisis (Contesse, 2020). The multiple missteps in reporting COVID data made individuals skeptical of the government's handling of the situation, and gave fodder to critics who saw a government effort to downplay the pandemic in order to prioritize economic reactivation over sanitary considerations.

Executive politicians not only seemed further out of touch with the hardships of large portion of the population—they seemed clueless in their management of the crisis. The administration clashed with the medical and scientific community, reporters, political opponents, and even members of their own coalition. Considering that the COVID-19 pandemic further underscored the inequalities of Chilean society—those from the poorest echelons of the country faired much worse than wealthy ones, both in economic and public health terms—this further exacerbated the feeling of aggravation that resulted in the 2019 protests. Arguably, if people did not take it to the streets this time it was because there was overwhelming public support for COVID-19 restrictions, but the scenario was one in which regulatory measures and governmental aid were implemented without political trust and with no reputational capital left.

Once it was clear that government's approach to manage the emergency was not working, the constant changes and improvisation further complicated things and increased the conflicts with medical experts and scientists. The insistence on a safe reopening of business was at odds with calls for self-isolation and the evidence that cases were nowhere near a plateau. Not surprisingly, things did not turn out well, as within a few weeks, Chile went from flattening the curve to being among the countries with highest per capita cumulative case rates, and the widespread perception that the government was neither prepared nor handling the situation successfully. Almost a year into the emergency, Piñera's approval remains low, the majority of Chileans think that the administration has been inefficient—if not negligent—in their management of the pandemic, and the economic and sanitary toll of the crisis has been high. With most media enduring their own crisis and struggling to hold authorities accountable, the resulting emergency has only deepened the political, economic, and social divisions within Chilean society.

The Chilean case underscores that a health crisis on top of a sociopolitical one does not improve popular support for a government. While a rally-round-the-flag effect for the Piñera administration was linked to fragmentation among different groups of citizens, our data show that people's response to the government measures to contain the spread of COVID-19 not only went along political cleavages. Rather, both supporters and opponents to the government were critical of how the pandemic was handled, as their expectations were not met. People considered pandemic-related restrictions either too hard or too soft, and the consensus was that the authorities did not respond appropriately to the challenges posited by the pandemic. Thus, in a largely fragmented society before the pandemic, this pandemic served to reinforce the division among different groups of citizens.

References

Allcott, H., Boxell, L., Conway, J. C., Gentzkow, M., Thaler, M., & Yang, D. Y. (2020). Polarization and public health: Partisan differences in social distancing during the Coronavirus pandemic. *National Bureau of Economic Research Working Paper* No. 26946. doi:10.3386/w26946

Araya, R. (2014). The global notion of journalism: A hindrance to the democratization of the public space in Chile. In M. A. Guerrero & M. Márquez-Ramírez (Eds.), *Media Systems and Communication Policies in Latin America* (pp. 254–271). London: Palgrave McMillan.

Bachmann, I. & Mujica, C. (2019). Exemplars as argumentative strategy in broadcast news: Analyzing the case of Chile. *Journalism Practice*, 13, 1042–1056. doi:10.1080/17512786.2019.1618198

Bargsted, M. & Maldonado, L. (2018). Party identification in an encapsulated party system: The case of postauthoritarian Chile. *Journal of Politics in Latin America*, 10, 29–68. doi:10.1177/1866802X1801000102

Bargsted, M., Somma, N., & Castillo, J. C. (2017). Political trust in Latin America. In S. Zmerli & T. van der Meer (Eds.), *Handbook of Political Trust* (pp. 395–417). Cheltenham, UK: Edward Elgar Publishing.

Bartlett, J. (2020, June 14). Chile's health minister quits over government response to Covid-19. *The Guardian*. Retrieved from https://www.theguardian.com/global-development/2020/jun/14/chiles-health-minister-quits-over-government-response-to-covid-19

Beaubien, J. (2020, July 3). How Chile ended up with one of the highest COVID-19 rates. *NPR*. Retrieved from https://www.npr.org/sections/goatsandsoda/2020/07/02/885207834/covid-19-exploits-cracks-in-chilean-society

Cabalín, C. (2014). The conservative response to the 2011 Chilean student movement: Neoliberal education and media. *Discourse: Studies in the Cultural Politics of Education*, 35, 485–498. doi:10.1080/01596306.2013.871233

Canel, M. J. & Sanders, K. B. (2016). Government communication. In G. Mazzoleni (Ed.), *The International Encyclopedia of Political Communication.* doi:10.1002/9781118541555.wbiepc190

Contesse, J. (2020). Responding to COVID-19 without public trust. *The Regulatory Review.* Retrieved from https://www.theregreview.org/2020/06/02/contesse-responding-covid-19-without-public-trust/

Criteria. (2020). Agenda Criteria Octubre 2020. Retrieved from https://www.criteria.cl/descargas/Agenda_Criteria_Octubre_2020-8htyd.pdf

Crozier, M. (2007). Recursive governance: Contemporary political communication and public policy. *Political Communication, 24,* 1–18. doi:10.1080/10584600601128382

Donoso, S. (2013). Dynamics of change in Chile: Explaining the emergence of the 2006 Pingüino Movement. *Journal of Latin American Studies, 45,* 1–29. doi:10.1017/S0022216X12001228

Elliott, L., & Bartlett, J. (2020, October 27). Chileans draw line under Pinochet era after referendum backs change. *The Times.* Retrieved from https://www.thetimes.co.uk/article/chileans-draw-line-under-pinochet-era-after-referendum-backs-change-n7gn3ghfx

Fuentes, V. (2020, July 23). Chile government concedes pension defeat after landmark bill. *Bloomberg.* Retrieved from https://www.bloomberg.com/news/articles/2020-07-24/chile-government-concedes-pension-defeat-after-landmark-bill

Fuentes, V., & Sanders, P. (2020, June 16). Once a Covid role model, Chile now among the world's worst. *Bloomberg.* Retrieved from https://www.bloomberg.com/news/articles/2020-06-16/once-a-covid-role-model-chile-now-among-the-world-s-worst-hit

Garcés, M. (2019). October 2019: Social uprising in neoliberal Chile. *Journal of Latin American Cultural Studies, 28,* 483–491. doi:10.1080/13569325.2019.1696289

Grassau, D., Valenzuela, S., Bachmann, I., Labarca, C., Mujica, C., Halpern, D., & Puente, S. (2019). *Uses and Attitudes toward News Organizations and Social Media during the 2019 Protests in Chile.* Santiago: School of Communications at Pontificia Universidad Católica de Chile. Retrieved from http://bit.ly/ChileMediaSurvey

Grassau, D., Valenzuela, S., Bachmann, I., Labarca, C., Mujica, C., Halpern, D. & Puente, S. (2020). *Comunicaciones, desinformación y emociones en la pandemia COVID-19 en Chile [Communications, Misinformation and Emotions in the COVID-19 Pandemic in Chile].* Santiago: School of Communications at Pontificia Universidad Católica de Chile. Retrieved from https://bit.ly/EncuestaCOVIDFComUC

González, R., & Morán, C. (2020). The 2019–2020 Chilean protests: A first look at their causes and participants. *International Journal of Sociology, 50,* 227–235. doi:10.1080/00207659.2020.1752499

Lin, Z., & Meissner, C. M. (2020). Health vs. wealth? Public health policies and the economy during Covid-19. *National Bureau of Economic Research Working Paper No. 27099.* doi:10.3386/w27099

Luna, J. P. (2016). Delegative democracy revisited: Chile's crisis of representation. *Journal of Democracy, 27,* 129–138. doi:10.1353/jod.2016.0046

Luna, J. P., Toro, S., & Valenzuela, S. (2021). El ruidoso silencio de los medios tradicionales [The loud silence of traditional media]. *CIPER Chile.* Retrieved from https://www.ciperchile.cl/2021/03/23/el-ruidoso-silencio-de-los-medios-tradicionales/

Lincoln, M. (2020). A special self-image is no defence against COVID-19. *Nature, 585,* 325. doi:10.1038/d41586-020-02596-8

Malinowski, M., Sanders, P., & Thomson, E. (2020, May 25). Social unrest is lurking in Latin America's new virus hotspot. *Bloomberg*. Retrieved from https://www.bloomberg.com/news/articles/2020-05-25/social-unrest-is-lurking-in-this-latin-american-virus-hotspot

Pew Research Center. (2020). Most Americans say state governments have lifted COVID-19 restrictions too quickly. Retrieved from https://www.pewresearch.org/politics/2020/08/06/most-americans-say-state-governments-have-lifted-covid-19-restrictions-too-quickly/

Sherwood, D. & Ramos, N. (2020, May 11). Chile surpasses 30,000 cases of coronavirus, braces for winter. *Reuters*. Retrieved from https://www.reuters.com/article/idUSKBN22N21X

Somma, N. M., Bargsted, M., Disi, R., & Medel, R. R. (2020). No water in the oasis: the Chilean Spring of 2019–2020. *Social Movement Studies*. doi:10.1080/14742837.2020.1727737

Thomson, E. (2020, July 5). Chile government adds stimulus with soft loans for middle class. *Bloomberg*. Retrieved from https://www.bloomberg.com/news/articles/2020-07-05/chile-government-adds-stimulus-with-soft-loans-for-middle-class

Valenzuela, S. (2013). Unpacking the use of social media for protest behavior: The roles of information, opinion expression, and activism. *American Behavioral Scientist, 57*, 920–942. doi:10.1177/0002764213479375

Valenzuela, S., Halpern, D., Katz, J. E., & Miranda, J. P. (2019). The paradox of participation versus misinformation: Social media, political engagement, and the spread of misinformation. *Digital Journalism, 7*, 802–823. doi:10.1080/21670811.2019.1623701

Van Bavel, J. J., Baicker, K., Boggio, P. S., Capraro, V., Cichocka, A., Cikara, M., ... Willer, R. (2020). Using social and behavioural science to support COVID-19 pandemic response. *Nature Human Behaviour, 4*, 460–471. doi:10.1038/s41562-020-0884-z

5

THE ITALIAN PRIME MINISTER AS A CAPTAIN IN THE STORM

The Pandemic as an Opportunity to Build Personalized Political Leadership

Gianpietro Mazzoleni and Roberta Bracciale

A Captain for the Storm?

Italy will be remembered as the first European country to be brutally hit by the COVID-19 pandemic. The lockdown, a totally unprecedented event that immobilized the lives of millions of citizens and crippled the economy for two months and beyond, the videos and images of dozens of coffins hauled out of the hospitals and delivered to cemeteries on military vehicles, all made the headlines of international media for weeks.

Among the several aspects of how the country as a whole confronted in 2020 with the pandemic worth of being investigated by academic research stands the communication conduct held by the national authorities throughout the crisis. This chapter attempts to analyze the patterns of the communication strategies that Italy's government pursued at various stages of the lockdown. In tune with the central questions of the book, we focus on how the central government headed by the Prime Minister Giuseppe Conte addressed the nation to cope with the public health issues and the growing anxieties.

Perhaps the most notable political communication phenomenon that evolved during the lockdown and in the subsequent phases was the consolidation of a tendency in domestic politics, that is of the personalization of public authority that accompanied the decline of traditional parties' grip on Italian political life. The tendency traces back to the PMs of the early 1980s and gained speed with the Berlusconi's premierships in the 1990s and 2000s. In Italy it has taken the shape of a mix of what in the scholarly literature are called "institutional personalization" and "centralized personalization" (Balmas, Rahat, Sheafer, & Shenhav, 2014). On the one hand there has been the "adoption of rules, mechanisms, and institutions that put more emphasis on the individual politician

DOI: 10.4324/9781003170051-6

and less on political groups and parties" (p. 38) and on the other hand there has been a centralization of political power in the hands of a few leaders at apical levels of the executive (PMs), a transfer of the ideological and political capital of the weakening parties to leaders with strong and charismatic personalities. The personalization of political leadership is by no means an Italian singularity, as it reflects similar trends in several mature democracies around the globe. In the case of Italy's pandemic emergency national and regional leaders, deliberately or unintentionally, strived to exploit the drama to enhance their personal and political footing. Whether the Italian way to personalization represented what Poguntke and Webb (2005) identify as "presidentialization", that is the increased capacity of political leaders to bypass their party machines and to appeal directly to voters is still to be fully assessed, given the indistinct political stature of the PM.

Mr. Conte, in fact, was an unknown law professor until he was handpicked after the general election of 2018 by the populist coalition Five Star Movement-League to lead the government. He gained media attention as he dribbled through the turbulent alliance and even managed to keep the post after the coalition collapsed in the summer of 2019. That ability to survive in the midst of political turmoil made pundits comment that Mr. Conte was all but a black horse of Italian politics, thus acknowledging he had the clout to emerge as a political leader, poised to novel adventures. For sure, the PM invested in building a personal image of serious, committed, compassionate and even stylish ruler. His trusted spokesman and spin doctor was Rocco Casalino, well known in the country's media circles, a half celebrity himself for having participated in the first edition of Big Brother's reality show, and famous for being inclined to play unchartered communication games on behalf of his employers (Loiacono, 2020). He pursued mainly three strategies:

1 Preferring live Facebook to publicly address the nation, instead of traditional speeches on joined TV channels. Even if the Facebook live speeches were also streamed by television channels, opting for a personal/direct use of the social network allowed an in-house management of the media event, aimed at showing a leader more intimately connected with the people at home.
2 Managing information by leaking to friendly media likely measures on the agenda of the council of ministers, to anticipate reactions of public opinion. The use of leaks as "trial balloons" is a well burned-in practice of news management by governments (Hess, 1984; Bovens, Geveke, & de Vries, 1995; Lieber & Golan, 2011). As we observe in the following pages, Mr. Conte's spokesman often leaked confidential information to a selected number of journalists, who were happy to anticipate it on their outlets, sometimes triggering unexpected consequences.

3   Resorting to several "PM's decrees" (the acronym "DPCM" becoming a popular buzzword). The resort to the DPCMs – more than two dozen from February to October – that carried detailed measures, regulations, and recommendations to contain the pandemic, involving restrictions to personal liberties and to economic activities, was intended to project an image of a leader in full control of an ailing country, fully engaged in the effort of healing it.

The almost compulsive' need of the PM to manage himself all steps in the enactment of his government's anti-COVID-19 policies needed, however, to be buttressed by a storytelling that could envelop and make more digestible the various measures listed in the decrees. This "meaning-making" is an essential part of crisis communication. Leaders tackling an emergency must "formulate a message that offers an authoritative definition of the situation, provides hope, shows empathy for victims, and gives assurances that the authorities are doing their best to minimize the consequences of the threat" (Boin, t' Hart, Stern, & Sundelius, 2016, pp. 78–79). A narrative of this kind ensures the keeping of consensus in leadership and in government. By means of an effective storytelling, the leader legitimizes himself as the "captain in the storm" and is able to rally public opinion in his support (Ventura, 2020, p. 50).

This strategy seems to have worked well. The polls would consistently register high confidence rates in the PM's leadership, and, at least in the most severe phase 1, Italian citizens showed high public compliance with the restrictions and acceptance of the several distresses that government had to impose (Braw, 2020; Johnson, Ghiglione, & Burn-Murdoch, 2020; Horowitz, 2020; Sylvers & Stancati, 2020).

As described in the next paragraphs, Mr. Conte's narrative showed discontinuities throughout the progression of the pandemic with significant effects on people's confidence in government.

The Phases of Government's Communication Vis-à-Vis the COVID-19 Pandemic

The identification of the phases has been carried out on the basis of two logical criteria. The first criterion is related to the periodization used by the government in DPCMs[1] (phases 1–3). The second is based on the spread of infections in Italy (ISS, 2020): phase 0, the detection of the first cases in Italy; phase 4, the second wave of contagion.

During the period of analysis of the phenomenon (February 2020–October 2020), the field of observation was delimited through three research strategies.

---

1 http://www.governo.it/it/coronavirus-normativa.

The first strategy was based on the analysis of the institutional communication through the study of the DPCMs and their presentation to the public that clearly identified the lockdown phases in Italy. The second strategy involved the analysis of newspapers and magazine articles, selected through the search engines alerts functions for specific keywords (Covid*, Virus*, Italy), focusing on the storytelling that accompanied the issuing of the DPCMs. The third strategy consisted of analyzing Mr. Conte's social media accounts and his posts, thanks to CrowdTangle (2020) and the Twitter APIs.

All the content was analyzed with an inductive approach based on the grounded theory method (Glaser & Strauss, 2017) to identify, by saturation, the most recurring categories that populated the main narrative strands.

Phase 0: "Italy Does Not Stop"

Phase 0 of the storytelling on coronavirus in Italy went between 30 January, the day when a Chinese couple of tourists tested positive for COVID-19 and was hospitalized in Rome, and 7 March, the date on which on the websites of the most important Italian newspapers appeared the breaking news that a lockdown for the Lombardy region and 14 other provinces of the center-north was going to be enforced by government. It was perhaps the most dangerous leak of a long series.

This phase was characterized by a communication strategy of minimizing the threat posed by the diffusion of the virus (Sturloni, 2020). Although it was already circulating in the country, the government's narrative on the spread of the infections remained reassuring for almost a month, tracing the problem mainly to those who had relations with China.

In this scenario the PM tried immediately to occupy a space of personal visibility. Mr. Conte's communication strategy followed two complementary lines: on the one hand, by reassuring the population about his ability to know how to keep in check the situation, mostly through disintermediated information; on the other hand, by playing the character of the man of action, distancing from the image of the dapper university professor, stripping from formal suits and rolling up his sleeves.

On social media, instead of using the official and institutional account (Palazzo Chigi, the seat of the government) he rather used his personal one in which he reached out to his followers day by day, describing his work in the first person and posting updates through pictures and livestream videos. Besides, the two accounts used a coordinated graphic style for pictures and infographics but in the personal one, he tended to add pictures with his face clearly visible and the Italian flag in the background.

The first interesting example of the strategy aimed at legitimizing a personal image as a political leader is a Facebook post of 3 February in which the PM was portrayed visiting the Spallanzani hospital in Rome, the clinic where the

Chinese couple was hospitalized and where the virus was isolated for the first time in Italy.

The photos with the entire hospital team, without any PPE (Personal Protective Equipment) or social distancing, testified a communication choice in which the concern for the pandemic was framed in a reassuring light: the problem was confined to China. The storytelling of the visit and the scientific discovery was so much comforting, in the photos as in the text of the post – "This afternoon I visited the staff of Spallanzani […] the Institute where the Coronavirus was isolated: doctors, researchers and healthcare professionals which represent excellence in the treatment of infectious diseases at national and international level […]" (Facebook, 3 February 2020[2]) – that it generated a great confusion in the population, convinced that Italy in a few days would be solving the problem of the global pandemic, as they had isolated the virus.

With the identification of the first Italian infected (21 February 2020) and the first deaths in Lombardy, the PM's communication activity escalated significantly. He intensified his television appearances and used all his social media profiles[3] in a coordinated manner to publish photos and videos of the meetings with "Protezione Civile" (the Emergency Management Agency) and scientists, to alert of the live press conferences, as well as to show his governing skills.

About the same time, a cycle of late afternoon press conferences kicked off on RAI public television networks in which the head of "Protezione Civile" and the experts of the Technical Scientific Committee provided daily updates on the course of the pandemic and answered questions of journalists and citizens. This was an event that kept millions of citizens watching television, confirming the key role of traditional media still played in keeping people abreast of what was going on around in the country. The centrality of television was also attested by the audience ratings indicating an increase in consumption of both entertainment and news. The coverage of the pandemic, moreover, occupied most of the TV news, going from an average of 35% in February to 80% in March, to then gradually decrease to 30% in June and rising again in October (AgCom, 2020a).

During phase 0, the use of the mask was advised, following recommendations from the WHO, only for people suspected of being sick or in case of assistance to sick people, thus not yet as a paramount tool to prevent the spread of the pandemic. The "mask mandate" was going to be in the following phases a point of controversy raised by political oppositions that targeted the mask as the icon of the government foolish measures. In this phase, the leader of the League, Matteo Salvini, often bullied the government by removing theatrically his mask in public spaces.

---

2 https://www.facebook.com/GiuseppeConte64/posts/836285903520043.
3 Facebook (3.4 million followers), Twitter (800,000 followers) and Instagram (1.6 million followers).

The coexistence of a plurality of institutional actors on the one hand and the conflicting indications of experts on the other fed a process of "infodemic" in the population – an informational pathology that makes it difficult to identify reliable information sources – and, driven by uncertainty and unable to detect reliable information, people begin to react based on the hype of the moment, as World Health Organization[4] (WHO) pointed out. Trending themes in social media, often triggered through memes, functioned as "self-fulfilling prophecies" in Italy as in the rest of Europe or in the USA. So, for example, when rumors of expected difficulties in the procurement of groceries spread online, people formed interminable lines outside supermarkets and pharmacies.

Against this state of growing concern among the population, further fueled by increasingly alarmist media headlines – such as "Italy is in lockdown", "The great fear", "Virus paralysis" – the PM tried to capture public attention on his doing. His media appearances became more frequent: he addressed citizens directly through TV and livestreams on social media, used slogans and the national flag, and initiated a narrative that stressed his institutional role as a problem solver, deserving public attention and approval.

In spite of signs that the situation might get soon worse, the non-alarmist parties were far from accepting the sustainability of a general lockdown and were still hopeful that Italy could avoid it. Leading figures of the parties close to the government as well as from the opposition stole the stage for a few days, launching a narrative that encouraged optimism, promptly picked up by the news media. To provide fuel were also statements of early "negationists" from the medical circles that in TV shows had stated that COVID-19 was nothing more than an ordinary flu. There were of course conflicting voices, but they were bound to remain minority at least for the rest of phase 0.

A couple of examples were bound to stir controversy and mutual accusations in the following months. On 27 February, underestimating the severity of the health situation in Lombardy, the epicenter of the spread of the virus, the mayor of Milan (Democratic Party) launched the #MilanoNonSiFerma (#MilanDoesNotStop) campaign on social media, to encourage the economic restart of the Lombard capital. With the blessing of the mayor, therefore, the reopening of shops and bars was celebrated by organizing aperitifs to which the population was invited to partake without any fear. In support of the initiative, Nicola Zingaretti, national leader of the Democratic Party, also arrived in Milan and was immortalized while drinking a spritz with a group of people, without any social distancing and without a mask.

It was the explosive growth of the infections that marked the turning point of the narrative frame on the coronavirus. From the underestimation of the problem to a "state of war" was a short step. In a few days the number of

---

4 https://www.who.int/news-room/spotlight/let-s-flatten-the-infodemic-curve.

recovered people in hospitals with serious risks of death skyrocketed, while the media reports were full of what ended up being contradictory statements by local and national authorities, scientists and self-proclaimed experts, who accused each other to have either over- or underestimated the virus.

Nevertheless, the fast and explosive growth of the infections and the increased number of people fallen sick led the government to issue a new DPCM. This time the "trial balloon" generated something unexpected. But on the evening of 7 March, the websites of the most important Italian newspapers leaked the news of the imminent lockdown for the entire Lombardy region and for other 14 provinces of the center-north. That information caused great agitation in the population to the point that Mr. Conte was forced to call a hasty press conference at 2:30 AM of 8 March. The DPCM that imposed the red zones only came into force the next day, which prompted thousands of workers – potentially COVID-19 positive – to flee from Lombardy to the regions of Southern Italy, with the risk of spreading the virus where it had not been yet detected.

The leaks seem too many to be unintentional.[5] In fact, the search for consensus by PM Conte involved the well-known strategy of the "trial balloon leaks" aimed (a) to pre-test the reactions of the population on the restrictive measures being envisaged by the government, and (b) to obtain a response of relief in the population when the restrictive measures were eventually less tough than anticipated by the media.

That nightly event signed a definite change in the narrative, from "Italy That Does Not Stop" to "Italy That Stays at Home".

Phase 1: "Italy Stays at Home"

Thanks to the acceleration caused by the mass flight to the south, on 9 March the prime Minister made a very tough and risky decision and, with a new DPCM, the entire country in lockdown starting from 10 March. That DPCM was named #IoRestoaCasa (#IStayAtHome) decree after the institutional campaign promoted by the Ministry of Health. The hashtag, to be found later in other countries, was largely adopted in official communications, documents, conversations, social media and the like, during the entire phase 1. Not surprisingly, the #IStayAtHome Decree was announced by Mr. Conte on Twitter, and then illustrated with a livestream on Facebook, with a strategy of moral suasion that shifted the weight of the emergency onto the sense of responsibility of citizens:

---

5 A first clue of this strategy was recorded on 25 February when the social media accounts of Giuseppe Conte, of Palazzo Chigi and of the Minister of Education jointly posted to rebuff the leak of an imminent closure of schools. A decision that, however, was to be made a few days later, on 4 March.

> The future of Italy is in our hands. We all do our part, giving up something for the good of the community. At stake is the health of our loved ones, our parents, our children, our grandparents. I have just signed the #IoRestoaCasa decree.[6]
>
> *(Twitter, 9 March 2020)*

The hashtag worked as a catalyst for individual responsibility and civic sense to which Mr. Conte repeatedly appealed in his communications, asking with a firm voice for solidarity and collective responsibility to stop the spread of the virus.

The collective responsibility frame was vigorously stressed in the weeks of the lockdown, so much to activate an almost obsessive form of social control for deviant behavior. It gained several front pages the case of runners in parks that were targets of "witch-hunts" and of public reproaches by people watching from their balconies.

Back in formal clothes, and aware of the emotional and empathic levers needed in a moment of extreme uncertainty, the PM was eventually portrayed with the Italian and European flags behind him, thus also iconically recalling the image of the captain holding firmly the rudder of the boat. The message coming from the PM was all but depressive. It was geared toward rallying "the people" around him and around the flag, because #AndràTuttoBene (#EverythingWillBeFine).

Italians shared wholeheartedly this narration and the balconies filled with banners with rainbows drawn by children with the catchphrase "everything will be fine"; jam sessions and karaoke were organized from the balconies, playing music from the Italian national anthem to pop songs; confined in their homes, they waved Italian flags from windows and balconies in the chilling silence of city streets and dedicated long applauses to doctors and nurses, hailed as heroes. This can be seen as an example of connective action (Bennett, & Segerberg, 2013) of people who shared on social media photos, videos, memes and messages, with the purpose to support each other, gathered all together around and in support of the "captain in the storm".

Thanks to a "rally-round-the-flag" effect (Mueller, 1970), which raises leaders' popularity ratings when unexpected and dramatic international events take place, Mr. Conte became the most welcomed prime minister in the past ten years (Demos & Pi, 2020). In fact, in March, 71% of Italians gave him a high level of confidence, compared to 52% he had in February.

The positive feeling toward Mr. Conte was also reflected in the pop narrations on social media where pages (e.g. Le Bimbe di Giuseppe Conte [Conte's babes]) dedicated to the "sexiest premier in Europe" were created, in which he was portrayed between hearts and stars. The Latin macho "Giuseppi"

---

6 https://twitter.com/GiuseppeConteIT/status/1237145779350929410.

(as Donald Trump called him) thus became the protagonist of a communication phenomenon that produced throughout the whole lockdown phase millions of memes, GIFs and videos that celebrated the alleged attractiveness of the leader. Mr. Conte became the subject of a transmedia storytelling in a circuit of references between social and mainstream media, which contributed to the process of personalization of political leadership, whether based in spontaneous, grassroots production or cunningly managed by image makers.

The 18 March is perhaps the most emblematic day of the deep crisis in which Italy is perceived as the "Wuhan of Europe". All the media were filled with photos of military trucks hauling coffins from the cemetery of Bergamo that could not take more to the crematoria of other regions. These disturbing scenes traveled around the world.

Following the exponential growth of infections, a new DPCM on 21 March tightened the already restrictive measures, with the complete shutdown of all the industrial activities.

The press conference in which the PM planned to explain the most delicate phase of the lockdown was scheduled for 22:45, but the Facebook livestream only started at 23:25, with a crescendo of tension for citizens and journalists. It is a sign of an initial screeching in the relations between the public opinion and the commander-in-chief.

The choice to broadcast yet another conference on the personal social profiles of the Prime Minister, with a livestream from his Facebook page instead of a public press conference, drew numerous critiques, including the one of the Parliamentary Press Association "Great disappointment for the umpteenth livestream on the personal Facebook page of the Prime Minister, who has completely cut off journalists, with no opportunity to ask questions to the Prime Minister" (Primaonline, 2020).

In this *modus operandi*, we find a recurring peculiarity of Mr. Conte's communication style:[7] the announcements made late in the evening, often at night and often postponed from minute to minute, with a communication that best exploited the livestreams on his social media. All his livestreams generated storms of posts with incomplete information that ended up causing confusion in the population. For his part, Mr. Conte saturated the media spaces. Between 1 March and 30 April, he appeared on TV for over 21 hours, while the opposition leaders Matteo Salvini and Giorgia Meloni occupied less than half the time (Agcom, 2020b). By making Mr. Conte's talking head the center piece of the narrative on every single channel, the media contributed to the focus on the leader and the initial rally around the flag effect.

---

7 https://www.repubblica.it/politica/2020/03/22/news/coronavirus_giuseppe_conte_facebook_matteo_renzi-251957928/.

Phases 2 and 3: "Together We Can Do It"

Thanks to strict containment measures, after 50 days of total lockdown, the spread of the virus in Italy slowed down and the curves of infections flattened, giving start to phase 2. The DPCM of 26 April provided for a progressive lessening of constraints, and later the restart of many businesses on 4 May.

Mr. Conte's storytelling in this phase focused on the "cohabitation" with the virus and highlighted three fundamental issues: social distancing, use of the PPE such as masks and social responsibility, summarized in the claim #InsiemeCeLaFaremo (#TogetherWeCanDoIt):

> Tomorrow, phase two of the emergency will begin, the one of cohabitation with the virus. It will be a new page that we all have to write together, with confidence and responsibility […]. We will need even more collaboration, civic sense, and respect for the rules on the part of everyone. We will always have to keep high the attention, continue to keep the interpersonal distance, to wear the mask when and where it will be necessary, and to wash our hands often and carefully […] I am confident, together we can do it.[8]
>
> (Instagram, 3 March 2020)

The PM abandoned livestreams on social media to return to traditional press conferences and his communications about coronavirus normalized and became less frequent.

In addition, phase 2 started with a lack of clarity on certain requirements. In particular, the term "kins" was used to indicate the permit to visit relatives. The term revealed very unclear and ambiguous, generating a controversy in the concrete interpretation. Did it include close friends? What about partners and fiancés living at different addresses? The same confusion characterized many other issues concerning the reopening, from the possibility to celebrate religious worships to the listing of allowed team sports, to the assured provision of surgical masks at the standard price of 50 cents, which were unavailable, and so on.

In this phase of reopening the clashes with the regions surfaced considerably. Tiresome negotiations between the central and regional governments were often cited as the cause of Mr. Conte's delays at press conferences in which he was due to illustrate the latest DPCM. The PM, in fact, constantly reclaimed political power to decide for the whole country but was opposed by the presidents of the regions, who were more inclined to stand as champions of their territories. Some exuberant staging of local officials became viral, thanks to a video, dubbed in English, that collected the best "sheriff's behaviors", such as threatening to use the flamethrower to curb private parties and social gatherings, or

---

[8] https://www.instagram.com/p/B_vAcIjAjWP.

the Hollywood-style chase of runners by city police. The compilation on social media became famous internationally, so much so that it was relaunched by several media outlets (e.g. *The Guardian*,[9] *CNN*,[10] *The Washington Post*[11]).

The insubordination of some regional presidents, driven by the pressure to accelerate the phase of relaunching local economies or by the opposed need to keep restrictive measures, crossed in a few cases party affiliations. Therefore, despite the effort by the PM to maintain national control, each region enacted local measures, adding to the confusion for people traveling from one region to the other for business or private reasons.

The return to a partial normality, thanks to the summer holidays and the new DPCM of 15 June that further loosened up the restrictions giving the start to phase 3, almost made COVID-19 disappear from the public agenda. In June the COVID-19 theme occupied in the main TV news less than 30% of the space vs. more than 80% in March (Agcom, 2020a), and the phase of "cohabitation" with the virus began with an epidemiological situation under sufficient control. Meanwhile, Mr. Conte's approval declined to 60% in June, compared to 71% in March (Demos & Pi, 2020).

Phase 4: "Wear a Mask, Wash Your Hands, and Keep Your Social Distance"

The end of the summer and the carelessness that accompanied the summer holidays triggered in Italy, as well as in many other European countries, the advent of a second wave of the virus. With the rise of infections and the nightmare of a new lockdown on the horizon, the PM adjusted once again his communication strategy, emphasizing also with his public comportment the worsening of the health situation. The mask became the item in the foreground of all his press conferences: for the first time since the beginning of the pandemic, Mr. Conte wore it while speaking in public. In addition, shortly before a new DPCM on 13 October, which re-introduced restrictive measures to businesses and to free movement of people, the PM changed his profile photo on social media to one in which he was wearing a mask. The background of his profile picture was replaced with a card in which his image appeared in the foreground with the three precepts anti-COVID-19: wear the mask, keep the distance, wash your hands. The issues of social distancing and PPE became central to public

---

9 https://www.theguardian.com/world/video/2020/mar/23/go-home-italian-mayors-rage-at-coronavirus-lockdown-dodgers-video.
10 https://edition.cnn.com/2020/03/23/world/italian-mayors-scolding-residents-coronavirus-lockdown-trnd/index.html.
11 https://www.washingtonpost.com/video/world/angry-italian-mayors-scold-people-ignoring-lockdown-rules/2020/03/24/f409c2f8-77d8-4269-85c1-7671a94fc5ac_video.html.

debate and were repeated to redundance. The young, less prone to wear masks, became targets of a campaign to make them abide to the rule. To achieve this goal, Mr. Conte resorted to "testimonials". He asked two influencers very popular among the youngest, Fedez and Chiara Ferragni, to produce a video, to encourage youngsters to wear masks. Other celebrities, such as the popular football player Ibrahimovic, were coopted by regional governments to convince people of the need to behave safely.

The exponential rise of the Rt index (measure of how fast the virus is spreading), however, called for the enforcing of more drastic measures on which the PM seemed to be less resolute than in earlier phases, allegedly for the need to hear all parties involved in the measures under consideration. The teetering of his popularity index urged Mr. Conte to be more cautious and to share the responsibility of hard decisions with the regional governments. That blurred to a certain extent his carved image of sole – and solely concerned – commander-in-chief. A close series of DPCMs were to follow in a few days, signaling a hasty and botchy crisis management, a stark departure from the earlier and more watchful decision-making.

Italy was divided into areas – yellow, orange and red – according to the gravity of the epidemiological situation, and different constraining measures entered into force in each zone. Italians, who heretofore had been keen to accept restrictions, if chaotic, started to show widespread unrest. A series of sectors staged protests and called for strikes (Camilli, 2020). The government tried to intervene quickly with economic relief measures, providing compensations in support of business penalized by the latest partial lockdowns, enforced by further DPCMs.

In response to public pressure, Mr. Conte's communication strategy accommodated elements that flashed some fear, something carefully avoided in the previous phases. The virus was compared to a high-speed train that had to be stopped:

> the virus now runs fast throughout the country and we must do everything in our power to stop it. These are not happy days for the red areas, but also orange and yellow areas are subject to restrictive measures, although differently graduated. We do not do this lightly. It is the only way we can fight COVID-19 and win this battle. We hope to win as soon as possible.[12]
>
> *(Instagram, 6 November 2020)*

At the end of autumn 2020, Mr. Conte's leadership, while maintaining a good popularity and public approval, showed evident signs of "communication

---

12 https://www.instagram.com/p/CHSKdZPMR8x/?utm_source=ig_web_copy_link.

fatigue", with a series of contradictory measures and confused messages vis-à-vis an exacerbation of the virus diffusion, that ignited irritation and discontent in many political circles. The PM came under a crossfire by the media, less prone to forgive government inadequacies, and by his political allies in the cabinet that few months later will put a stop to his leadership for the time being and replace the "captain in the storm".

Conclusion

Our analysis of Italy's government communication in the pandemic of 2020 highlights contradictory processes at work in Italian political communication, which are embodied in the trajectory of Prime Minister Giuseppe Conte.

Institutional and centralized personalization, of the kind described by Balmas et al. (2014), was attained by Mr. Conte's leadership, who gained some political stature, although challenged by his adversaries, and in spite of several failures scored in the ten months of piloting the ship in the country's troubled waters. He could rely on a professional communication know-how that helped to boost his media presence and public approval. However, the professionalization of the communication was gradually more criticized as too strategic and cynical to be of effectual help to the public image of the PM in the long run.

The evidence offered by the Italian way the pandemic was managed reveals also a number of things about the domestic political communication environment. The rise of a leader such as Mr. Conte was made possible by a political system that allows non-political outsiders to gain and exercise power without going through an electoral contest. That happened before, as in the case of Mr. Mario Monti, back in 2011. In both cases at the core of their initial success there was the task of governing a country in deep distress.

The pandemic has been an opportunity for Mr. Conte to build his political leadership. Although it discounted an expected decrease in popularity, associated with the rally-around-the-flag effect, passing from the very high approval of 71% recorded in March 2020 to 58% of October, his approval remained relatively high. However, dark clouds were piling up on the horizon of his government.

A further lesson from the pandemic in 2020 is the stronger polarization of political struggle. One could tell that the tensions between the regionals and the national governments over the measures to keep the spread of the virus under control were more dictated by partisan standings than by legitimate diverse visions and opinions on the best policies to adopt. In fact, to stand up against the center-left governing coalition were mostly the presidents of the regions controlled by right-wing parties. A dramatic emergency such as the COVID-19 pandemic would have called all political factions to lay down their partisan weaponry and cooperate to respond to the crisis. This was made impossible by the personal ambition of the prime minister to be the (only) captain in the storm – highlighted by the use of DPCMs – and by the stand-off with the former allied party, the far-right League of Matteo Salvini, that also constrained the moderate components of the right-wing opposition.

The outcome of such a political deadlock, which was going to have serious developments in the following phases of the pandemic, can also be seen against the backdrop of a media system that traditionally mirrors the polarized political spectrum. Mainstream media did not stand out in challenging the government's handling of the pandemic from a citizens' advocacy standpoint. They would rather hammer out the government's spin, thus confirming the deeply rooted "press-party parallelism" that still marks Italy's political communication landscape (Hallin & Mancini 2004).

References

AgCom. (2020a). *Tempo di argomento dedicato al tema Coronavirus in Tv e in Radio*. https://www.agcom.it/dati-monitoraggio-covid-19.

AgCom. (2020b). *L'informazione nei programmi Televisivi*. https://www.agcom.it/documents/10179/18706755/Dati+monitoraggio+20-05-2020/76ed5ee1-e123-44e3-8800-ab98161b406c.

Balmas, M., Rahat, G., Sheafer, T., & Shenhav, S. R. (2014). Two routes to personalized politics: Centralized and decentralized personalization. *Party Politics*, *20*(1), 37–51. doi:10.1177/1354068811436037.

Bennett, W. L., & Segerberg, A. (2013). *The logic of connective action: Digital media and the personalization of contentious politics*. New York: Cambridge University Press.

Boin, A., t' Hart, P., Stern, E., & Sundelius, B. (2016). Meaning making: Constructing a crisis narrative. In *The politics of crisis management: Public leadership under pressure* (pp. 78–101). Cambridge: Cambridge University Press.

Bovens, M. A., Geveke, H. G., & de Vries, J. (1995). Open public administration in the Netherlands: The politics of leaking. *International Review of Administrative Sciences*, *61*(1), 17–40. doi:10.1177/002085239506100103.

Braw, E. (2020, September 23). How Italy snatched health from the jaws of death. *Wall Street Journal*. https://foreignpolicy.com/2020/09/23/italy-mismanagment-covid-19-health-pandemic.

Camilli, A. (2020, February 2). Da dove viene la rabbia di chi protesta a Napoli. *Internazionale*. https://www.internazionale.it/reportage/annalisa-camilli/2020/11/02/napoli-proteste-lockdown.

CrowdTangle Team. (2020). *CrowdTangle*. Facebook, Menlo Park, California, United States. https://apps.crowdtangle.com/search/.

Demos & Pi. (2020). *90°Atlante Politico*. http://www.demos.it/2020/pdf/5500ap90_20201030.pdf.

Glaser B. G., & Strauss A. L. (2017). *The discovery of grounded theory*, Routledge, New York.

Hallin, D. C., & Mancini, P. (2004). *Comparing media systems: Three models of media and politics*. New York: Cambridge University Press

Hess, S. (1984). *The government/press connection: Press officers and their offices*. Washington: Brookings Institution Press.

Horowitz, J. (2020, July 20). How Italy turned around its coronavirus calamity. *The New York Times.* https://www.nytimes.com/2020/07/31/world/europe/italy-coronavirus-reopening.htm.

ISS (Istituto Superiore di Sanità). (2020). *Prevenzione e risposta a COVID-19: evoluzione della strategia e pianificazione nella fase di transizione per il periodo autunno-invernale.* Roma: Ministero della Salute, Istituto Superiore di Sanità. https://www.iss.it/documents/20126/0/COVID+19_+strategia_ISS_ministero+%283%29.pdf/e463c6e7-6250-109c-1c74-d2f8262f5056?t=1602672178859.

Loiacono, M. (2020, October 3). Riecco la tecnica Casalino per far crescere l'audience di Conte. *ItaliaOggi.* https://www.italiaoggi.it/news/riecco-la-tecnica-casalino-per-far-crescere-l-audience-di-conte-2483124.

Lieber, P. S., & Golan, G. J. (2011). Political public relations, news management, and agenda indexing. In J. Strömbäck, & K. Spiro (Eds.) *Political public relations: Principles and applications* (pp. 54–74). New York-London: Routledge.

Mueller, J. E. (1970). Presidential popularity from Truman to Johnson. *The American Political Science Review, 64*(1), 18–34. doi:10.2307/1955610.

Johnson, M., Ghiglione D., & Burn-Murdoch J. (2020, September 23). Italy's harsh lessons help keep second wave at bay. *Financial Times.* https://www.ft.com/content/6831be3e-2711-4ea3-8f62-daa82cf9ca11.

Poguntke, T., & Webb, P. (2005). *The presidentialization of politics: A comparative study of modern democracies.* Oxford: Oxford University Press.

Sylvers, E., & Stancati, M. (2020, September 22). As covid-19 fatigue fuels infections in Europe, Italy resists second wave. *The Wall Street Journal.* https://www.wsj.com/articles/as-covid-fatigue-fuels-infections-in-europe-italy-resists-the-second-wave-11600772400.

Sturloni, G. (2020, April 20). Chi ha sbagliato di più: tutti gli errori della gestione italiana della crisi coronavirus. *Wired.* https://www.wired.it/attualita/politica/2020/04/20/coronavirus-errori-emergenza-governo-regioni/

Ventura, S. (2020). La pandemia e la crisi della leadership: come il Covid-19 può cambiare le democrazie. In A. Campi (Ed.). *Dopo. come la pandemia può cambiare la politica, l'economia, la comunicazione e le relazioni internazionali* (pp. 49–58) Soveria Mannelli: Rubbettino.

Primaonline. (2020, March 22). Conte e la diretta (in ritardo) su Facebook scatena le reazioni di stampa e politici. Mentana: non può essere tutto comunicazione. *Primaonline.* https://www.primaonline.it/2020/03/22/303513/conte-e-la-diretta-facebook-in-ritardo-scatena-le-polemiche-mentana-non-puo-essere-tutto-comunicazione/.

PART 2
Media Coverage

6
INTERACTIVE PROPAGANDA

How Fox News and Donald Trump Co-produced False Narratives about the COVID-19 Crisis

Yunkang Yang and Lance Bennett

Introduction

During the summer of 2020, a group calling themselves "America's Frontline Doctors" took to the steps of the US Supreme Court claiming that the antimalaria drug hydroxychloroquine was a cure for COVID-19. Even though one of these doctors, Stella Immanuel, had a history of making outlandish claims about alien DNA and demon sperms, many radical right media organizations including Fox News stood by her (Gertz, 2020). Despite her questionable credibility, Immanuel and many other dubious medical experts became useful sources for the false yet politically useful narrative that COVID-19 could be cured effectively treated by hydroxychloroquine, a widely available and inexpensive anti-malaria drug. If such a miracle cure did exist, then the economy could be reopened, and Donald Trump would have a better chance to be reelected.

The parade of pseudo experts appearing on right-wing news and interview programs helped spread and legitimize claims that Trump had been making since March that hydroxychloroquine (hereafter HCQ) was a cure for COVID-19. This false narrative was widely repeated within the radical right media sphere, which we define as a media ecosystem in which a variety of outlets produce and spread a mixture of conventional and fake news, political propaganda, and public mobilization activities (Yang, 2020).[1]

A casual observer might conclude that the outlets in this sphere, centered around Fox News (as shown below), were just amplifying Trump's

---

[1] The radical right media sphere is not monolithic, but organizations typically mix partisan journalism with networked propaganda aimed at achieving strategic political goals (Benkler, Faris, & Roberts, 2018; Yang, 2020).

DOI: 10.4324/9781003170051-8

disinformation. However, it would be a mistake to conclude that they were merely following his lead. After gathering and creating timelines for a comprehensive collection of statements by Trump and various Fox personalities on various topics related to COVID-19, we detected a more interesting pattern: at different times, and on different issues, each side (i.e., Trump and Fox) took the lead in framing issues, and then adopting and amplifying the other's framing. This co-production of disinformation was sustained over many months in a coordinated propaganda campaign aimed at minimizing the seriousness of the disease. The many elements of this campaign included claims that the virus was no more serious than the regular flu; death totals were being inflated; leaving churches, schools, and businesses open would not make things worse; wearing masks violated personal freedoms; "herd immunity" could be achieved with minimal social and economic disruption; and HCQ was a cure.

From this preliminary analysis, we generated several research questions. First, what is the evidence that Trump and Fox alternately took the lead in promoting various kinds of COVID-19 disinformation? Second, in what ways did the resulting disinformation display the degree of coordination, persistence, and goal orientation to qualify as propaganda? And, if we can call it propaganda, does this form represent a break with traditional models of propaganda as top-down communication, typically flowing from government to media and other societal echo chambers? Third, what does a preliminary model of this process look like? And, related to this, what might account for two independent organizations in a democracy (namely a presidential administration and a news organization) co-producing systematic disinformation?

We try to answer these questions via case analysis of coverage and communication about HCQ using Fox program content, Trump's Twitter feed, other public statements by Trump, and outside news reporting on the relationship between Fox and Trump over the year 2020. We chose to look at HCQ both because of its long-running importance in the right-wing corona propaganda campaign in the USA, and because it was far more reliable to track empirically than other terms in the large and noisy media corpus on COVID-19. More concretely, we apply our preliminary model to a fine-grained analysis of how the Fox-to-Trump side of the interaction worked. Finally, in the conclusion we assess this co-production process as one possible path for transition toward an illiberal regime in which the state forms partnerships with important media outlets.

To begin with, we address the question of why we look primarily at Fox. During the period under study (March–November 2020), Fox drew by far the largest audiences of any cable news network during the time of the Trump administration, with an average of 3.6 million viewers in primetime programs hosted by "personalities" such as Sean Hannity, Laura Ingraham, and Tucker Carlson (Richwine, 2020). This not only made Fox the most viewed cable outlet during the pandemic, but it was also the central node in a large networked

Interactive Propaganda   **85**

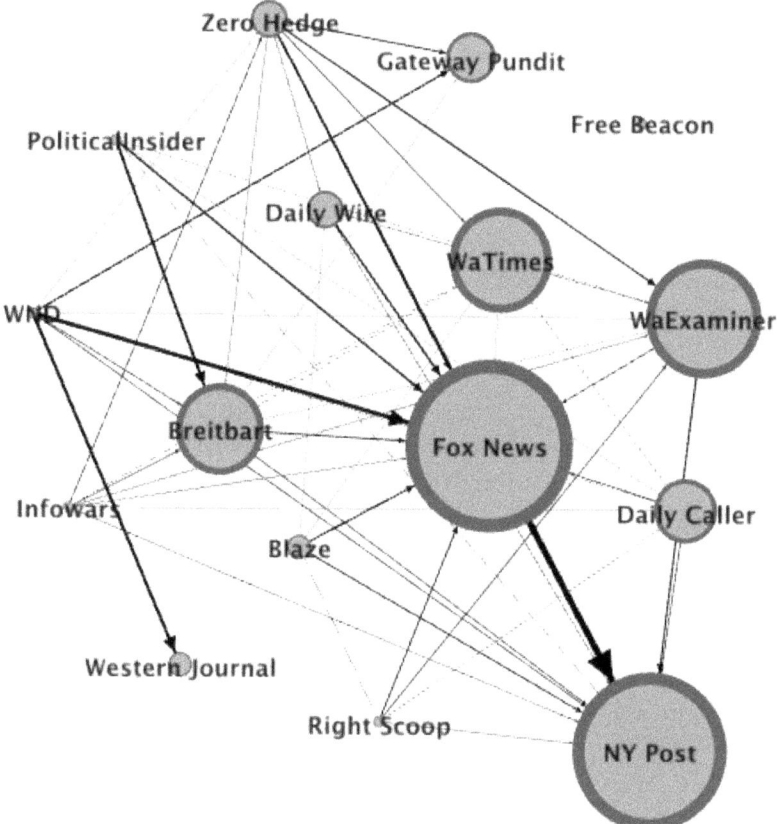

FIGURE 6.1 Hyperlink network of 16 major radical right media outlets based on their coverage of HCQ (March 15–August 15, 2020).
Source: Media Cloud.

COVID-19 propaganda sphere on the radical right, as shown in the hyperlink network in Figure 6.1. This began to change after the November election when the Fox News division called the state of Arizona early for Joe Biden, and Fox anchors and hosts acknowledged Biden as the President, leading an angry Trump to point his followers to other media outlets.

Qualitative Evidence of Co-production between Fox and Trump

From the beginning of the pandemic, the Trump administration pursued the strategy of misleading the public by minimizing the severity of the virus. After being briefed by his National Security Advisor on January 28 that the coronavirus would be the largest national security threat to his presidency

(Woodward, 2020), Trump declared in public two days later that "we have it very well under control" (Kiely, Robertson, Rieder & Gore, 2020). In the early months, both Trump and Fox personalities compared COVID-19 to the annual flu. On February 14, Trump even suggested that the virus would disappear in April (McDonald, 2020). At the same time, Trump privately acknowledged the lethality of the virus, saying in an interview with journalist Bob Woodward on February 7 that "it's also more deadly than … your strenuous flu" (Woodward, 2020).

Fox personalities repeated most of these claims coming from the Trump administration (Evanega, Lynas, Adams & Smolenyak, 2020). For instance, the day after an early Trump comparison of the virus to the flu, Fox host Sean Hannity suggested on his show that the virus is even less lethal than the common flu (Hannity, February 27, 2020). In the following week, Fox host Jeanine Pirro told her viewers that "all the talk about coronavirus being so much more deadly [than the flu] doesn't reflect reality" (Pirro, March 7, 2020); and Fox News medical correspondent Marc Siegel declared that "at worst – worst case scenario – it could be the flu" (Hannity, March 6, 2020).

While Fox News regularly echoed Trump's message, it also produced propaganda materials "in house," many of which were later repeated and amplified by President Trump. Many falsehoods ranging from "miracle cures" (e.g., HCQ) to "herd immunity" theories that were peddled by President Trump actually came from Fox personalities. Once manufactured, Fox's "in house" propaganda was often quickly tweeted by Donald Trump himself (Gertz, 2018). For instance, hours after Fox News host Steve Hilton railed against economic shutdown and said "You know that famous phrase – the cure is worse than the disease" on March 22 (Hilton, 2020), Trump tweeted "We cannot let the cure be worse than the problem itself."

By mid-March, the development of the pandemic reached a point where denialism simply wouldn't work. COVID-19 turned out to be far more serious than the flu and showed no signs of disappearing. Yet the overall communication plan was to continue to minimize the severity of the virus, keep the economy open, and proclaim victory over the still soaring problem. In less than ten days after Trump declared a national emergency in March, he pushed for reopening the economy when many states were still in the beginning stages of shutdown (Stelter, 2020). On July 6, Trump declared on Twitter that "schools must open in the fall!"

As the national health-care system became strained and COVID-19 deaths continued to rise, the co-production of disinformation was routinized through a variety of activities, including Trump's regular appearances on Fox programs, coordinated information leaks, coordinated attacks on public health officials, and through regular contacts between Fox personalities and Trump. For example, in July, the White House sought to damage the reputation of the nation's leading infectious disease expert Dr. Anthony Fauci, by leaking a memo to Fox and other media outlets, highlighting alleged contradictions in Fauci's statements (Faulders & Santucci, 2020). Meanwhile, Scott Atlas, a neuroradiologist with no expertise in public health, caught Trump's attention through his appearance on Fox News. Atlas soon joined Trump's inner circle and became the only medical advisor in the White House that Trump consulted regularly (Dawsey & Abutaleb, 2020). Atlas soon began to spread various falsehoods about mask wearing, COVID-19 vaccine, and perhaps the most dangerous of all "herd immunity," the idea to achieve population-level immunity by allowing the virus to spread quickly (Abutaleb & Dawsey, 2020). In a September town hall event, Trump cited Atlas and floated "herd mentality" as one option to make the virus disappear in the absence of a vaccine (Bump, 2020b).

Trump's tweeting Fox content was one publicly visible and measurable example of propaganda[2] moving in unconventional directions. Beyond Trump and Fox personalities monitoring and amplifying each other, there were also a number of private channels through which Fox personalities influenced Donald Trump's communication strategies. Those private channels were built on personal relationships. Jeanine Pirro, for instance, was a decades-long friend of Trump who spent holidays with him, traveled on his jet, and dined with him at the White House (Ellison, 2019). Before leaving office, Trump even pardoned Pirro's ex-husband on tax fraud charges. Another top rated Fox personality, Sean Hannity was dubbed Trump's "shadow chief of staff" who counseled Trump at all hours. These close relationships gave Fox hosts personal access to the US President to promote their agendas.

Some of the Fox input from Fox personalities was aimed at tempering Trump's bizarre disregard for evidence-based reality. Even hosts who often vouched for Trump occasionally pushed back. In the early stage of the pandemic, the Fox host Tucker Carlson became concerned about Trump's minimization of the risk of the virus, in part due to the safety and liability risks associated with relaying that information to an audience of senior citizens. Encouraged by Fox's owner Rupert Murdoch[3] and a White House aide, Carlson personally visited Trump at Mar-a-Lago to express his concerns on March 7 (Ellison & Barr, 2020; Stelter, 2020). When Trump continued to compare the virus to the flu on Twitter on March 9, Carlson delivered a veiled criticism of Trump and the government's incompetence in handling of the virus, stressing that "it's definitely not just the flu" on his show (Carlson, March 9, 2020). Carlson's show reportedly influenced Trump's decision to declare national emergency on COVID-19 four days later (Costa, 2020).

---

2 We define this form of propaganda more fully in the next section, but for now offer the provisional definition as *the saturation of a media sphere with strategically coordinated disinformation*.
3 Murdoch also reportedly sent Fox's parent company News Corp. CEO Robert Thomson to speak to Trump about the risk of the virus in March (Ellison & Barr, 2020).

This suggests that interactions between Trump and Fox News were not without friction, as one might expect when independent organizations with different agendas seeking areas of convergence. Beyond the occasional efforts of talk show hosts like Carlson to introduce a modicum of reality in the president's often unhinged performances, there were also some journalists anchoring news programs who tried to create the appearance of independence. Chris Wallace, Neil Caputo, and Shepard Smith[4] were among a few at Fox known for occasionally fact-checking Trump or asking him tough questions. They often found themselves under attack by Trump and his followers, who were a large share of the Fox audience. When Fox host Neil Cavuto contradicted Trump's narrative on HCQ (Cavuto, May 18, 2020), Trump retweeted personal attacks on Cavuto and threatened to look for a new media outlet (Choi, 2020). This was not the only time that Trump threatened to abandon Fox News. Trump publicly attacked Fox at least 11 times before the 2020 election, for various acts of disloyalty, from mild criticisms of his bizarre White House briefings (Derysh, 2020), to allowing Democrats to appear on its shows, and for showing that he was trailing in the polls. Beyond the negotiated co-production process, what other aspects of this novel relationship qualify for considering this a new form of propaganda?

How Interactive Propaganda Differs from More Conventional Forms

There are really two questions here: Why talk about propaganda and not just disinformation? and What distinguishes interactive propaganda from more conventional varieties? First, as shown in the quantitative analysis below, the collaboration between Trump and Fox was not just an episodic case of lying or deception, but a sustained campaign waged over months to minimize the severity of the pandemic and promote the larger objectives of keeping a strong economy going to elect Trump to a second term. Second, the interactive production of such a sustained propaganda campaign deviates in many ways from classical patterns of propaganda that tend to be more top-down and centrally managed.

Propaganda generally refers to the strategic uses of disinformation (half-truths, lies, hate, conspiracies) interspersed with selected legitimizing "facts" to confuse, disorient, and/or influence public opinion and behavior. The origins of modern propaganda in the USA can be traced to the early twentieth century with the selling of World War I and various campaigns to improve the images of big businesses and capitalist "robber barons" (Ewen, 1996; Hamilton, 2020). The term gained popularity thanks to the book by the same name written by

4 Shepard Smith left Fox News in 2019 and joined CNBC in 2020.

Edward L. Bernays (Bernays, 1928). However, the Nazi regime in Germany gave propaganda a bad name, and Bernays applied the tools of his trade to rebrand the new field with the more democracy-friendly name of public relations (Bernays, 1945). Until recently, state propaganda has been largely episodic and top-down, as when the Bush administration sold the Iraq War to much of the US media in 2002–2003 (Bennett, Lawrence, & Livingston, 2007). More benign forms of political PR and advertising have been used in top-down campaigns to sell particular policies or to market politicians in elections (Blumler & Kavanagh, 1999).

One might draw a modern-day distinction between PR and propaganda based on the ratio of truth to lies, with propaganda often using small truths to promote big lies, and PR selecting facts to support strategic messages and images. The volume of sustained false information in the Trump-Fox collaboration clearly places it in the category of propaganda. But what distinguishes it from more conventional forms is that the government regularly received active input from Fox. This was made possible by Fox's transition from a partisan journalism operation in the late 1990s to a hybrid organization that added political activism and audience mobilization to its mission (Yang, 2020). That shift in mission began after 2009 when the network became an organizing beacon for the Tea Party. Fox personalities attended political rallies, and the network website hosted membership signups (Skocpol & Williamson, 2011).

Since that time, many other right-wing media sites have emerged, often with even greater emphasis on political activism and mobilization. This has led to reclassifying much of the radical right sphere less as conventional partisan journalism, and more as a networked (Benkler et al., 2018; Bennett & Livingston, 2020) or hybrid (Chadwick, 2017; Yang, 2020) propaganda sphere producing content for strategic purposes of promoting fear, anger, division, distraction, and confusion. As shown in the network analysis in Figure 6.1, Fox content was not restricted to its own audience, but became widely shared among other organizations in this radical right media ecology. Our extension of the work on networked propaganda introduces an interactive dynamic: two-way content cueing and amplification of flows between state actors and independent media organizations. This variety of propaganda involves a different balance of power between media and state than typically found in conventional propaganda models.

A Preliminary Model of Interactive Propaganda

To summarize the argument so far, interactive propaganda during the COVID-19 crisis resulted from a two-way negotiation between Fox and Trump. The calculations on both sides of the negotiation involved several factors: the overlap in both the Trump administration and Fox agendas to keep the economy going; the overlap between Fox's audience and Trump's base;

Trump's need to appeal to his voting base through appearances on Fox and by having his messages amplified by key personalities; and Fox's periodic assessments of various risks associated with spreading false information that might put its audience and, by extension, its business at risk.[5]

A preliminary model that expresses the dynamics of this relationship involves the following stages: (1) both Trump and Fox actively monitoring the information environment to identify propaganda materials (e.g., doctors advocating the use of HCQ); (2) Trump and/or Fox cueing the other with the manufactured disinformation; (3) both sides monitoring and amplifying each other; and (4) both addressing criticism and adjusting for areas of conflicting interest. At the core of the model is the growing importance of media for political organization, with both politicians and media organizations gaining the most important asset in the attention economy, continuous public engagement.

Before he was de-platformed from Twitter for promoting the lie about the 2020 stolen election, Trump had about 88 million Twitter followers. However, based on Gallup data we estimate that roughly 10 million Americans of voting age regularly read his tweets.[6] This means that Trump still needed intermediaries to reach the rest of his voters, who numbered more than six times his regular US Twitter consumers. In addition to reaching its own viewers, Fox propaganda spread over a large right-wing media network (Figure 6.1). The echo chamber effect of multiple media reproducing and translating the same content also created conditions for reinforcement effects among self-selected audiences (Bennett & Iyengar, 2008).

Generally speaking, it was in Fox's business interest to align with Trump, who had driven Fox's ratings since the 2016 election. As Fox producers noted, their ratings dropped whenever they said something negative about Trump (Drezner, 2018). When Trump boycotted Fox News' Republican presidential debate in Des Moines in early 2016, Fox's viewership declined by 50% compared with the previous presidential debate where Trump participated (Mahler & Rutenberg, 2019). Many Fox hosts and commentators privately admitted that they felt immense pressure to please their audiences because most were also part of Trump's base (Stelter, 2020). Indeed, Fox ratings and audience share plunged after the November election in 2020 when the news division and even some of the primetime personalities were reluctant to promote Trump's big lie that the election was somehow stolen from him. However, many primetime

---

5 One study showed that early programing on *Hannity* that played down the risk of the virus resulted in greater infection and death toll than *Tucker Carlson Tonight* which gave the virus a more serious treatment (Leonardo, Rao, Roth, & Yanagizawa-Drott, 2020). Hannity later tempered his message and tried to give a revisionist impression that he had always treated the virus seriously (Hannity, March 18, 2020).

6 According to a 2018 Gallop poll, about 4% of American adults said they followed Trump Twitter account and regularly read his tweets (Newport, 2018). Based on the US Census Bureau's estimation of the size of voting population in America, we estimated that 10 million Americans of voting age regularly read Trump's tweets.

hosts adopted the line that since so many people (including most of their audience) felt the election was stolen, their concerns should be taken seriously.

By contrast, over the many months when COVID-19 was the top story, Fox played to its largely pro-Trump audience and (misguidedly) tried to solidify Trump's reelection bid by painting a rosy picture of the public health crisis with the aim of keeping the economy open. Even when programs resisted the worst of Trump's denialism, the focus was on good news: human interest stories about patient recovery, people attending church, and the promise of economic rebound. Much of the happy news was about miracle cures – drugs promoted as effective in treating COVID-19 without any scientific proof. Many of those stories portrayed Trump as a strong leader trying to cut the red tape to speed up the distribution of a cure. It was in this context that HCQ became politically useful for both Trump and Fox.

A Networked Propaganda Study of Fox and Hydroxychloroquine

The Trump administration pressured the Food and Drug Administration (FDA) to approve HCQ as a treatment for the virus. An emergency use authorization was granted on March 28, and the government distributed the Strategic National Stockpile of HCQ to hospitals and clinical trials. Moreover, the White House sidestepped the FDA and shipped some of the stockpile to pharmacies in a dozen states for treatment outside hospital and clinical trial settings in April (Rowland, Cenziper, & Rein, 2020; Taylor & Roston, 2020). All of this happened despite the lack of reliable scientific evidence that HCQ could effectively treat COVID-19. Even worse, on April 24, the FDA issued a caution that the drug could lead to sudden cardiac death. As reports of problems grew, the FDA revoked its use authorization in June, and again cautioned against HCQ due to issues such as heart rhythm problems and kidney injuries (FDA, 2020). On July 4, the World Health Organization discontinued its clinical trials of HCQ based on the finding that the drug produced little or no reduction in the mortality of hospitalized COVID-19 patients when compared to standard care (WHO, 2020).

Through this entire period and beyond, Trump continued to vouch for the drug in his press briefings, tweets, and interviews – by our count, more than 30 times between March and August. How did he become so personally invested in promoting the drug? How was the propaganda around HCQ sustained despite constant pushback from public health experts? It turns out that Fox led Trump in this misdirection and helped spread the resulting propaganda across a large right-wing media sphere.

We gathered data on the networked spread of disinformation about HCQ from Media Cloud,[7] a digital content database. We extracted all the online

---

7 Media Cloud is sponsored by multiple institutions including the Berkman Klein Center for Internet & Society at Harvard University.

articles mentioning HCQ published by 16 major radical right media outlets[8] between March 15 and August 15. We found that Fox received the highest attention within the network. Figure 6.1 shows the hyperlink network of 16 major radical right media based on their coverage of HCQ.[9] The node size in Figure 6.1 corresponds to the number of times an outlet was linked to by different media sites in the network. Fox News received the most media links, drawing attention from other outlets such as the Daily Caller, the *Washington Examiner*, the Daily Wire, and Breitbart News, which are all regular part of the US radical right media sphere as described above.

The disproportionate attention to the drug on Fox becomes clear when we compare it to mainstream TV networks. We counted the times that HCQ and chloroquine appeared in Fox programs based on Factiva's collection of TV transcripts.[10] We did the same search for CBS and NBC.[11] Figure 6.2 is a plot of the number of mentions of HCQ and chloroquine on Fox, CBS, and NBC.

CBS and NBC, while offering much smaller volumes of mentions, followed similar peaks in the weeks of March 19, May 18, and July 26. Based on our close readings of their transcripts, we found that the three peaks were respectively driven by Trump's first public comment on HCQ on March 19, his revelation that he was taking the drug on May 18, and the America's Frontline Doctors event in late July. Yet, Fox's coverage looked different. First, its initial coverage was earlier than that of CBS and NBC. Second, Fox devoted significantly more attention to the drug overall. Third, Fox's coverage was heavily concentrated in March and April and then spread across every week throughout the five-month period including June and July where there was no coverage by CBS or NBC for several weeks.

In keeping with our earlier point about areas of friction in the co-production process, not every Fox program spread disinformation about HCQ. For example, in *Your World with Neil Cavuto*, Fox host Cavuto warned his audience that the drug "will kill you" if "you are in a risky population … and are taking this as a preventative treatment" (Cavuto, May 18). In *Special Report with Brett Baier*, Fox's senior managing editor for health news Manny Alvarez called Trump's promotion of the drug highly irresponsible (Baier, May18, 2020).

8 We followed Yang (2020)'s work in identifying the 16 major radical right media in the USA.
9 The 16 media outlets are Fox News, Washington Free Beacon, *the Washington Times*, the *Washington Examiner*, the Daily Wire, the Daily Caller, WND, *the Western Journal*, Political Insider, the Gateway Pundit, the Blaze, Zero Hedge, the Right Scoop, Infowars, Breitbart News, and *the New York Post*.
10 Our Fox News collection includes The Story with Martha MacCallum, Tucker Carlson Tonight, Fox News Sunday, Hannity, Special Report with Brett Baier, the Five, the Ingraham Angle, Live Events, and Your World with Neil Cavuto.
11 Our CBS collection includes 60 Minutes, CBS This Morning, Evening News, and Face the Nation. Our NBC collection includes Today, Nightly News, and Meet the Press.

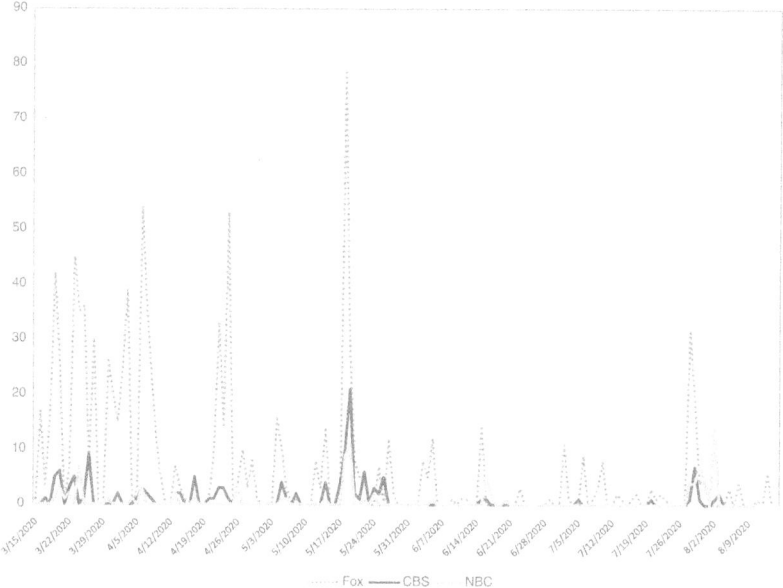

FIGURE 6.2 Word counts of hydroxychloroquine and chloroquine in the news and opinion programs of Fox, CBS, and NBC between March 15 and August 15, 2020.

Source: Factiva.

Fox's hybrid mode of straight news reporting and propaganda warrants a more granular analysis at the program level. We counted the number of mentions of the drug in five of Fox's weekday programs including the two aforementioned straight news programs and three top opinion shows (i.e., the Ingraham Angle, Hannity, and Tucker Carlson Tonight). We found that Fox's disproportionate focus on HCQ was mainly driven by its opinion shows, which accounted for roughly 70% of all its mentions. Ingraham's show alone mentioned the drugs 450 times between March and August. By contrast, Fox's straight news programs had a pattern similar to the broadcast networks: far lower than Fox primetime opinion programs and peaking at the time of Trump's announcement that he was taking the drug. We can better explain these patterns by fitting them into the preliminary model of interactive propaganda introduced earlier.

Explaining How Fox Cued Trump Using the Interactive Propaganda Model

The flow of HCQ content on Fox's opinion programs reflects all four essential components of interactive propaganda introduced earlier, namely: (1) both Trump and Fox News actively monitored the information environment to identify propaganda materials (e.g., doctors advocating the use of HCQ); (2) Trump and/or Fox cued the other with the manufactured disinformation;

(3) both sides monitored and amplified each other; and (4) both addressed criticism and adjusted for mutually conflicting interests. The following sections use the model to explain the Fox side of the interaction with an analysis focusing on Laura Ingraham's show, both because she covered the drug much more often than the other opinion hosts, and because she played a key role in shaping President Trump's personal promotion of the drug.

Monitoring and Gathering (Dis)information

The first component of the model is monitoring the information environment and identifying politically useful, even if factually incorrect claims. Previous research shows that Fox's disinformation comes from a board range of sources including politicians, right-wing think tanks, and social media (Benkler et al., 2018). According to researchers from First Draft, the false narrative about HCQ as a coronavirus treatment originated from the French doctor Didier Raoult who declared the drug had a 100% cure rate against COVID-19 (Gallagher, 2020). Yet, it was through a blockchain enthusiast named Gregory Rigano that Fox found that disinformation. On March 13, Rigano and others created a Google Doc on the use of chloroquine for COVID-19 treatment (Bump, 2020a; Sayare, 2020). The Google Doc quickly gained traction within Silicon Valley and caught the attention of Raoult who shared his research results with Rigano before publishing his study on March 20. On March 16, Rigano appeared on Ingraham's show as a spokesperson for the French study, claiming that HCQ can prevent the virus from attaching to the body and could get rid of COVID-19 completely. "That's a game changer" Ingraham declared (Ingraham, March 16). In the following day, Rigano appeared on Tucker Carlson's show and claimed that Raoult's study showed a 100% cure rate (Carlson, March 18, 2020).

To convert this piece of disinformation into a sustained propaganda campaign, Ingraham kept surfacing new anecdotal evidence on her show. Our data reveal that Ingraham brought at least five different patients on her show to offer their personal accounts, interviewed more than thirteen different doctors who vouched for the drug, and cited four "scientific studies" to buttress her argument. Ingraham's sustained efforts to gather and present fresh materials kept the propaganda campaign alive even during June and July when little major news about the drug broke on broadcast TV. For example, between June 25 and July 25 Ingraham interviewed five different doctors, promoted a new study that showed benefits of the drug, and pushed out a series of talking points (Ingraham, July 2, 2020; Ingraham, July 20, 2020). Both the study and the talking points were later tweeted repeatedly by Trump. Ingraham had turned sketchy disinformation into breaking news that was taken up by Trump.

Cueing the Trump Administration with Manufactured Information

The next step following the identification and promotion of disinformation is to channel it to the government. Knowing that Trump was their most influential audience, many Fox hosts spoke directly with and to the President on their shows. Ingraham directly addressed President Trump multiple times in her show and claimed credit for bringing HCQ to Trump's attention (Ingraham, March 19, 2020). We also found that Ingraham actively tried to channel the disinformation to other Trump officials. For instance, in March Ingraham invited administration health officials Anthony Fauci and Alex Azar to her program and informed them of the studies that showed benefits. And Fox White House correspondent John Roberts touted the drug during a March 18 briefing by Dr. Deborah Birx, the White House Corona Virus Response Coordinator. The next day, Trump promoted the drug at the daily White House briefing.

Over the next weeks Fox personalities fed Trump a steady supply of talking points. For example, on April 7 Trump said he learned from Laura Ingraham's show that a Democratic congresswoman from Michigan used HCQ and recovered from COVID-19. More generally, we examined all of Trump's tweets ($N = 23$) about HCQ over the five-month period and compared their content as well as timing to those of various Fox shows. We found that at least 11 of Trump's tweets[12] were direct or indirect responses to Fox content. Based on those tweets, we also found that Fox cued Trump with at least three talking points: a study in the *International Journal of Antimicrobial Agents* reporting promising results, a study from the Henry Ford Health System claiming that HCQ reduced COVID-19 death rate, and an on-air medical expert who claimed that it could save up to 100,000 lives if the US government distributed its stockpile. Besides the on-air cueing, Fox personalities communicated with Trump and other administration officials both personally and through backchannels. For instance, on April 3, Ingraham brought two doctors from her "medical cabinet" to the White House to advise Trump personally on HCQ.

Monitoring and Amplifying the Government Response

After Ingraham and other Fox hosts cued the president, they amplified his messages, which, in fact, were largely theirs. In March, Trump promoted the drug at five different public events. While NBC News only covered one of those events, Laura Ingraham covered all the five, including Trump's March 19 statement about HCQ as a very powerful drug, the March 20 statement about him being a big fan of the drug, the March 27 statement about him pushing the FDA to green-light HCQ, the March 30 statement about him receiving

---

12 Two tweets criticized Fox and nine promoted Fox's content.

donations of the drug from pharmaceutical companies, and the March 31 statement about him getting the approval from the FDA (which was later revoked).

Addressing Criticism and Adjusting for Areas of Conflicting Interest

Given the volume of false information in this campaign, it is not surprising that Fox faced scrutiny by fact-checkers, public officials not aligned with Trump, and mainstream media outlets. The day after Laura Ingraham spread the disinformation about HCQ on March 16, Dr. Fauci claimed that the evidence from the French study was only anecdotal. After the FDA was pressured to issue an emergency use authorization for the drug in hospitals and clinical trials on March 28, more scrutiny and warnings came from public health experts. One reason why Ingraham's coverage peaked and concentrated in March and April and tailed off after that may be due to the large volume of criticism from public health experts and mainstream media. In Table 6.1, we listed the sources of criticism and paraphrased Ingraham's responses to criticism during March and April.

As Table 6.1 shows, Ingraham began to counter criticism on the day that Trump first touted the drug in public. To defend herself and Trump, Ingraham framed skepticism toward the drug as anti-Trump hatred and attacked government agencies (FDA and CDC), public health officials (Fauci), the scientific community, and the mainstream media. Her countering of criticism continued into June and July when Ingraham called on the FDA to rescind its warning and resume authorization of the drug. Ingraham eventually turned

TABLE 6.1 The Ingraham Angle's Responses to Criticism

Date	Source	Content	Response
3/19	MSNBC	President should not tout the drug.	He should.
3/20	Fauci	The evidence was only anecdotal.	We don't have time to wait for better evidence.
3/26	Fauci	We need controlled clinical trials.	We don't have time to wait for better evidence.
3/31	Fauci	We need controlled clinical trials.	We don't have time to wait for better evidence.
4/9	CDC director	We should be cautious about the drug.	We don't need the CDC director.
4/13	Fauci	The evidence was only anecdotal.	Fauci is dismissive.
4/22	CNN, WaPost, NYT, and AP	Experts urged caution against the drug. A new study showing potential harms of the drug.	Mainstream media is a joke. The study was flawed.
4/24	FDA, CNN	FDA issued warning against the drug.	FDA is dismissive.

4/27	Doctors	Johns Hopkins Medicine pulled back from using the drug due to heart issues.	We don't believe it.
4/28	Arizona governor	Arizona governor restricted the use of the drug.	Politicians should not get in between patients and doctors.
4/29	Fauci	We should start trials on the drug Remdesivir.	Fauci could be financially motivated to dismiss HCQ and promote Remdesivir.

Source: Factiva.

her attention to developing new elements of the propaganda campaign, such as opening schools in the fall.

Conclusion

The co-production of disinformation about HCQ was just one chapter in the long propaganda battle against the coronavirus on the radical right led by Fox and Donald Trump. The various elements of this campaign followed the four elements that we have identified as constituting the co-production process: mutual monitoring and identifying disinformation, alternate media cueing of government or government cueing of media, each side echoing the uptake of cues by the other, and countering criticism while adjusting for diverging interests. In the last section, we formulated this process from the standpoint of the media outlet, Fox, but a parallel analysis can easily be done from the standpoint of the Trump administration.

Like many other messages about COVID-19 that were both wrong and dangerous, HCQ was eventually replaced by other co-produced lines of propaganda. Underlying the continuing resistance to protecting public health were concerns that the virus would kill the economy and damage Trump's reelection chances. Following that misguided logic, Trump alternately ignored the growing problem, mocked its prominence in mainstream news, and dismissed statements by opponent Joe Biden, whom Trump mocked for wearing such big masks. Trump returned to holding large public campaign rallies featuring packed crowds with few masks in sight. Those super-spreader events caused alarm among health experts, but Fox spun it all away with criticisms of Biden for hiding in his basement during the campaign. Due in part to the misdirection from the president and trusted information sources on the right, the virus reached new records in its spread by the final stages of the 2020 presidential election campaign. That surge of illness was ironically led by the Red or Republican states that were liberated from worrying about the problem, partly due to being primary targets of the propaganda.

Such production of interactive, networked propaganda is a novel and unfortunate development in the role of media in a struggling American democracy. Had Trump won the election, it is likely that both sides would have continued their mutually beneficial relationship, at the cost of steering the country in an increasingly authoritarian direction. It bears watching what will happen if Trump's post-election popularity fades and other radical right politicians such as senators Ted Cruz or Josh Hawley try to inherit his movement. Will they attempt to develop similar relationships with Fox and other outlets in the right-wing media ecology? Will they escalate attacks on independent journalism, as has happened in other polarized societies with leaders seeking to create illiberal regimes? Whether or not current levels of hostility toward science, public institutions, and liberal values continue to grow, large numbers of Americans will continue living in alternative realities that both produce and create strong demand for disinformation. An interactive propaganda system may become a stable communication model in a divided nation that continues to call itself a democracy.

References

Abutaleb, Y., & Dawsey, J. (2020, August 31). New Trump pandemic adviser pushes controversial herd immunity strategy, worrying public health officials. *The Washington Post.*

Baier, B. (2020, May 18). *Special Report* [Transcript]. Fox News Channel. Retrieved September 3, 2020, from Factiva database (Dow Jones).

Benkler, Y., Faris, R., & Roberts, H. (2018). *Network propaganda: Manipulation disinformation, and radicalization in American politics.* Oxford University Press.

Bennett, L., & Iyengar, S. (2008). A new era of minimal effects? The changing foundations of political communication. *Journal of Communication, 58*(4), 707–731.

Bennett, L., Lawrence, R., & Livingston, S. (2007). *When the press fails: Political power and the news media from Iraq and Katrina.* University of Chicago Press.

Bennett, L., & Livingston, S. (2020). A brief history of the disinformation age. In W. L. Bennett & S. Livingstone (Eds.), *The disinformation age.* Cambridge University Press.

Bernays, E. (1928). *Propaganda.* Horace Liveright.

Bernays, E. (1945). *Public relations.* Bellman.

Blumler, J. G., & Kavanagh, D. (1999). The third age of political communication: Influences and features. *Political Communication, 16*(3), 209–230.

Bump, P. (2020a, April 24). The rise and fall of Trump's obsession with hydroxychloroquine. *The Washington Post.*

Bump, P. (2020b, September 16). The problem with Trump's herd mentality line isn't the verbal flub. It's the mass death. *The Washington Post.*

Carlson, T. (2020, March 9; March 18; July 6). *Tucker Carlson Tonight* [Transcript]. Fox News Channel. Retrieved September 3, 2020, from Factiva database (Dow Jones).

Cavuto, N. (2020, May 18). *Your World with Neil Cavuto* [Transcript]. Fox News Channel. Retrieved September 3, 2020, from Factiva database (Dow Jones).

Chadwick, A. (2017). *The hybrid media system.* Oxford University Press.

Choi, M. (2020, May). Trump goes after Fox News host, and the network, in Twitter flurry. *Politico.*

Costa, R. (2020, March 17). As much of America takes drastic action, some Republicans remain skeptical of the severity of the coronavirus pandemic. *The Washington Post.*
Dawsey, J., & Abutaleb, Y. (2020, October 31). A whole lot of hurt: Fauci warns of Covid surge, offers blunt assessment of Trump's response. *The Washington Post.*
Derysh, I. (2020, April). Trump attacks Fox News reporter for asking about disbanded pandemic team: Are you working for CNN. *Salon.*
Drezner, D. (2018, January 17). The Fox News effect. *The Washington Post.*
Ellison, S., & Barr, J. (2020, October 29). What happens to Fox News if Trump loses? Rupert Murdoch is prepared. *The Washington Post.*
Ellison, S. (2019, June 23). The judge who speaks Trump's language. *The Washington Post.*
Evanega, S., Lynas, M., Adams, J., & Smolenyak, K. (2020). Coronavirus misinformation: Quantifying sources and themes in the COVID-19 infodemic. Working paper. Cornell University.
Ewen, S. (1996). *PR! A social history of spin.* Basic Books.
Faulders, K., & Santucci, J. (2020, July 13). White House seeks to discredit Fauci in memo leaked to reporters. *ABC News.*
FDA. (2020). FDA cautions against use of hydroxychloroquine or chloroquine for COVID-19 outside of the hospital setting or a clinical trial due to a risk of heart rhythm problems. US Food and Drug Administration.
Gallagher, F. (2020, April 22). Tracking hydroxychloroquine misinformation: How an unproven COVID-19 treatment ended up being endorsed by Trump. *ABC News.*
Gertz, M. (2018, January). I've studied the Trump-Fox feedback loop for months. It's crazier than you think. *Politico.*
Gertz, M. (2020). *Top right-wing media figures rally around "demon sperm" doc.* Media Matters.
Hamilton, J. M. (2020). *Manipulating the masses: Woodrow Wilson and the birth of American propaganda.* LSU Press.
Hannity, S. (2020, February 27; March 6; March 18). *Hannity* [Transcript]. Fox News Channel. Retrieved September 3, 2020, from Factiva database (Dow Jones).
Hilton, S. (2020, March 22). *The Next Revolution with Steve Hilton.* [Transcript]. Fox News Channel. Retrieved September 3, 2020, from Factiva database (Dow Jones).
Ingraham, L. (2020, March 16; March 19; March 20; April 4; July 2; July 20). *The Ingraham Angle* [Transcript]. Fox News Channel. Retrieved October 9, 2020, from Factiva database (Dow Jones).
Kiely, E., Robertson, L., Rieder, R., & Gore, D. (2020). *Timeline of Trump's COVID-19 comments.* Fackcheck.org.
Leonardo, B., Rao, A., Roth, C., & Yanagizawa-Drott, D. (2020). Misinformation during a pandemic. *SSRN Electronic Journal.* https://doi.org/10.2139/ssrn.3580487
Mahler, J., & Rutenberg, J. (2019, April 3). How Rupert Murdoch's empire of influence remade the world. *The New York Times.*
McDonald, J. (2020). Will the new coronavirus go away in April. *Fackcheck.org.*
Newport, F. (2018). Deconstructing Trump's use of Twitter. *Fackcheck.org.*
Pirro, J. (2020, March 7). *Justice with Judge Jeanine* [Transcript]. Fox News Channel. Retrieved September 3, 2020, from Factiva database (Dow Jones).
Rowland, C., Cenziper, D., & Rein, L. (2020, October 31). White House sidestepped FDA to distribute hydroxychloroquine to pharmacies, documents show. Trump touted the pills to treat COVID-19. *The Washington Post.*
Richwine, L. (2020, December 29). Fox News extends streak, sets cable news records in 2020. *Reuters.*

Sayare, S. (2020, May 12). He was a science star. Then he promoted a questionable cure for COVID-19. *The New York Times*.

Skocpol, T., & Williamson, V. (2011, December 21). The Fox in the Tea Party. *Reuters*.

Stelter, B. (2020). *Hoax: Donald Trump, Fox News, and the dangerous distortion of truth*. Simon & Schuster.

Taylor, M., & Roston, A. (2020, April 4). Exclusive: Pressured by Trump, US pushed unproven coronavirus treatment guidance. *Reuters*.

WHO. (2020). WHO discontinues hydroxychloroquine and lopinavir/ritonavir treatment arms for COVID-19. World Health Organization.

Woodward, B. (2020). *Rage*. Simon & Schuster.

Yang, Y. (2020). *The political logic of the radical right media sphere in the United States* (Order No. 27957926). Available from Dissertations & Theses at University of Washington WCLP; ProQuest Dissertations & Theses Global (2437414567). Retrieved from https://search.proquest.com/docview/2437414567?accountid=14784

# 7

STOOGES OF THE SYSTEM OR HOLISTIC OBSERVERS?

A Computational Analysis of News Media's Facebook Posts on Political Actors during the Coronavirus Crisis in Germany

Thorsten Quandt, Svenja Boberg, Tim Schatto-Eckrodt, and Lena Frischlich

Introduction

News media frequently cover crisis situations, from military conflicts, natural disasters, and terrorist attacks to large-scale effects of man-made accidents. Some of these are unexpected and practically without a build-up (like the Chernobyl disaster or 9/11), but some of them evolve (like hurricane seasons), and some fall somewhere in-between (like structural conflicts between nations that lead to sudden military actions). For most types of crises (Nord & Strömbäck, 2006), journalism has developed specific routines and practices (e.g., Olsson & Nord, 2015). Preparation and rules, as well as rituals (Durham, 2008; Riegert & Olsson, 2007) help in dealing with unexpected events or unfolding situations that fall outside the coverage of "normal" times. Part of this is driven by informational goals that are inherent to journalism, but part of it is an urge to establish authority in societal communication under non-normal conditions (ibid.).

The coronavirus crisis, however, seems to have caught many news organizations off-guard; the coverage during the initial spread of the virus in early 2020 was scarce (see also Boberg et al., 2020) and many news media around the globe made the false assessment that the outbreak would either not affect countries other than China or that the virus was less dangerous than the flu (e.g., Henry & Hauck, 2020). Coverage did not take off until the consequences for the respective nations became apparent and experiential. When the virus and its effects reached the national populations, though, the news output on the virus threat seemed to explode, and journalism switched to full "crisis mode."

Critics, including journalism researchers, noted multiple issues with this reaction, identifying deficits in the coverage and journalism's functioning. In the

DOI: 10.4324/9781003170051-9

case of Germany, which is the country of analysis of this chapter, communication scholars noted a limited set of expert voices and "court circular"[1] for some media (Jarren, 2020), a lack of distance and critique, not enough variance, and "horse-race reporting" with regard to national comparisons of infection numbers (Meier & Wyss, 2020). Many of these critical observers found the coverage to be too close to the actions of the political elite and in unquestioned support of governmental decisions. The anecdotal evidence has yet to be tested against empirical research, and it remains to be seen whether there is support for the more general observation of previous research that the coverage in crisis situations turns to "pseudo-journalism" (Nord & Strömbäck, 2006, p. 105) and "reporting more, informing less" (ibid., p. 85), i.e., a systemic failure.

To address this research interest, we will analyze the posts of journalistic media on Facebook during the first nine months of the coronavirus crisis in Germany, using various forms of computational content analysis. In particular, we will focus on the presence of (political) elite actors: how they were connected to specific topics and strategic roles in the coverage, and how this has changed during the various phases of the pandemic. The choice of Facebook news is deliberate: virtually all journalistic media in the country do offer near-time news via their Facebook channels, so this is a useful tool for observing the news flow. By analyzing the news items there, we can give a comprehensive overview of the crisis response of the journalistic system in one country (i.e., it serves as an indicator of what is covered in news media in general). Furthermore, Facebook is also used as a primary news source by many users, and as such, it is a highly relevant distribution channel for news media in its own right: 21% of the German population above the age of 14 use it daily (in contrast to highly researched Twitter, which is only used by 2%) (Beisch et al., 2019). Before turning to the analysis, though, we will briefly recap previous research on crisis journalism and its relations to political actions.

Crisis Journalism

Crisis coverage has been subject to journalism research for decades, often in relation to specific events. In particular, in the aftermath of the 9/11 attacks and other terrorist events and the military conflicts that directly or indirectly followed it, there has been a rising interest in the analysis of the journalistic response and performance throughout extraordinary times (Lund & Olsson, 2016). While a major block of this research focused on armed conflict and shocking events tied to terrorism, some of the findings may be helpful in understanding the coronavirus crisis coverage. Naturally, differing qualities of

---

1 In German, "Hofberichterstattung" (court circular) means news of the court and the royal family, but it is also used to denote uncritical reporting on the political elite and their decisions.

the respective cases under analysis still need to be kept in mind, in particular, with regard to time-based developments and the existence of tangible conflict groups and interests (or the lack thereof). Also, there are more or less severe crises, and it has been shown that the journalistic handling very much depends on such qualities. In particular, so-called "frame breakers" (Lund & Olsson, 2016), that is, the "worst events (...) that are genuinely unprecedented and shocking," which cannot be "anticipated, and challenge even the most established journalistic practices" (ibid., p. 358) can lead to inadequate responses.

Such works on frame breakers (Boin et al., 2005; Lund & Olsson, 2016) are following Weick's (1993) characterization of "cosmology episodes" that shatter the universe's order (in a figurative sense) and also the means to piece that order together again. Journalism research has identified and analyzed multiple such events, like terrorist attacks and wars (Lund & Olsson, 2016; Nord & Strömbäck, 2006). In particular, research has focused on the importance of norms, standards, roles, and routines in channeling events that are unknown and untypified when they enter journalistic processing in crisis situations (Olsson & Nord, 2015). Expecting the unexpected is, in many ways, part of the modus operandi of journalism under normal conditions, but as research shows, even for extraordinary events, the level of disruption can be reduced by having appropriate work routines in place. Other studies have focused on rituals in journalism (Durham, 2008; Riegert & Olsson, 2007). They argue rituals to be essential to journalism's operation in crisis (Couldry, 2003; Durham, 2008), as "media rituals can be said to function as a way for media organizations (...) to establish authority by playing a key part in society's healing process" (Riegert & Olsson, 2007, p. 147). Based on the analysis of broadcast journalist's decision-making during two crises (9/11 and the Anna Lindh murder in 2003), Riegert and Olsson (2007, p. 143) conclude that "in times of crisis, the roles of psychologist, comforter and co-mourner should be considered journalistic role conceptions especially in a live, 24-hour news culture."

Naturally, there are limitations to applying the patterns as observed in armed conflicts and attacks on the civil society to the pandemic situation. German virologist and government advisor Christian Drosten called the pandemic a "natural disaster in slow-motion" (NDR Info, 2020). In terms of news-related properties, this characterization is quite fitting. Many of the previously analyzed crises are structured around "events" that happen at specific points of time. The time span of the relevant trigger events is often minimal, without a lengthy build-up, and the effects are directly apparent and severe (like in the case of terror or military attacks, volcano eruptions, or tsunamis). The pandemic, however, evolved over a longer period of time, with no publicly observable trigger event, and there were no immediately observable and strong effects directly following the initial first infections.

In line with these considerations, Nord and Strömbäck (2006), in their analysis of Swedish news media in multiple crises, noted that *time* is a key component in the way media operate in crises. Their study hypothesized that the performance of journalistic reporting in crisis is "dependent on both the existence of media routines and the possibility for the media to make adequate preparations" (ibid., p. 89), further typifying crises along these two dimensions (media preparations and media routines). Taking the expansion of online information channels in recent years and the corresponding changes in the news flow into account, the pressure to "fill empty space" under time constraints has plausibly increased considerably in the context of the unforeseen and unprecedented crisis situation, challenging journalistic work processes even more.

New Platforms and News Bursts

The efforts to report on extraordinary events in the shortest possible time predate the Internet by far, and to be as up-to-date as possible has always been relevant for news production (Lewis & Cushion, 2009). However, news media were bound to deadlines, due to fixed production and publication rhythms. The arrival of 24-hour TV news channels changed this considerably, as the threshold for the immediate coverage of "breaking news" was lowered systematically (Lewis & Cushion, 2009; Rosenberg & Feldman, 2008). The Internet and online news media further contributed to the evolution of journalism – the "online first" dissemination of news in a continuous process ushered in a new "era of fluid deadlines" (Buhl et al., 2019, p. 911). New platforms like Facebook and Twitter further added to this, as they are built for constant information flows; the timeline logic, extremely short messages, and a culture of pushing texts in an evolving stream have all contributed to a further compression of time and journalistic processes, and even a vanishing of deadlines (Karlsson & Strömbäck, 2010).

Journalism research has focused on the effects of such rapid news diffusion processes. For example, Harder, Sevenans, and Van Aelst (2017) applied a "news story" approach to the analysis of intermedia agenda-setting processes in hybrid media systems. Buhl and colleagues (2018, 2019) showed that specific event features lead to extremely fast reaction times and stories by a high number of media. They labeled this phenomenon "news bursts." This empirical research stresses not only the effects of online media and platforms on virtually immediate news diffusion processes, but also the complexities of information distribution in a still-evolving hybrid media system (Chadwick, 2017). Further, it reveals that information in such a system seems to partially spread in a viral, uncontrolled logic; at the same time, event features are relevant, and actors (like news media) still play an active, partially steering role. With regard to the crisis state of journalism, we therefore ask:

RQ1: How did the coronavirus news flow evolve over time?

Coverage of Political Actors in Crisis

Studies on the representation of political actors in crises are relatively rare. However, critics noted a very limited focus on very few key figures in the coronavirus crisis, and a heroization of seemingly omni-present individuals, for example, leading medical experts and virologists (see the introductory section). From the long-standing tradition of personalization research, we know that news media, especially in the political realm, use personalization as a tool for telling stories via individual actors (Boumans et al., 2013). However, systematic reviews of personalization research show that the thesis of increasing personalization cannot be universally confirmed (Adam & Maier, 2010), at least when the concept is understood in a very broad sense. Therefore, Van Aelst and colleagues (2012) call for a division of the concept into the dimensions "privatization" and "individualization." In the current study, we refer to personalization not in the sense of "privatization" (i.e., the focus on the private or even intimate life and characteristics of political actors), but in the form of individualization. Individualization is defined as the increased focus on individual politicians at the expense of other political actors (i.e., institutions). A further distinction is made here between *general visibility* and *concentrated visibility*.

General visibility is referred to as the increased presence of individuals as opposed to parties and organizations. In German election campaigns, there has been an increasing visibility of individual politicians, with parties focusing on the presentation of their top candidates and fading into the background as an organization; this process has increased especially with the advent of TV debates (Esser & Hemmer, 2008). However, the increasing focus on individual politicians cannot be observed consistently, or rather reached its saturation (Kriesi, 2012). Crisis journalism also seems to focus more on individual action takers than on the organizations to which they are affiliated (Denner et al., 2020). Therefore, we examine the extent to which this is also the case in the coverage of the pandemic:

RQ2: Is the corona coverage focusing on individual actors or instead organizational actors?

In fact, focusing on people can be useful from the user's perspective and help reduce the complexity of reporting – as long as the acceptance of others as legitimate speakers is not affected. This phenomenon is addressed in the concept of concentrated visibility, meaning the shifting focus to few leading actors and top politicians (Van Aelst et al., 2012).

A common example of this is the incumbency bonus. Politicians who are currently in (higher) offices generally attract more media attention than regular (oppositional) politicians. The extent to which this bonus is granted depends on various factors such as the power structure in the country and the journalism culture (Hopmann et al., 2011; van Dalen, 2012). In Germany – in contrast to other consensus democracies, where the focus on political elites is traditionally less pronounced than in majoritarian democracies – the reporting mainly focuses on a few individual figures. However, a constant prominence of the chancellor does not equal an advantage in the evaluation (Esser & Hemmer, 2008). In the context of the pandemic, a strong (though possibly critical) spotlight on political elites could prevent other voices, such as the opposition, from being heard. We address this problem in the following research question.

RQ3: Is the corona coverage concentrated on a limited number of elite actors?

This does not mean, however, that this form of storytelling causes issues to disappear from view. Indeed, another facet of the concept of personalization is whether specific actors can be associated with particular issues in the media coverage. This has so far been observed during election campaigns (Günther et al., 2017). However, crises can offer special opportunities for actors, as they can show expertise and distinguish themselves as problem solvers. This is an especially relevant aspect in Germany, as multiple regional elections and federal elections are held in 2021. Thus, the candidates' crisis management is occasionally discussed as a trial by fire on the way to chancellorship (Wiegand, 2020). Therefore, it is consequential to examine central actors and their strategic role in media coverage during the pandemic:

RQ4: In what topical contexts do the prominent political actors show up and how does this change over the course of the pandemic?

Method

Sample

In the subsequent analysis, we address the Facebook posts of news outlets during the first nine month of the coronavirus crisis, beginning with January 7, 2020, the day Chinese authorities first isolated the new type of virus, until October 6, 2020. As part of Facebook's transparency initiative, we were able to collect the data via CrowdTangle, a platform that tracks the public content from verified Facebook profiles and pages.

For the collection of news media posts, we relied on an updated version of an earlier overview of German mainstream newspapers (Frischlich et al., 2019). The procedure followed a multi-level triangulation approach identifying online media sites with more than 500,000 unique users (AGOF, 2020), then detecting online newspapers within this database following the existing literature (Buhl et al., 2018; Schütz, 2012). Hereby, we identified 77 national and regional online newspapers that ran an active Facebook page during our analysis period and collected a total of 578,551 news media posts. In order to detect all coronavirus-related posts, we applied a dictionary including most frequent terms that are associated with the coronavirus, the resulting disease COVID-19 or measures taken to prevent infections (e.g., "Maskenpflicht," obligation to wear masks), resulting in 159,422 coronavirus-related posts.

Preprocessing

CrowdTangle allows for a typical set of metadata like timestamps, page likes, engagement metrics, and information on linked URLs in the posts (including embedded headlines and teaser texts of the linked sites or articles).

To make the data ready for analysis, we used a pipeline of preprocessing steps that were demonstrated in previous studies (Boberg et al., 2018), which included removing fragments of html markup, URLs, mentions, and hashtags, punctuation, and stop words. The ambiguous use of words was disentangled by annotating named entities with the Python software library spaCy (Honnibal & Johnson, 2015) and adjusting them manually. This included the merging of different terms for the same actor (e.g., "the US-president" and "Donald Trump"), but also the differentiation of terms used in varying contexts (e.g., "government," "German government," or "US-government").

Analytical Approach

With regard to RQ1 we identified and counted the coronavirus-related posts over time and the number of preprocessed named entities. In order to inspect the most central actors (RQ2 and RQ3) and the contexts in which they are discussed (RQ4), a co-occurrence analysis was conducted (Bordag, 2008), which counts the number of times two words occur in the same document. The pairwise count was computed on the whole sample of corona-related posts and then filtered by the 20 most frequently named political actors as annotated during named entity recognition. These included professional politicians, as well as political parties and institutions (i.e., the German Government or the European Union). The co-occurrence network of actors and associated terms was then visualized as a force-directed graph using the R package igraph (Csardi & Nepusz, 2006).

Results

The (Coronavirus) News Flow

During the course of the nine months – or 274 days – of analysis, the news outlets published 578,551 news pieces, which equals more than 2,000 items per day (see Table 7.1 for an overview). More than 70% of this news output was contributed by regional outlets, which also means that their individual daily output was slightly higher than the average.

TABLE 7.1 News output and interactions according to media type

Media Type	Pages	Page Likes		Posts		Total Interactions	
		Total	Per Page	Total	Per Page	Total	Per Post
Nationwide (liberal)	8	5,420,096	677,512	56,874	7,109	28,038,049	493
Nationwide (conservative)	4	3,148,001	629,600	37,148	7,430	24,184,443	651
Tabloid	8	3,389,416	423,677	49,913	6,239	22,764,877	456
Regional	52	4,376,107	84,155	412,550	7,933	37,4722,86	91
Other	5	617,121	123,424	22,066	4,413	1,248,988	57

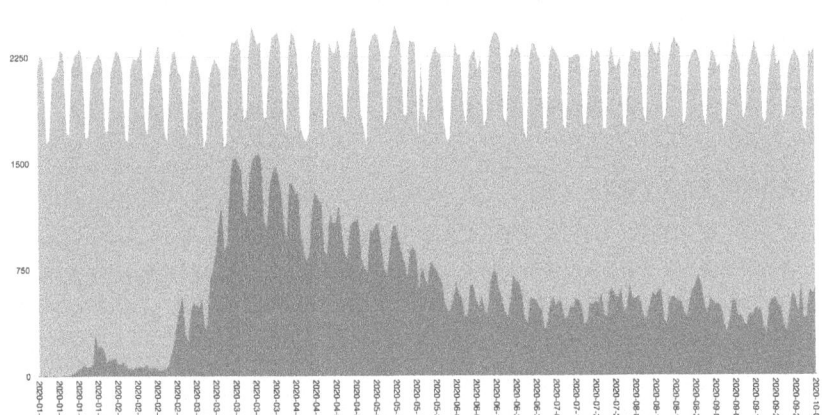

FIGURE 7.1 News flow during the first nine months of the pandemic (N=578,551)

While these aggregated numbers allow for a comparison of media type's performance across the first nine months of the crisis, they do not reveal how the overall system reacted to the crisis over time, and how the coverage evolved. Plausibly, one would expect the news flow to grow (at least in the beginning of the crisis), as media ramp up production to cope with the heightened interest and the additional need for information.

Indeed, and in contrast to the plausible expectation, there are just limited adaptions in the overall output (see Figure 7.1; light gray). There were some more "busy" weeks in March and April (with peak outputs being over the average), which was the time of the school closures and contact restrictions, i.e., the first "lockdown," and some "high output" days throughout the year (mostly due to individual "breaking news"). However, all in all, the news flow is surprisingly stable. Notable are the weekend production dips, hinting at typical production routines being not affected by the pandemic at all (even though some news outlets had to rely on home office work for some time throughout the year, depending on national or regional/local measures).

In contrast to the overall numbers, the output of coronavirus-related posts changes much more dynamically throughout the year. There is a first, smaller burst of messages early on in the year, when there were first infections in Germany. As the situation seemed to be contained at first, the coverage quickly diminished. There was a second burst at the end of February, when there were new and hard-to-trace infection chains. The first deaths in Germany, a growing number of infections, the loss of control over the situation, and the decision of strong restrictions ("lockdown") contributed to a massive growth of COVID-19-related messages. Indeed, the crisis coverage took over much of the news output in March, and was still the dominant topic in April. We see the curve to flatten in May, and stay at a relatively constant level throughout the rest of the analysis period. Even the beginning growth of infection numbers after the summer holidays (which heralded the "second wave") is not reflected in the stable output. One can interpret this as a "normalization" of the crisis, with a certain base of messages focusing on the coronavirus citation, but a large portion of the coverage dedicated to other topics (like the US election campaigns). In that sense, we see several phases of development here that deserve further inspection – and that may correspond with different time-based types of crisis reactions, as also implied by previous literature.

The Visibility of Political Actors

The current study focuses on the coverage of actors in the crisis, the respective personalization in the form of individualization. All of these aspects are plausibly indicative of a specific type of crisis coverage close to the power elite and the government.

In line with previous research (i.e., during elections), there is support for the assumption that journalism in crisis is concentrating on a limited set of elite actors (see Figure 7.2): the distribution follows a power logic, with a very small set of actors dominating the coverage, and a large number of others being very rarely covered in a "long tail."

Within the group of most frequently covered actors, we find a few unexpected or atypical actors. Most conspicuously, the most frequently mentioned actor in the crisis is not even a domestic one: it's the US President Donald Trump. There are other US-American actors in the long tail (like the democrat Joe Biden and the director of the National Institute of Allergy and Infectious Diseases, Anthony Fauci), but the leading position of Trump in the news is not necessarily just due to the "typical" reporting on the United States as the

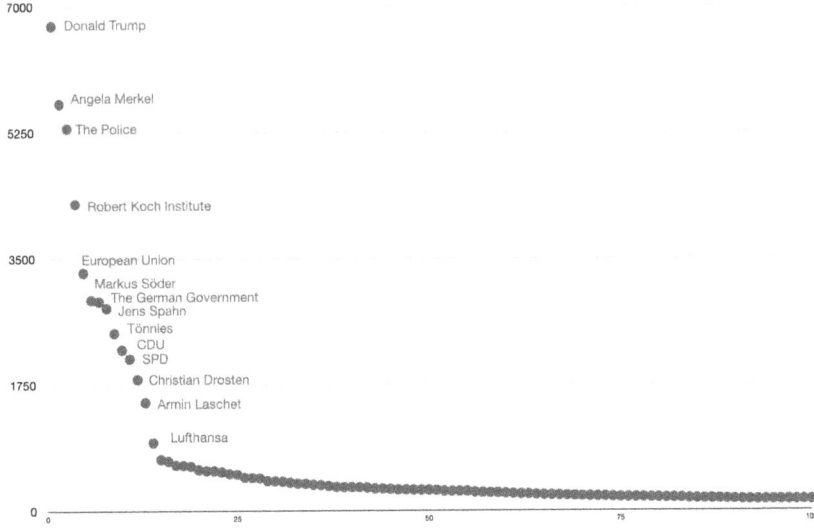

FIGURE 7.2 100 most frequent actors (N=24.260)

relevant superpower for politics in Germany. Trump himself has been object to a mixture of fascination and disapproval in the German press, and there has been a very strong personalization of US politics, which were virtually equated with the actions of the US president even before the crisis.

Unsurprisingly, the second most frequently mentioned actor is the German chancellor, Angela Merkel. Other politicians among the top actors include the Bavarian minister president, Markus Söder, the minister of health, Jens Spahn, and the North Rhine-Westphalian minister president, Armin Laschet – they were all involved in various governmental decision processes on containment measures. So their presence is in line with previous studies addressing concentrated individualization (for example, Günther et al., 2017), yet the reduction to just a handful of elite actors is still striking. Similarly, our analysis also reveals a very sharp focus on just a few medical experts who serve as "elite scientists": the virologists Christan Drosten and Hendrik Streeck, as well as the politician and health expert Karl Lauterbach. In particular, Drosten and Streeck were portrayed as opponents in some media (for example in the tabloid BILD), with Drosten symbolizing a strict approach to containment, and Streeck symbolizing a more liberal approach. Individualization is extreme here, and these actors "signify" a specific position in the debate.

However, we can also identify numerous institutional actors as being relevant in the coverage, like the police and the national institute for disease control, the Robert Koch Institute (RKI), the parties in the governmental coalition (SPD, CDU), and large companies that were heavily affected by the economic effects of the coronavirus measures (Lufthansa, Karstadt, TUI, etc.) or virus outbreaks (Tönnies, Webasto, Wiesenhof). With regard to RQ2, the coverage is not fully "individualized," with the economy being rather portrayed from an organizational or systemic perspective, while the political sphere is being reduced to the actions of individuals.

Finally, it is important to also mention what we do *not* see in the top list of the most frequently mentioned actors: the politicians of the parliamentary opposition are largely missing from the picture. The leading representatives of the Green Party receive less than 200 mentions, and the leader of the liberals (FDP) is not even among the top 100. As a comparison, conspiracy theorists (like the former TV cook and influencer Attila Hildmann, who early on warned of an impending "coronavirus dictatorship") and other fringe actors received more attention than the actors of the political opposition. These findings regarding RQ3 are congruent with the assumed concentration of political coverage on a few governmental elite actors in national crises, which has been observed by other scholars before.

Pandemic Phases and Changes in Actor Constellations

As outlined above, one of our main interests is the analysis of personalization during the crisis, in order to see how journalism covered political (elite) actors. While we identified main (political) actors already, we still do not know *how* they were portrayed in the media. To make the changes over time more tangible, we decided to apply a term-based network analysis according to phases, following our above analysis of the news flow over time. The above temporal news flow analysis already implied three phases of coverage throughout the crisis: (1) a first phase predating and leading to the national outbreak, (2) a second phase of dominant coverage during the national lockdown (with a relatively quick decline after the lockdown ended), and (3) a third phase of a stable plateau, with the coronavirus coverage being a central, but somewhat "normalized" topic.

Phase 1: Outbreak (7 March–21 March 2020)

As noted above, the virus spread wasn't perceived as a threatening event during the first weeks of the pandemic, until there were several uncontained outbreaks within the country. When this happened, the situation quickly got out of hand, and the government then intervened with strict measures. In this phase, we can identify several main actors: Chancellor Merkel, Health Minister Spahn, Bavarian Minister President Söder, and US President Donald Trump. Further relevant actors include institutional actors like the government (Bundesregierung) and the RKI. The network of connected terms reveals these actors to be clearly defined in political roles or in relation to specific events. Merkel is

112 Thorsten Quandt et al.

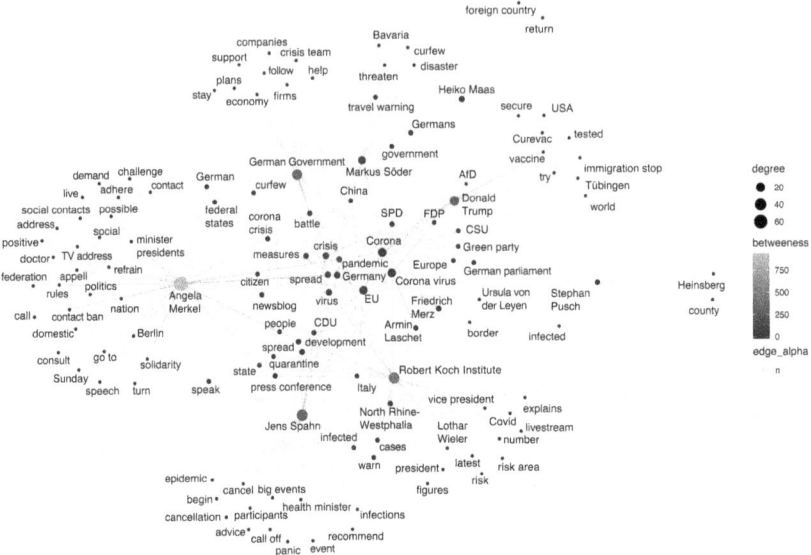

FIGURE 7.3 Phase 1: Co-occurrences of 20 most frequent political actors (n=24,437)

closely linked to terms that are indicative of her TV address to the nation on the imminent lockdown measures at the end of the analysis period, plus terms referring to her crisis talks with the minister presidents of the individual states. Spahn is linked to warnings about the infection, and several press conferences and interviews where he explained the severity of the beginning pandemic. In contrast to Spahn, who is linked to terms related to the health and medical side, Söder is placed in the context of terms referring to specific containment measures like border closures and curfews. This is indicative of different roles the three main German actors occupied in the first phase: Merkel as the stateswoman and leader of the country, Spahn as the expert and "annotator" of the epidemic, and Söder as the guarantor for security and stability. This division of tasks is perfectly mirrored in the coverage, which reproduces the political action of the government and political elite.

As mentioned above, Donald Trump plays a special role in the coverage, as he's very prominent *in general* throughout the pandemic. However, in the first phase, we find several connections to a specific news story: as media reported, Trump planned on buying the German company Curevac in Tübingen that was working on a vaccine (which in turn lead to reactions by the German administration). Interesting enough, Trump is also closely placed to the German right-wing party AfD in the network analysis, something we will also see in the subsequent phases. This means that Trump is connected to similar terms and topics in the German coverage, i.e., the news media imply direct or indirect topical connections between the two.

Phase 2: Lockdown (22 March–19 April 2020)

After the build-up phase, we can see a very dominant coverage of the crisis, with coronavirus-related news accounting for the majority of news during that time. During this phase, the country was mostly in lockdown, so the virus spread and debates surrounding containment measures are central topics. We see a shift in the focal actors of the network: the importance of Health Minister Spahn is fading, while Merkel is still very prominent as a decision maker and chief negotiator in meetings with the minister presidents of the states. EU politics are featured prominently during the lockdown as well, as financial aids for countries like Italy were subject to a controversy in the union. Due to his infection we see UK's Prime Minister Boris Johnson to be core of a sub-network. The sub-network being only weakly linked to the central network of political terms indicates that he's less depicted as an acting politician here, but more as a "celebrity patient."

It needs to be noted that the coverage here has to be understood in light of the omnipresence of coronavirus-related news during that phase. So not only does our analysis reveal a strong focus on political action, with Chancellor Merkel being the dominant individual and just a few individual elite persons

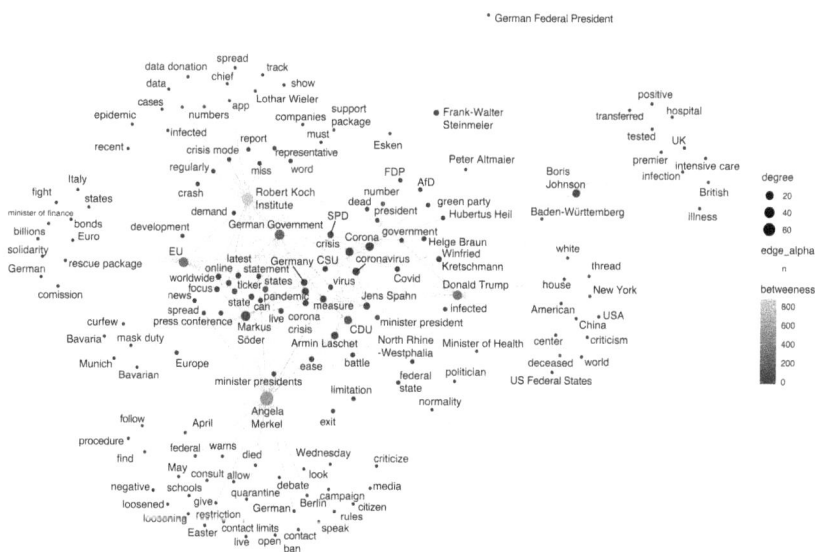

FIGURE 7.4 Phase 2: Co-occurrences of 20 most frequent political actors (n=35,338)

defining the political core of this network – it is also remarkable that the absolute amount of political news tied to well-defined elite actors was skyrocketing during that phase. In that sense, we see clear signs of strong individualization in sync with an extreme reduction of the overall news spectrum to crisis coverage. In many ways, the coverage equates the actions of elite politicians, the government, and state institutions during that time. So during the lockdown, media in the country were primarily telling the story of governmental decision makers managing the crisis – again, and remarkably, with no signs of the main protagonists of the political opposition.

Phase 3: Normalization (April 20–October 6, 2020)

After the lockdown, the number of coronavirus-related posts was going down considerably, staying at a relatively constant plateau level during summer and fall. In terms of the output, we already noted this as being a "normalization" of the crisis. With the loosening of lockdown measures, we can see a broadening of topics, also in the coronavirus coverage. There is a notable focus on the development of infection numbers and individual super-spreading events (e.g., at the Tönnies meat factory), which can be seen as an alerted monitoring of the situation. Further, we see new virus related topics and terms, like holidays, traveling, and protests against coronavirus measures (which were linked to the right-wing AfD and a number of fringe actors and conspiracy theorists

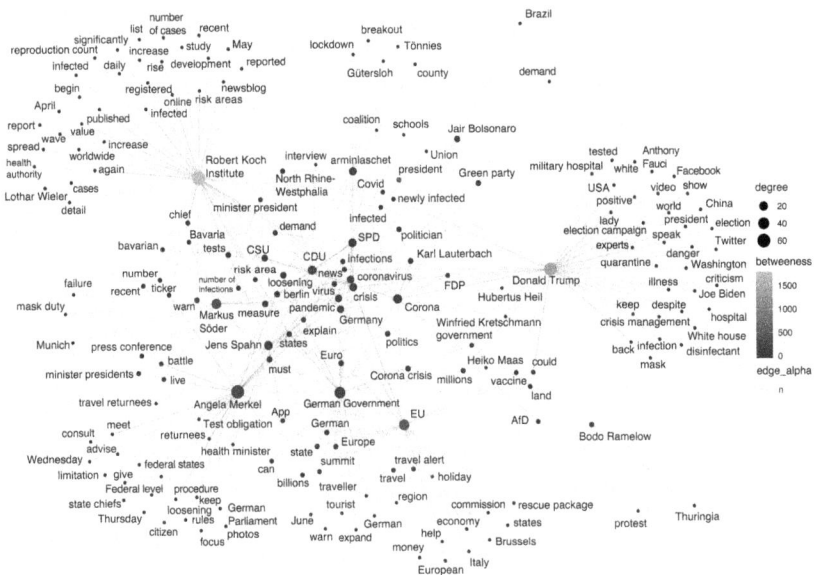

FIGURE 7.5 Phase 3: Co-occurrences of 20 most frequent political actors (n=99,647)

who do not show up in the network, as they didn't make it above the relevance thresholds for inclusion in the graph). Last but not least, there is a focus on the mismanagement of international political actors like Jair Bolsonaro and, more prominently, Donald Trump. Indeed, Trump is very visible here, and this is also related to the upcoming US elections.

In short, this last phase of the analysis period is more diverse, in both topics and (political) individuals covered in the news. Naturally, we can still identify a few key actors (like Merkel) and institutions (like the German government and the RKI). However, this needs to be seen in sync with the much lower (relative) level of pandemic-related news as opposed to the previous phase. So not only do the news media focus less on the crisis, they also do it in a different way, with a much broader selection of voices. The previous immense individualization and focus on primarily a handful of "decision-making" elite actors has been replaced with a more plural composition of the news flow.

Discussion

It is an equally frequent and mundane observation that the coronavirus crisis is an unprecedented event. Indeed, there are no recent examples of such impactful, global pandemics. However, despite this uniqueness, some observations from previous research on crises may apply. Journalism studies, for example, have analyzed previous large-scale crises (like wars or hurricanes) and sudden events in relation to the interplay of politics and journalism, and in particular with empirical studies on journalistic coverage and performance, journalistic rules and routines, news bursts, and personalization/issue ownership in crisis situations. These studies identified multiple occasions where journalism ramped up the output of news in crisis and reverted to individualization and a storytelling along selected political elite actors, which resulted in partially uncritical reporting in support of the "national interest."

Based on this research tradition, we focused on the news flow, the individualization of (political) actors, and the topical embedding of these actors. In general, we were wondering: can we identify the same patterns in journalistic coverage during the coronavirus crisis as pointed out by previous research?

Indeed our analysis revealed several of the characteristics as observed in previous crises: an explosive growth of the related coverage when the crisis became a domestic threat and a stark individualization of political coverage, with just a handful of elite politicians showing up as the main actors in the phase of the "hot" crisis. These elite persons were portrayed as actors in the actual sense of the word, i.e., as active managers of the crisis. Interestingly, other societal systems were not reduced to the actions of individuals, but described in a more functional way – for example, the economy was primarily represented by companies and institutions, and, as such, was appearing to be a more passive "object" of the crisis.

So from a more general viewpoint, one may come to the conclusion that the media did not perform well, and reverted to well-known, but problematic patterns of coverage: following Nord and Strömbäck (2006), the above features may be indicative of "reporting more, informing less" situation and a reduced diversity of voices. It is crucial to remind, though, that these authors differentiated crises according to the existence of routines (i.e., did the event happen before or is it new/unprecedented) and preparation (could the media prepare for this, was there an expectation of something to happen). *Theoretically*, media should perform well when the preparation time is there and the event is known. As Nord and Strömbäck have shown, though, this theoretical performance is *empirically* limited by media's resources (personnel, money, time, etc.), which in turn need to be seen in light of the "news hole" they have to fill, and the number of news media trying to do so. In short, if many media report in a near-instant competition to fill a large news hole, this will plausibly reduce the performance.

As our analysis further shows, there was a period where the coronavirus-related output was growing exponentially, and took over most of the output of the overall journalistic system: during the lockdown, the pandemic clearly dominated the coverage. So it is no surprise that in particular during that phase, we can observe a high level of individualization and a reduction of the coverage to the actions of well-defined governmental lead actors. Further, we also observe a lack of parliamentary opposition and alternative viewpoints. This can be theoretically explained by Nord and Strömbäck's earlier observations: the event was unprecedented, just partially expectable and without much build-up time (although one may argue that there was some preparation time in January and February), there was a huge gap to fill as there was such a huge public interest, and nearly all media devoted most of their publication space to the event.

However, the later phase of the pandemic shows a reduction of coronavirus coverage, and a broader spectrum of actors. So the political elite was no longer the sole proprietor of the main issues in the crisis, and other actors became more relevant. In that sense, we can observe a "normalization" of the crisis coverage here, with the system apparently adapting to the situation and turning COVID-19 into a relevant, but not fully dominant topic. While it needs to be seen whether this normalization holds true in the subsequent months and the second wave of the pandemic in Germany beginning in October 2020, this is already proof that there is no general, "one size fits it all" logic that applies to all phases of the crisis under analysis.

We have to stress that our analysis has limitations here, so the above conclusions are certainly preliminary and should be subject to further examination. For a more comprehensive analysis, one would need reference measurements from "normal" times in opposition to various types of crises, and preferably continuous measurements. This would allow for a more detailed view of changes over time, and it would offer comparative data from various types of crises and the respective reactions in the system. Also, the indicators used here are still surface level, and sketch the situation in broad strokes. More intricate analyses of sentiments and language as well as more complex analysis of latent patterns in the material, evolving over time, may uncover further regularities in crisis coverage of political action.

Correspondingly, research needs to further refine its models and come up with nuanced and time-based models that take emergent features of crises into account. As noted above, preparation time, routines, the amount of public interest and the related volume of the respective coverage, as well as the competition play a crucial role here. However, crises are not just "happening" at a specific point, and then the track for the coverage is set and cannot be changed: as the analysis of the German case shows, the coverage evolves and the system may adapt to the situation, for example by "normalizing" the crisis. In that sense, we need to not only observe crises as monolithic events from an overview perspective, or observe their beginning as determining their further course, but track their emergence and evolution, in order to develop phase-based typologies and better explain why the system struggles at some points – and why and how it may recover from such problems.

References

Adam, S., & Maier, M. (2010). Personalization of politics a critical review and agenda for research. *Annals of the International Communication Association, 34*(1), 213–257. https://doi.org/10/ghm4vf

AGOF. (2020). *Monatsberichte zur daily digital facts.* https://www.agof.de/studien/daily-digital-facts/monatsberichte/

Beisch, N., Koch, W., & Schäfer, C. (2019). ARD/ZDF-Onlinestudie 2019: Mediale Internetnutzung und Video-on-Demand gewinnen weiter an Bedeutung. *Media Perspektiven, 9,* 374–388.

Boberg, S., Quandt, T., Schatto-Eckrodt, T., & Frischlich, L. (2020). Pandemic populism: Facebook pages of alternative news media and the corona crisis – A computational content analysis. *ArXiv:2004.02566 [Cs].* http://arxiv.org/abs/2004.02566

Boberg, S., Schatto-Eckrott, T., Frischlich, L., & Quandt, T. (2018). The moral gatekeeper? Moderation and deletion of user-generated content in a leading news forum. *Media and Communication, 6*(4), 58–69. https://doi.org/10/gf5bpt

Boin, A., t' Hart, P., Stern, E., & Sundelius, B. (2005). *The politics of crisis management: Public leadership under pressure.* Cambridge University Press.

Bordag, S. (2008). A comparison of co-occurrence and similarity measures as simulations of context. *International Conference on Intelligent Text Processing and Computational Linguistics,* pp. 52–63. https://doi.org/10.1007/978-3-540-78135-6_5

Boumans, J. W., Boomgaarden, H. G., & Vliegenthart, R. (2013). Media personalisation in context: A cross-national comparison between the UK and the Netherlands, 1992–2007. *Political Studies, 61*(S1), 198–216. https://doi.org/10/gbcxgg

Buhl, F., Günther, E., & Quandt, T. (2018). Observing the dynamics of the online news ecosystem: News diffusion processes among German news sites. *Journalism Studies, 19*(1), 79–104. https://doi.org/10/gddjrp

Buhl, F., Günther, E., & Quandt, T. (2019). Bad news travels fastest: A computational approach to predictors of immediacy in digital journalism ecosystems. *Digital Journalism*, 7(7), 910–931. https://doi.org/10/gf4tcg

Chadwick, A. (2017). *The hybrid media system. Politics and power.* Oxford University Press.

Couldry, N. (2003). *Media rituals: A critical approach.* Routledge.

Csardi, G., & Nepusz, T. (2006). The igraph software package for complex network research. *InterJournal, Complex Systems*, 1695(5), 1–9.

Denner, N., Koch, T., & Senger, S. (2020). Faces of companies: Personalization of corporate coverage in crisis and non-crisis periods. *Journalism*, 17. https://doi.org/10.1177/1464884920901615

Durham, F. (2008). Media ritual in catastrophic times: The populist turn in television coverage of Hurricane Katrina. *Journalism*, 9(1), 95–116. https://doi.org/10/bsn8mk

Esser, F., & Hemmer, K. (2008). Characteristics and dynamics of election news coverage in Germany. In J. Strömbäck & L. L. Kaid (Eds.), *The handbook of election news coverage around the world*, pp. 289–307. Routledge.

Frischlich, L., Boberg, S., & Quandt, T. (2019). Comment sections as targets of dark participation? *Journalists' Evaluation and Moderation of Deviant User Comments*, 20(14), 2014–2033.

Günther, E., Domahidi, E., & Quandt, T. (2017). Mediale Sichtbarkeit der WahlbewerberInnen und der Themen der Bundestagswahl 2013. Eine automatisierte Analyse der Online-Berichterstattung. *Studies in Communication and Media*, 6(3), 262–299. https://doi.org/10/ggw4j7

Harder, R. A., Sevenans, J., & Van Aelst, P. (2017). Intermedia agenda setting in the social media age: How traditional players dominate the news agenda in election times. *The International Journal of Press/Politics*, 22(3), 275–293. https://doi.org/10/gbk7cx

Henry, M., & Hauck, G. (2020). Coronavirus is scary, but the flu is deadlier, more widespread. *USA Today*. https://eu.usatoday.com/story/news/health/2020/02/01/coronavirus-flu-deadlier-more-widespread-than-wuhan-china-virus/4632508002/

Honnibal, M., & Johnson, M. (2015). An improved non-monotonic transition system for dependency parsing. *Proceedings of the 2015 Conference on Empirical Methods in Natural Language Processing*, pp. 1373–1378. https://doi.org/10/gf3gvw

Hopmann, D. N., de Vreese, C. H., & Albaek, E. (2011). Incumbency bonus in election news coverage explained: The logics of political power and the media market. *Journal of Communication*, 61(2), 264–282. https://doi.org/10.1111/j.1460-2466.2011.01540.x

Jarren, O. (2020). Im Krisenmodus: Das öffentlich-rechtliche Fernsehen in Zeiten von Corona. *Epd Medien*, 13, 3–6.

Karlsson, M., & Strömbäck, J. (2010). Freezing the flow of online news: Exploring approaches to the study of the liquidity of online news. *Journalism Studies*, 11(1), 2–19. https://doi.org/10/cb8vv5

Kriesi, H. (2012). Personalization of national election campaigns. *Party Politics*, 18(6), 825–844. https://doi.org/10/fdqpzj

Lewis, J., & Cushion, S. (2009). The thirst to be the first: An analysis of breaking news stories and their impact on the quality of 24-Hour news coverage in the UK. *Journalism Practice*, 3(3), 304–318. https://doi.org/10/fdndbg

Lund, M. K., & Olsson, E.-K. (2016). When routines are not enough. Journalists' crisis management during the 22/7 domestic terror attack in Norway. *Journalism Practice*, 10(3), 358–371.

Meier, K., & Wyss, V. (2020). Journalismus in der Krise: Die fünf Defizite der Corona-Berichterstattung. *Meedia Online*. https://meedia.de/2020/04/09/journalismus-in-der-krise-die-fuenf-defizite-der-corona-berichterstattung/

NDR Info. (2020). *Wir müssen jetzt gezielt handeln*. 11. https://www.ndr.de/nachrichten/info/11-Wir-muessen-jetzt-gezielt-handeln,audio651406.html

Nord, L. W., & Strömbäck, J. (2006). Reporting more, informing less. A comparison of the Swedish media coverage of September 11 and the wars in Afghanistan and Iraq. *Journalism*, 7(1), 85–110. https://doi.org/10/d3x964

Olsson, E.-K., & Nord, L. W. (2015). Paving the way for crisis exploitation: The role of journalistic styles and standards. *Journalism*, 16(3), 341–358. https://doi.org/10/f2z8kx

Riegert, K., & Olsson, E.-K. (2007). The importance of ritual in crisis journalism. *Journalism Practice*, 1(2), 143–158. https://doi.org/10/ds67f7

Rosenberg, H., & Feldman, C. S. (2008). *No time to think: The menace of media speed and the 24-hour news cycle*. Continuum International.

Schütz, W. J. (2012). Deutsche Tagespresse 2012. Ergebnisse der aktuellen Stichtagsammlung. *Media Perspektiven*, 11, 570–593.

Van Aelst, P., Sheafer, T., & Stanyer, J. (2012). The personalization of mediated political communication: A review of concepts, operationalizations and key findings. *Journalism: Theory, Practice & Criticism*, 13(2), 203–220. https://doi.org/10/chdp2g

van Dalen, A. (2012). Structural Bias in Cross-National Perspective: How Political Systems and Journalism Cultures Influence Government Dominance in the News. *The International Journal of Press/Politics*, 17(1), 32–55. https://doi.org/10.1177/1940161211411087

Weick, K. E. (1993). The collapse of sensemaking in organizations: The Mann Gulch disaster. *Administrative Science Quarterly*, 628–652. https://doi.org/10/cp2wrw

Wiegand, R. (2020, May 8). Die Krisenmanager. *Sueddeutsche Zeitung*. https://www.sueddeutsche.de/leben/coronavirus-politik-merkel-spahn-soeder-1.4898115

8

MORE THAN "A LITTLE FLU"

Alternative Digital Journalism and the Struggle to Re-Frame the Brazilian Government's Response to the COVID-19 Outbreak

Stuart Davis

Introduction

In profound ways, the federal response to the COVID-19 outbreak in Brazil represents one of the starkest examples of what journalist Kate Aronoff calls epidemiological denialism (Aronoff, 2020). As the country exhibited the highest exponential growth curve in terms of daily deaths in the world in May 2020, President Jair Bolsonaro has received global attention as the national leader most virulently opposed to imposing public health interventions to stem the virus' spread. Since initial cases manifested, he has repeatedly engaged in activities aimed to minimize the severity of both the breakout and the virus's impact on individuals. From calling it "a little flu" [uma gripezinha] to arguing that leftist activists are burying empty coffins to amplify the mortality rate, he has consistently downplayed the danger of COVID-19. Bolsonaro's flippant attitude represents the farcical extreme of a general trend: the country has spent a negligible number of resources on either comprehensively mitigating the spread of COVID-19 or offering policy solutions like unemployment insurance to help encourage social distancing. Compounding the problem, preliminary demographic data show that following similar patterns to other nations with large outbreaks, the most sizable concentrations of these cases in Brazil have been in areas with poor existing health infrastructure or among historically vulnerable groups.

Perhaps the most useful way to understand the situation of political communication regarding the COVID-19 crisis in Brazil is the metaphor of an "information war" as actors mobilizing digital networks against each other in an attempt to persuade audiences that their version of the narrative bears epidemiological veracity (Janowicz, 2020). However, and crucially, this information

DOI: 10.4324/9781003170051-10

war is not merely about establishing an appropriately scientific epistemological framework for understanding COVID. For dissident journalists and community activists, it is more fundamentally a struggle over how the Bolsonaro government and its allies have exacerbated a long-standing economic situation in which the poorest members of society are underserved by the privatization of public health, increased defunding of public institutions, the failure of human rights protection, and the incessant prioritization of economic austerity measures over the public good.

Drawing on a qualitative thematic analysis of the published materials from three alternative digital news projects, Brasil 247, Brasil Wire, and Coletivo Papo Reto, this chapter presents an analysis of how these outlets went against both President Bolsonaro's mishandling of the virus and the larger system of social, economic, and racial oppression it supports. The first project, Brasil 247, is a national daily news site launched in 2011 in order to provide an online space for progressive voices within Brazil. During the COVID-19 pandemic, this site dedicated a specific section for providing an alternative narrative of the corona virus outbreak, including combating Bolsonaro's denialist rhetoric. Brasil Wire, launched in 2014, is inspired by Latin American leftist social movements and focused on the struggle between these forces and the rising right wing exemplified by politicians like Bolsonaro (Meir, 2020). In this spirit, its coverage of the government response to the COVID-19 outbreak explicitly focuses on how Bolsonaro's administration fits within larger patterns of structural oppression against Afro-Brazilian, indigenous, and other historically marginalized groups within Brazil. The final project, O Coletivo Papo Reto ([The "Straight Talk Collective"], often shorted to "Papo Reto"), is a social media-based collective situated in one of the largest favelas (or unincorporated urban peripheries) of Rio de Janeiro. Started in the wake of the 2013 national protests as a watchdog against police brutality, during the pandemic the group has acted as a source of public health information for favela residents across Rio as well as a voice of advocacy for favela residents. For each of these outlets, all stories with thematic content focus on COVID-19 published between March 20, 2020 and February 1, 2021 were first identified. Within this body of stories, several characteristics were coded such as major themes and area of focus (i.e., local/neighborhood level, state level, and national/international level). This initial coding facilitated a larger qualitative thematic analysis of trends in published material that oriented the discussion in this chapter.

These projects were identified for inclusion in this chapter because they provide powerful cases of "alternative" digital journalism in the way conceptualized by Atton (2002) and Forde (2011) through both their oppositional stance toward the Brazilian government and mainstream media and by their attempts to provide a voice for populations generally not included within Brazilian news coverage. Key differences exist between the three in terms of scope: Brasil 247 is national in coverage, Brasil Wire is national/international, and Papo Reto focuses on the local level. However, all of these sites provide alternative perspectives on the COVID-19 outbreak in Brazil that move attention away from the president's antics and toward understanding how the national government failed to address the more systemic impacts of the pandemic on the country's most marginalized communities.

Background: Bolsonaro's COVID-19 Denialism

This quote from a November 9, 2020 press conference by Jair Bolsonaro captures his administration's response to the COVID-19 outbreak:

> Everything now is the pandemic. We have to put a stop to that. I'm sorry for all those who have died...all of us are going to die one day. Everyone is going to die. There is no point in escaping from that, escaping from reality. We have to stop being a land of pussies.
>
> *(quoted in Kertman, 2020)*

Beyond the callous and uncouth nature of the statement, two key elements of his (non)-response surface. The first is a frustrated downplaying of the seriousness of COVID-19 symptomology and its epidemiological footprint within Brazil. Connectedly (and also similar to Trump), Bolsonaro's rejection of the scientific and public health communities has proliferated within and beyond the social media networks that grew on Facebook, WhatsApp, and other platforms during the 2018 election.

As this chapter's title indicates, Bolsonaro's response to the novel coronavirus has consistently minimized its potential epidemiological impact. Most iconic by riding a horse through a crowd of unmasked supporters at a rally for hydroxychloroquine, Brazil's president has engaged in a series of erratic behaviors that all serve to downplay the COVID-19 outbreak's impact. Resonating with Trump's messaging, he has levied a number of specious claims including that mask wearing leads to an increase in criminal activity, that the boredom of social distancing and self-quarantining is "as dangerous as COVID" (Maghalaes and Forero, 2020), and that because of air and water pollution Brazilians already have the necessary antibodies to fight COVID-19 (Friedman, 2020). Also echoing Trump, Bolsonaro has promoted experimental treatments like zinc and chloroquine to the point of expressing unhappiness with Donald Trump when the US president did not take these medicines after contracting COVID-19. Finally, Bolsonaro has joined Trump in both condemning China for originating the coronavirus and arguing Chinese companies attempting to collaborate with Brazilian researchers engaged in subterfuge bordering on espionage (Preissler Iglesias, Adghrini, and Rosler, 2020).

Bolsonaro's rhetorical denialism has produced a significant impact in creating confusion and delegitimizing the work of the national public health infrastructure and state governments in combating the virus. It has also actively pushed citizens to ignore guidance regarding preventive measures. A number of cross-disciplinary epidemiological studies have shown strong correlations over time between presidential rhetoric and the rise in cases. Two recent studies vividly illustrate that whenever the president minimized the pandemic, the rate of social isolation decreases, and more people became infected and died (Garcia, 2020; Ricard, 2020). Not coincidentally, the Pan-American Health Organization (the Latin American wing of the WHO) published a statement accusing both Bolsonaro and Trump of producing "the worst case of infodemia" in the Americas, pushing followers to ignore mask mandates and to refuse to follow public health guidelines (Pan-American Health Organization [PAHO], 2020).

The president's attempts to downplay COVID-19 and obfuscate the virus' larger social impact create the acute problem of epidemiological credibility. If the president does not behave in a coherent and medically sound manner, the national-, state-, and local-level responses risk falling into chaos. More potentially hazardous, however, is the way Bolsonaro's behavior obfuscates the systemic ramifications of the COVID-19 outbreak on the health of those communities already marginalized by patterns of racial or class-based oppression. The rest of this chapter will discuss digital media projects that provide counter-frames to the forms of COVID denialism propagated by Bolsonaro.

Theoretical Framework: Counter-Framing and Networked Power

Tracking the response to Bolsonaro within alternative media outlets raises theoretical questions related to how activists *provide counter-framing narratives* (Chong and Druckman, 2007) to Bolsonaro's trivialization of the pandemic and *mobilize different constituencies around these counter-frames*. The conceptual coupling of "framing/counter-framing" offers a useful theoretical framework for understanding both how the messaging strategies political elites utilize around highly controversial issues like COVID-19 to the wider public and how media actors push back on these messaging strategies. While recognizing rigorous debates around the concept (e.g., Cacciatore, Scheufele, and Iyengar, 2016), we adopt Entman's definition of framing as "the process of culling a few elements of perceived reality and assembling a narrative that highlights connections among them" (2007, p. 164). The operation of narrative assemblage is characterized by power struggles between competing groups attempting to exert influence including governments or other "official" actors, political elites, journalists, and the public (Entman, 2003). With wide-scale public health crises or other phenomena of national relevance, the first framing is driven by the federal government in contention with mainstream media. The story's development from its initial framing instigates a cascading process through which the first frame might shift in response to contestation from other elite actors (including pundits and ex-officials), journalists, constituencies of the public, and interest groups (ibid.; Hanley, 2010). Crucially, the cascading process presents opportunities for what Chong and Druckman have called "counter-framing", or the act of providing later interpretations that contrast or conflict with previous frames. For example, when conservative news outlets in the USA present a federal publicly funded healthcare as program as "socialized medicine", they are offering a counter-frame (Chong and Druckman, 2013). Counter-framing provides a powerful conceptual tool for journalists and activists to challenge representational frames produced by federal governments and other political elites.

In circulating counter-frames of the COVID outbreak, digital media producers are offering a corrective to Bolsonaro's denialism and mainstream media coverage while also mobilizing audiences who receive their stories. The ability of digital media activists to reconfigure dominant political frames in the service of political mobilization fits closely with some of the key features of networked digital activism delineated by Manuel Castells, particularly the notions of programming/reprogramming and switching. Theoretically resonant with the "framing/counter-framing" coupling, "programming/reprogramming" refers to the manner in which narratives are produced and distributed. At the macro-level, news organizations, political parties, or influential figures "program" the "dominant regimes of codes" within a social order. In contesting these codes, activists can engage in a number of tactics. "Reprogramming" refers to attempts to create a counter-hegemonic response to the dominant code: "radical reprogramming comes from resistant movements aimed at altering the fundamental principle of the network or the kernel of the program code" (Castells, 2009, p. 48). Reprogramming is linked to the attempt to produce a sweeping counter-hegemonic position against dominant codes. Switching, however, refers to the link of points where previously unlinked networks might overlap with each other. In the context of social movement, organizing switches act as connecting points or interfaces between different strategic networks which can then cooperate, combine resources, and pursue common goals. These two tactics reinforce each other. The linking work of switches is crucial in the accretion of sufficient collective power to reprogram dominant codes. Reading these two approaches together, Castells' focus on the ability of digital activists to reprogram news frames through organization and collective action adds an explicitly social justice-oriented dimension to the broader process of counter-framing.

National Alternative Digital Journalism: The Reprogramming Work of Brasil 247 and Brasil Wire

The first group of projects to be discussed here are those that engage in "reprogramming" the COVID response in Brazil at the national or even international levels. These two projects work toward providing a counter-frame to the depiction of the COVID-19 outbreak produced by Bolsonaro's denialism and the mainstream media response preoccupied with Bolsonaro's erratic behavior. When discussing the COVID outbreak, many high-circulation national newspapers like O Globo and corporate sites like www.G1.com and Noticias UOL have heavily emphasized the eccentricities of Bolsonaro's response. Recent studies by Albuquerque and Gagliardi (2021) and others depict a mainstream response to the virus that highlights either the grotesquely comical elements of Bolsonaro's mishandling or conflicts between Bolsonaro, federal public health officials, or other political elites such as São Paulo governor João Doria. In highlighting Bolsonaro's mishandling of the outbreak, these sources potentially serve to provide an avenue for public frustration with the president. However, they do not shift the framing of the COVID-19 outbreak away from Bolsonaro himself. This mainstream media frame might be encapsulated by the statement: "The problem with the COVID outbreak is that Bolsonaro is an incompetent leader who does not listen to science". Though appropriate given the outrageousness of his behavior, this counter-frame lacks a more systematic investigation of how the COVID outbreak is exacerbating pre-existing social problems within Brazil.

Brasil 247 and Brasil Wire, digital native outlets that each arose out of an explicit attempt to create a space for perspectives not covered within the mainstream press, provide a more sustained attempt to build a counter-frame that situates the COVID-19 outbreak in the context of larger social dynamics including enduring legacies of racism and racialized inequality, the defunding of public health infrastructure, and increasing socio-economic disparities. The content produced by each of these outlets about COVID since March 2020 is consistently characterized by stories that move from the global to the national to the extremely local. Each of these outlets attempts to counter the narratives regarding the crisis propagated by the federal government through a combination of providing a counter-narrative through national- and international-level coverage and reporting on the impacts of COVID-19 within specific socio-economically, racially, and geographically vulnerable populations. Each of these outlets dedicated significant coverage of the outbreak through specific sub-sections within the larger site. Within these sections, Brasil 247 published 205 stories while Brasil Wire published 64. The wide range in the number of stories reflects the nature of each site: Brasil 247 is designed to serve as a daily source of breaking news while the other two outlets feature longer form investigative stories. Comparing the ways these outlets frame the administration's response to COVID-19 provides a comprehensive counter-hegemonic narrative against epistemological denialism while also providing a systemic interrogation of the larger structural issues enflamed by the virus outbreak including legacies of systemic racism, underfunding of public infrastructure, and the threat of a paradigmatic shift back to military-style authoritarianism within the Brazilian government.

The remainder of this section will address the counter-frames developed by these two projects to broaden and sharpen the analysis of the pandemic's impact.

Brasil 247

Brasil 247 was launched in 2011 by Editora 247, a publishing company started by investigative journalist Leonardo Attuch, as the first news site specifically designed for mobile devices. Modeled after American political blogs like Alternet and the Daily Kos, Brasil 247's founders intend the site to serve a watchdog function that "broke with the link between corporations and governments" ("Sobre Brasil 247"). Aiming to develop a comprehensive alternative news coverage on a broad range of topics, Brasil 247 capitalized on its position as the "first digital native news outlet in Brazil" to receive significant foundation funding and private investment, including from major public corporate social responsibility organs including the Bank of Brazil and public oil corporation Petrobras. As the site grew, its progressive outlook and funding connections to the national government fostered attacks from the mainstream media as well as high-profile conservative activists—including many who would later become key Bolsonaro supporters (Observatorio da Imprensa, 2019).

Brasil 247's coverage of the COVID outbreak reflects two intertwined objectives: creating a critique of Bolsonaro's handling of the pandemic as part of a larger structural defunding of Brazilian public health institutions and providing a robust counter-narrative to Bolsonaro's demonization other nations—particularly China. Given its aspirations to become a comprehensive national progressive outlet and its embattled relationship with the political right, it is characteristic that Brasil 247's coverage adopted this dual approach on fighting the right and providing copious documentation of the nationwide attempt to fight the virus.

Within the 205 stories on coronavirus, 40% were either critiques of Bolsonaro or the federal pandemic response. Though Brasil 247 mirrored Jornal O Globo and other mainstream media in covering Bolsonaro's own bouts of COVID-19 (and comical associated behavior), its interventions often tended to be focused more on the deleterious impacts of his behavior on the capacity of the government to respond. For example, a story from March 25, 2020 interviewed a former cabinet member of the administration who was leading an initiative in congress to freeze discretionary spending on public credit cards in possession of the Bolsonaro family for the duration of the COVID outbreak—cards that had accrued 4.6 million Reais in charges in 2019 ("Joice quer bloquear gastos do clã Bolsonaro com cartão corporativo durante a pandemia"). Another recurring element of Brasil 247's coverage is the attempt to illustrate how the defunding of public infrastructure worsens the suffering associated with the virus. A story from April 2 publicized data from a research study illustrating that the lack of federal stimulus resulted in food insecurity for 76% of favela households in the Sao Paolo area. Finally, in one of the clearest parallels between Bolsonaro's COVID-19 response and Donald Trump, Brasil 247 published 18 stories on how the Bolsonaro administration has attempted to exert control over the Oswaldo Cruz Foundation (FIOCRUZ), Brazil's national public health center. Since March FIOCRUZ has critiqued the president for downplaying the significance of the virus and for refusing to collaborate with other nations in developing vaccines and therapeutics. In response, Bolsonaro has attacked FIOCRUZ on social media and attempted to fire key researchers. Brasil 247 has covered this story at length, acting as a voice piece for the public health researchers. Of particular note, a story titled "Doctors denounce federal government interference in FIOCRUZ, who tried to put it in Bolsonarista command" (November 7) explicitly stages the institute's doctors against Bolsonaro's agenda.

The second central trend in Brasil 247's coronavirus coverage (40 stories or 19% of the total coronavirus coverage) is an attempt to fill a perceived information gap in public knowledge regarding the relationship between the virus outbreak in Brazil and other nations. As it introduces its first story in the COVID-19 section, its coverage is designed to "provide a picture of the COVID outbreak in Brazil and across the world that you would not get from the mainstream". Though the USA, Spain, India, and other nation-states were covered, China was most oft referenced. Like Bolsonaro, Brasil 247 is vociferously focused on China. However, the way the site frames China is radically different. Unlike the president and his retinue, the site's published stories on China depict it not as a threat but as a potential partner in fighting the coronavirus. The site's second story published on coronavirus from March 23, 2020 illustrates this cooperative position. Titled "Governors of Amazon States Ask China for Support in Stopping New Coronavirus", the story discusses how governors of the state of Amapá and Amazonas requested to the Chinese Ambassador to Brazil for respirators, PPE, and other equipment needed to mitigate viral spread. Another story from April 1 warns Brazilian audiences that Chinese public health officials are worried that asymptomatic spread is much more prevalent than they previously believed. Eleven stories from October and November 2020 focus on the Butantan Institute's work on the COVID vaccine in coordination with Chinese medical researchers. These stories reflect a support for the collaboration that is specifically pitched in a cosmopolitan understanding of Brazil and China's links as part of a larger international project against the virus. This positive depiction of China's role raises the question of whether Brasil 247 goes too far in re-framing the role of the Chinese government in a way that paints too rosy a picture and thus misses potential mishandling of the virus outbreak. However, as the stories on China tend to focus on either providing warnings for Brazilian audiences about COVID-19 or discussing collaborative work toward creating a workable vaccine, the site's coverage can be characterized as offering a counter-frame of Bolsonaro's Sinophobia that narrows the discourse on China to topics relevant to combating the pandemic.

Through its coverage Brasil 247 rewrites the narrative on COVID-19 by foregrounding Bolsonaro's missteps in the larger context of neoliberal privation of public programs and anti-scientific rhetoric while also creating a more complex and more cosmopolitan picture of the COVID crisis and the global collective response.

Brasil Wire

Brasil Wire was launched in 2014 by Daniel Hunt and Brian Mier, American and British expatriate journalists living in São Paulo. Publishing most stories in both English and Portuguese, Brasil Wire started specifically as a digital space for capturing "movements of the poor, of Afro-Brazilians, and of other marginalized populations that are pushing from below" (Interview with Mier, May 22, 2020). The project's internationalist perspective is baked into its origins as both Mier and Hunt have worked as correspondents internationally—specifically with progressive or leftist outlets: the former with the TeleSUR (Venezuela) and Fairness in Accuracy in Reporting (USA); and the latter with Tribune (UK). In a similar fashion to the way TeleSUR views its mission as "developing a hemispheric communication strategy" (Burch, 2007, p. 227), Brasil Wire explicitly attempts to situate Bolsonaro's COVID non-response within larger geopolitical movements and patterns. As an admittedly socialist outlet, Brasil Wire presents its coverage of the corona crisis in Brazil in a level of abstraction that sacrifices in-depth local coverage in favor of making global links. Two of these links will be discussed in this section: the transnational slave trade and "black genocide" as a framing device for understanding the impact of COVID-19 on Afro-Brazilian communities; and the role of the US military, intelligence agencies, and corporations in attempting to leverage the crisis for geopolitical gains.

Following its mission to align with Brazilian social movements, Brasil Wire has published extensively on Afro-Brazilian activism ranging from histories of the Brazilian Black Movement to regular profiles of Afro-Brazilian activists murdered under questionable circumstances. During the COVID outbreak, the site drew international attention from organizations including the Democratic Socialists of America (DSA) and the World Federation of Trade Unions, by publishing the translation of a polemic essay by activists Felipe Milanez and Samuel Vida. The essay, "The Pandemic, Racism and Indigenous/Black Genocide in Brazil: Coronavirus and Extermination Policy", linked the disproportionate numbers of deaths of people of color during the COVID outbreak in Brazil to a larger extermination narrative around communities of color. The essay presents a sweeping narrative that places the disproportionate mortality rate among communities of color as not a matter of abnegation but of design:

In a society historically structured by socio-racial disparities that cross differences of social class, defining different degrees of recognition and access to basic social, civil and political rights, the primary victims of this genocide are, fundamentally, Black communities, both urban (favelas, invasion settlements, tenements, occupations, etc.) and rural (quilombos, subsistence communities and other traditional forms of land occupation), and the diverse ethnic groups of originary peoples, who also live in urban contexts and in rural and forest areas

(Milanez and Vida, 2020)

Connecting dots, the piece argues that structural racism embedded in the way capitalism developed as an economic and political system in both the USA and Brazil produced the conditions for mass death that were then ignited by the COVID outbreak. In this way the essay explicitly links racial marginalization with mortality. In the wake of this essay, Brasil Wire published a series of stories profiling different Afro-Brazilian and indigenous communities ravaged by the corona crisis. This piece's counter-framing of the pandemic echoes Marxist social critic Mike Davis's argument that the monstrous nature of pandemics arises not only from their virology but from the combustible situations which they inhabit: subpar living conditions created by lack of investment. This confluence of environmental and human factors "offers perfect environments for the evolution of flu virulence" (2012, p. 152).

Though the scathing deployment of black genocide as a framework for interpreting the large socio-politics of COVID-19 diagnoses a persistent if not overt connection between racialized capitalism in the USA and Brazil, Brasil Wire's discussion of American involvement in the Brazilian pandemic is more instrumental. Two examples prove illustrative. The first, "How the Generals Took Out the Captain" (April 6, 2020), presents an argument from investigative journalist Luis Nassif about how General Walter Braga Netto, Bolsonaro's chief of staff, began to take functional control of the national COVID-19 response, usurping Bolsonaro's authority. The piece ends with the speculative claim that this move ushers in a "post-Bolsonaro and post-Trump" era that would harmonize Brazil's administrative branch with the wills and desires of American government and business. The second, "U.S. Expands Influence in the Brazilian Amazon During Pandemic" (August 24, 2020) by Bolivian/Brazilian Santiago Navarro F., details the way that the US government has taken advantage of the virus outbreak in the Amazon to expand its geo-strategic position. The article details at length both the way the US military (through Southern Command and US AID) and American businesses have mobilized within the Amazon to provide "aid". Questioning their motives, the piece forcefully asks: "If the coronavirus in the U.S. has mostly impacted poor, Latino, and African American people because there's no public health system, are they really interested in poor and Indigenous people in the Amazon?" (Navarro F., 2020).

Navarro F.'s piece points to the larger counter-framing agenda of Brasil Wire: to situate the COVID-19 response in Brazil within an "inter-imperialist rivalry" (Calinicos, 2009) between the USA and China. An editorial from Mier makes this point starkly: "The COVID crisis shows that Brazil has become a kind of battlefield in the full spectrum war between the United States and China" (Mier, 2020). This statement offers the site's most globally angled understanding of the damage wrought by the COVID crisis in Brazil: Bolsonaro and his allies in the USA working against Brazilian scientists and activists and potential allies in China.

Local Alternative Digital Journalism: Digital Mutual Aid and Community Health Justice

The remainder of the chapter will focus on the digital media activist project Coletivo Papo Reto, arguing that this group's work offers a form of "digital mutual aid" that works. Papo Reto represents in some ways the other side of the coin of projects like Brasil 247 and Brasil Wire. Whereas the first two attempt to "reprogram" the narrative around the COVID-19 outbreak at the national level, Papo Reto is focused on linking mutual aid work done within marginalized communities in one Brazilian favela with wider audiences. As numerous research projects during the pandemic document, practices of mutual aid have supplemented if not supplanted public health interventions attempted by the state in many areas (Spade, 2020; Stirken and Sembrar, 2020). Mutual aid, a concept developed within the anarchist tradition, links local intervention to broader social critique. As a practice grounded in the empowerment of local communities (particularly marginalized communities) and an explicit critique of the state's failures to its subjects, mutual aid links local struggles with a larger political project. The practice of "digital mutual aid" (Milan, 2015) investigates the manner in which the medium-specific characteristics of digital media facilitate the amplification and expanded distribution pathways for mutual aid practices, providing the fibers connecting mutual aid projects in on area with others. In Castells' terminology, digital media projects employed in the service of sharing mutual aid practices serve a *switching* function—they create opportunities for connection between community-based projects.

The Papo Reto collective was founded in 2014 in the Complexo do Alemão group of favela communities by a group of residents interested in providing a tool for their communities to document violence and civil rights abuses against residents—particularly at the hands of the city's Unidades de Polícias Pacificadoras ["Pacifying Police Units"], or UPPs (WITNESS, 2017). Growing out of a larger activist milieu that developed during the 2013 nationwide protests, Papo Reto became a powerful voice for both documenting police violence within its community and working to connect victims of police violence with lawyer's organizations and human rights organizations in Brazil.

Although in the words of both its co-founders and within press coverage of its work, Colletivo Papo Reto is primarily defined as a digital media project by and for community residents of Complexo de Alemão, it performs important connective work as a facilitator of other favela-based activist groups. During the COVID-19 outbreak Papo Reto adopted the role of a "switcher" by engaging in two forms of linking practice: first, providing space both digitally through social media and in-person for community organizations working on mutual aid projects in favelas to both advertise and coordinate service provision; second, participating in digital strategizing sessions with human rights organizations in other parts of Latin America and beyond to address how to use digital media advocacy as a tool for aiding marginalized communities during the pandemic.

The first form of digital mutual aid offered by Papo Reto came almost out of necessity. As the health crisis began to intensify in the favelas in April 2020, it became clear that the city would not be able to provide preventive materials, PPE, or other supplies that residents might need. This led Papo Reto and two other community organizations to launch the Gabinete de Crisis de Alemao ["Alemao Crisis Cabinet"], a collective aiming to mitigate the COVID-19 situation. The cabinet began to work with local businesses and the meagerly supplied public health clinics in the neighborhood to both assess resident issues and attempt to organize distributions. Within this process, Papo Reto served as simultaneously the mouthpiece for community residents to discuss their needs and as an advertising tool for alerting residents to mutual aid activities ranging from frozen meat distribution to community trash pickups to COVID-19 testing. In April 2020 Papo Reto's mutual aid practices moved into music with the creation of the "Funk Cabinet against COVID". Produced in collaboration with local *baile funk* musicians, this project launched a series of public service announcements that played on the group's social media channels and community radio within Alemão. Pivotally, the Funk Cabinet framed its message to residents as a critique of the government's inaction. As the project's slogan indicates: "Without government action the Funk Cabinet intervenes!" (de Melo, 2020).

Turning to the local, Papo Reto has also acted as an outward-facing advocacy tool for favela residents during the corona crisis. Since its inception Papo Reto has had an eye toward what Keck and Sikkink call the "advocacy boomerang", a practice where grassroots activists reach out to transnational advocacy networks for support that will then be reinvested in local projects. Co-founder Raul Santiago's participation in a roundtable on September 22, 2020 on "The Panopticon of Public Space: COVID and Authoritarian States during the Pandemic". This panel, organized by UN Habitat, offers a particularly illustrative example of its engagement with transnational support networks. Santiago is able to make links from his group's local interventions to a much wider group of activists and support networks.

Conclusion

Put in opposition to Bolsonaro's COVID-19 denialism, these three alternative digital journalism projects replace the callous dismissal with a multi-faceted, multi-level response. Projects like Brasil 247 offer an alternative narrative for the history of the battle against the virus while Brasil Wire links national antagonisms within larger global patterns of exploitation. Finally, Papo Reto serves to amplify struggles within some of Brazil's poorest communities in an attempt to cultivate solidarity. The aim of this chapter is that these responses present a series of counter-frames for the COVID-19 outbreak in Brazil that are internationalist and cosmopolitan in scope and attuned to local experiences within the nation's poorest communities. Read together, they present a powerful indictment of the Brazilian response to the COVID outbreak as well as potential paths forward built on collaboration and a sense of collective solidarity…if only they could reach a wider audience. As counter-frames in competition for public attention, these narratives miss a key element: there is no indication that they resonate with larger audiences in Brazil. Returning to Entman's model of cascading activation, the ability of a counter-frame to significantly challenge a dominant frame to the point of potentially replacing it depends on a number of factors, including elite discord and resonance with larger audiences. While there is elite discord (as evidenced by the growing discontent with Bolsonaro), the ability of the frames provided by the projects mentioned in this chapter to exert wider influence points to a fundamental problem with digital activism of this sort. If alternative media producers are to provide a sufficient political will to combat Bolsonaro's ability to rile up his support networks through his political communication practices on social media and beyond, the question of scalability is key. Sources like Brasil Wire and Brasil 247 provide a message that is resonant with the kind of mutual aid promoted by Papo Reto. However, the anti-imperialist agenda runs the risk of missing coordination at the local level.

The difficulty of coordination reflects a longstanding problem facing alternative journalists. By presenting stories focusing on topics ignored or marginalized by mainstream media, the reach of alternative media producers is often limited to smaller and self-selective audiences (Downing, 2003). Consequently, even when published in readily accessible digital formats, the ability of these outlets to reach and potentially influence wider segments of population is limited. During the Brazilian coronavirus outbreak, the limited ability of these alternative outlets to reach a larger audience meant that their counter-framing of the pandemic was eclipsed by those presented by mainstream media. Thus, while Bolsonaro's public approval rating has declined significantly during the outbreak (see Chapter 1), the framing of his response as part of a larger set of systemic problems has not taken hold among the general population, political elites, or the mainstream press.

The limited influence of the counter-framing attempts initiated by these three outlets reflects potential limitations of this chapter. Our focus on the content of the counter-frames mobilized against the denialist narrative propagated by the president only addresses one element of counter-framing. Subsequent analyses could address in more nuanced fashion the critiques of Bolsonaro's COVID response proffered by mainstream media as well as critiques of the president provided by other elite actors including former Health Minister Luiz Henrique Mandietta or São Paulo state Governor João Doria. Beyond the immediate context of the coronavirus, a broader avenue of investigation could examine the political economic and organizational factors that have prevented social movements representing marginalized populations from exerting influence within Brazilian politics. As Souza (2016) and Davis and Straubhaar (2019) have tracked, the confluence of forces that framed the economic problems felt in the early 2010s as a result of corruption within the leftist Workers Party and ushered in the rise of the radical right in Brazil was well funded and well organized; without this network Bolsonaro's denialism would probably never have flourished. If an oppositional movement is going to grow on behalf of the poor, ethnic minorities, and other marginalized populations ravaged by pandemic, the question of how to mobilize around counter-frames produced must be addressed.

References

Albuquerque, A., and Gagliardi, J. (2021). Blame it on populism! COVID-19 and Bolsonaro in *O Estado de São Paulo*'s editorials. Paper presented at the International Communication Association 2021 Meeting.

Aronoff, K. (2020, April 27). "Believe science" Is a bad response to denialism. *The New Republic*. Available at https://newrepublic.com/article/157442/believe-science-bad-response-denialism

Atton, C. (2002). *Alternative Media*. Thousand Oaks, CA: Sage.

Burch, S. (2007). Telesur and the new agenda for Latin American integration. *Global Media & Communication* 3 (2): 227–232. DOI: 10.1177/1742766507078419

Cacciatore, M., Scheufele, D., and Iyengar, S. (2016). The end of framing as we know it…and the future of media effects. *Mass Communication and Society* 19: 7–23. DOI: 10.1080/15205436.2015

Calinicos, A. (2009). *Imperialism and Global Political Economy*. London: Polity Press.

Castells, M. (2009). *Communication Power*. New York: Oxford University Press

Chong, D., and Druckman, J. (2007). Framing theory. *Annual Review of Political Science* 10(1): 103–126.

Chong, D., and Druckman, J. (2013). Counter-framing effects. *The Journal of Politics* 75(1): 1–16.

Davis, M. (2012). *The Monster at Our Door: The Global Threat of Avian Flu*. New York: The New Press.

Davis, S. and Straubhaar, J. (2019). Producing Antipetismo: Media activism and the rise of the radical, nationalist right in contemporary Brazil. *International Communication Gazette* 82(1): 82–100. DOI: 10.1177/1748048519880731

De Melo, J. (2020, April 12). Sem ação do governo, Alemão cria gabinete de crisis com funk contra Corona. *Noticias UOL*. Available at: https://noticias.uol.com.br/cotidiano/ultimas-noticias/2020/03/21/coronavirus-alemao-cria-gabinete-de-crise-com-funk-da-prevencao-e-doacoes.htm

Downing, J. (2003). Audiences and readers of alternative media: The absent lure of the virtually unknown. *Media, Culture, & Society* 25: 625–645.

Entman, R. (2003). Cascading activation: Contesting the White House's frame after 9/11. *Political Communication* 20(4): 415–432.

Entman, R. (2007). Framing bias: Media in the distribution of power. *Journal of Communication* 57: 163–173.

Forde, S. (2011). *Challenging the News: The Journalism of Alternative and Community Media*. New York: Red Globe Press.

Friedman, U. (2020, March 27). The Coronavirus denial movement now has a new leader. *The Atlantic*. Available at https://www.theatlantic.com/politics/archive/2020/03/bolsonaro-coronavirus-denial-brazil-trump/608926/

Garcia, D. (2020, October 12). "Efeito Bolsonaro" sobre alta nos casos de coronavirus surpreende pesquisadores. *Folha de S.Paulo*.

Hanley, R. (2010). Cascading activation: Bush's 'war on terrorism' and the Israeli—Palestinian conflict. *Journalism* 11 (4): 445–471. DOI: 10.1177/1464884910367595

Janowicz, N. (2020). *How to Lose the Information War*. London: IB Tauris.

Kertman, R. (2020, June 06). Bolsonaro: dos braços do povo para a lixeira da história. *Revista ISTOE*. Available at: https://istoe.com.br/bolsonaro-dos-bracos-do-povo-para-a-lixeira-da-historia/

Magalhaes, L., and Forero, R. (2020, April 2). 'Go back to work': Bolsonaro dismisses risks of deadly Coronavirus in Brazil. *The Wall Street Journal*.

Mier, B. (2020, April 21). Covid-19: Bolsonaro's lack of control is Brazil's best chance. *Brasil Wire*.

Milan, S. (2015). Mobilizing in times of social media: From a politics of identity to a politics of visibility. In Dencik, L., and Leisert, O. (eds.) *Critical Perspectives on Social Media and Protest*. Lanham: Rowman and Littlefield.

Milanez, F., and Vida, S. (2020, June 06). Pandemic, racism, and indigenous/black genocide in Brazil: Coronavirus and extermination policy. *Brasil Wire*. Available at: https://www.brasilwire.com/pandemic-racism-and-indigenous-and-black-genocide-in-brazil-coronavirus-and-extermination-policy/

Navarro, F.S. (2020, August 24). U.S. expands influence in the Brazilian Amazon during pandemic. *Brasil Wire*. Available at: https://www.brasilwire.com/u-s-expands-influence-in-the-brazilian-amazon-during-pandemic/

Observatorio da Imprensa. (2019, September 8). Os dez posts mais compartilhados no Facebook sobre as manifestações de 15 de maio. *Observatorio da Imprensa*.

Pan-American Health Organization. (2020). Infodemia tem tornando resposta às emergências de saúde ainda mais difícil, afirma OPAS em aula inaugural de pós-graduação de comunicação em saúde. White Paper, August 12, 2020. Available at: https://www.paho.org/pt/noticias/14-8-2020-infodemia-tem-tornando-resposta-emergencias-saude-ainda-mais-dificil-afirma-opas

Preissler Iglesias, S., Adghrini, S., and Rosler, A. (2020, August 1). Bolsonaro's erratic behavior is making his military backers nervous. *Bloomberg News*. Available at https://www.bloomberg.com/news/articles/2020-07-31/bolsonaro-s-military-backing-stokes-growing-unease-in-army-ranks

Ricard, J. (2020). Using misinformation as a political weapon: COVID-19 and Bolsonaro in Brazil. *The Harvard Kennedy School (HKS) Misinformation Review*, 1 (2). Available at: https://dash.harvard.edu/handle/1/42661741

Souza, J (2016). *Radiografia do Golpe: Entenda Como e Por Que Cocê foi Enganado*. São Paulo: Casa da Palavra.

Spade, D. (2020). *Mutual Aid: A Primer*. New York: Verso Books.

Stirken, M., and Sembrar, C. (2020). *Pandemic Solidarity: Mutual Aid during the COVID-19 Crisis*. London: Pluto Press.

WITNESS. (2017). Coletivo Papo Reto: Combating police violence. WITNESS Blog. Available at: https://www.witness.org/coletivo-papo-reto-combating-police-violence-in-brazil/

9
WHEN A POLARIZED MEDIA SYSTEM MEETS A PANDEMIC

Framing the Political Discord over COVID-19 Aid Campaigns in Turkey

Gizem Melek and Emre İşeri

> Such attempts [opposition municipalities' fundraiser campaigns for COVID-19] have been tried by [terror] organizations such as FETÖ and PKK in the past.
> Turkish President Recep Tayyip Erdoğan (20 April 2020)

Introduction

With the advent of the COVID-19 pandemic around the globe, many scholars have begun to question whether the pandemic bridges political divides in polarized countries (e.g., Brazil, Italy, the USA, Hungary, Indonesia, Poland, Turkey; Carothers & O'Donohue, 2020; Mudde, 2020; Müller, 2020). Given that those studies have mainly focused on trust in and support for political leaders, they have neglected many other aspects of how pandemic stories have been discussed and framed in the media.

This study aims to explore the stances of mainstream media, alternative media, and a public broadcasting outlet during the pandemic in Turkey's polarized media system under a newly established executive presidency signifying an authoritarian drift. (Akman & Akçalı, 2017; Çalışkan, 2018). Recent studies regarding Turkish media show a sharp polarization in news coverage according to news outlets' affiliations with certain socio-political camps (Panayırcı et al., 2016; Çarkoğlu et al., 2014; İşeri et al., 2019; Yıldırım et al., 2020). Given the existence of an already deep polarization in the media regarding national issues, will there be a convergence in news reporting about a global health crisis? The COVID-19 pandemic provides a solid basis to examine how a global crisis impacts the editorial policies of media outlets in a highly polarized media system. We explore the degree of disparity in terms of the media's framing strategies in this crisis. More concretely, we

DOI: 10.4324/9781003170051-11

use populist[1] frames as tools to analyze the pro-government affiliated media, public broadcasting organizations, opposition media, and alternative media outlets' news coverage of the political discord between the government and the main opposition party over the COVID-19 aid campaigns. First, the opposition mayors of the capital, Ankara (Mansur Yavaş), and the largest city, İstanbul (Ekrem İmamoğlu), organized donation campaigns to help citizens in economically difficult conditions, especially those who are unable to work or go out or those who are unemployed due to the pandemic. Therefore, the mayors announced fundraisers for the victims of the pandemic. Second, the President Recep Tayyip Erdoğan of the incumbent Justice and Development Party (AKP) launched a "National Solidarity Campaign" with the slogan "We don't need anyone, but each other, my Turkey" a day after the municipalities' campaigns. He announced that the Presidency started a donation campaign to help those in need; he donated seven months of his salary to the campaign and later called on everyone to follow him and donate.

Turkey is an exemplary case of "competitive authoritarianism," which describes regimes that are neither "democratic" nor "authoritarian" (Bogaards, 2009). By the same token, Levitsky and Way (2010) have emphasized on the unequally designed democratic playing field (e.g., the abuse of state power, the capture and discipline of opposition media) to conduct electoral campaigns and win elections (Levitsky & Way, 2010). Recent studies regarding the period around election in Turkey show that, in competitive authoritarian regimes, press-party parallelism backs ruling parties, and as a result, the incumbents accumulate critical media advantages (Yıldırım et al., 2020). Regardless of this unfair playing field, the main opposition party, the secular social democrat Republican People's Party (CHP), has managed to put an end to the predominant[2] pro-Islamist AKP's 18 years of dominance at both the local and central levels with the 2019 mayoral elections. Along with the capital city of Ankara, the landslide victory of the CHP in Istanbul, as the largest city and the economic center of Turkey, in the initial election on 31 March 2019 and following the unjustified annulment in the repeated election on 23 June 2019 was a highly symbolic one. In the context of the country's competitive authoritarian regime, with its polarized and restricted media, the municipal-level incumbency provided golden opportunities for the mayors of the opposition CHP to directly

---

1 As a "buzzword," the concept of populism has been utilized to capture various types (e.g., left-wing, right-wing, progressive, authoritarian) in distinct geographies and contexts. Drawing on an ideological-discursive approach (Mudde and Kaltwasser, 2012), this paper conceives of populism as a thin-centered ideology separating society into two homogeneous and antagonistic camps (i.e., "the pure people" versus "the corrupt elite") with the claim of the "pure people's" sovereignty.

2 The predominant-party system is defined as one "where a single party is consistently supported by a winning majority of voters ... and thus is able to monopolize power" (Sartori, 1976, p. 196).

connect with the urban poor, which constitutes the ruling AKP's electoral base (Korkmaz, 2020).

The political conflict over COVID-19 aid campaigns began when the Ankara mayor, Mansur Yavaş, and later the İstanbul mayor, Ekrem İmamoğlu of the main opposition CHP, and several other municipalities launched fundraisers to aid those in need due to the pandemic. Later, President Erdoğan of the ruling AKP launched the "National Solidarity Campaign," suggesting that all the aid would be collected in a single fund by the presidency, and he blamed municipalities for having "a logic of state within a state" (Sayın, 2020). Next, the Interior Ministry issued a decree calling the opposition municipalities' fundraiser campaigns illegal, and consequently, the municipalities' fundraiser accounts were frozen (Sayın, 2020) and criminal probes against İmamoğlu and Yavaş were launched (Sade, 2020). These political struggles received a significant volume of news coverage in the Turkish media.

Populism and the Media: Mediatization of Politics versus Politicization of Media

Due to the context-dependent interaction of various socio-economic factors (Mounk 2018; Norris & Inglehart, 2019), populist politics have resurged around the world and could be either a "threat" or a "corrective" to democracy (Kaltwasser, 2012). With "the rise of personalized politics," the stability of the given system has become contingent on the popularity of "strong" leaders elected through democratic means. In Turkey, Recep Tayyip Erdoğan is a populist leader who has adjusted democratic rules and institutions to strengthen his political position in a way that is similar to other strong leaders (e.g., Vladimir Putin in Russia, Victor Orban in Hungary, and Jarosław Kaczyński in Poland). Those leaders have adopted authoritarian policies and a populist rhetoric undermining democratic institutions (Kendall-Taylor et al., 2017; Esen & Yardımcı-Geyikçi, 2019), thereby, posing a "threat" to democracy.

Why do the media support populist actors and disseminate their political discourses? One strand of the literature, mainly dealing with Western democracies, emphasizes the process of the "mediatization of politics" (Mazzoleni & Schulz, 1999; Esser & Strömbäck, 2014; Meyen et al., 2014). This refers to how the media adopts the criterion of marketability to determine which political figures and issues should be covered. Accordingly, the growing literature on "mediated populism" (Mazzoleni, 2008; Chakravartty & Roy, 2015) and/or "media populism" (Mazzoleni et al., 2003; Krämer, 2014) proposes that the media's logic is inclined to cover more conflictive and scandalous aspects of politics due to commercial interests, which prompt those outlets to align with the political logic of populists, who are in dire need of the "oxygen of publicity" (Aalberg et al., 2017, p. 4). Nonetheless, there is insufficient empirical evidence to support the claim that there is a convergence of media logic and populist discourses (Manucci, 2017, p. 592).

An alternative answer to the question is the "politicization of media" as a peculiar feature of "polarized pluralist" societies, in which competing political parties instrumentalize the media (i.e., "press-party parallelism") in their ideological struggles (Hallin & Mancini, 2004, p. 61). Seymour-Ure (1974, p. 157) has used the term "press-party parallelism" to describe the mass media's degree of partisanship. Later, Hallin and Mancini (2004) have defined "press-party parallelism" as a crucial dimension in their typology of media systems, next to the development of the newspaper industry, professionalization of journalism, and the state's role. Drawing on those four dimensions, Hallin and Mancini (2004) have identified three types of media systems: (1) the democratic corporatist model, (2) the liberal model, and (3) the polarized pluralist model.

The Polarized Media System of Turkey

The Turkish media's characteristics mostly align with the "polarized pluralist model," with high levels of press-party parallelism (Kaya & Çakmur, 2010; Çarkoğlu et al., 2014; Panayırcı et al., 2016; Yıldırım et al., 2020) under a competitive authoritarian regime that governs media through "coercive capture and discipline" that targets oppositional outlets (Yeşil, 2018). Within a context of high levels of political parallelism under a regime with authoritarian tendencies, low levels of journalistic professionalism and media commercialization set the stage for commentary-oriented partisan journalism to dominate the Turkish media landscape (İşeri et al., 2019). On 15 July 2016, a faction of the Turkish army, allegedly linked to the Fethullah Gülen movement, executed a plot to overthrow the AKP government by creating a chaotic environment. Labeling heightened coercive measures against dissident media in the aftermath of "the coup attempt" as "the final layer of increased media control by the AKP," Akser (2018, pp. 95–96) has suggested two outcomes: (1) the government's increasing adoption of political and economic means to censor critical views and (2) conglomerates (e.g., Kalyon, Demirören) with patronage links to the government adoption of further internal censorship (if not solely covering pro-government content) in their news media coverage. In this light, one could safely presume that the heightened "politicization of media" under a "competitive authoritarian regime" has largely tasked the Turkish media landscape with covering the government's words and actions without much critique. Hinging on the significance of the media system type in the resurgence of populisms, Erdoğan and Erçetin (2019, p. 67) have found that the polarized media system of Turkey offered significant advantages for populist forces (i.e., Erdoğan and his AKP) during the constitutional referendum in 2017—after which the parliamentary system was abolished and the new executive presidency was established—particularly for those in power, allowing them to communicate directly with voters, while opponents were deprived of such communication opportunities. Therefore, the context of the pandemic offers scholars an ideal way to assess how the Turkish media landscape provides alternate realities for their audiences through their different (populist) frames and source adoptions (cf. O'Donohue et al., 2020; Gürhanlı, 2020).

Media plays a critical role in spreading information to the public about many issues, but with high-concern environments such as a global health crisis like COVID-19, this role is even more significant (Uluçay et al., 2020). Even though the public mainly relies on the information the media provides, many citizens are highly skeptical of the media in Turkey (O'Donohue et al., 2020). The results of a recent survey indicate that a total of 30% of respondents trust the media, while 70% believe that it is biased and untrustworthy (O'Donohue et al., 2020). Among the respondents, the highest percentage of citizens who trust the media are supporters of the ruling AKP (51%) and its coalition partner, the far-right MHP (37%), whereas trust among the opposition supporters (CHP, 13% and İYİP, 18%) and pro-Kurdish HDP (6%) is much lower (O'Donohue et al., 2020). During the early days of the COVID-19 pandemic, however, a study in Turkey showed that the public found the media slightly more reliable in terms of data sharing (above 50% in many instances), even though the respondents were mainly opposition-minded, and their political ideology was predominantly left-leaning (Uluçay et al., 2020).

At the same time, Turkey had a brief period of political unity regarding the national response effort of the COVID-19 battle, but after the onset of the pandemic, the sharp dispute between the ruling AKP and the opposition CHP over the aid campaigns swiftly ended this initial cooperation (Aydın-Düzgit, 2020). The polarization also sharpened when President Erdoğan declared that his political and media opponents were "akin to the coronavirus" due to their critical statements and coverage of the government's measures; heavy fines from Turkey's official media regulation authority, the Radio and Television Supreme Council (RTÜK), followed for opposition TV networks (Aydın-Düzgit, 2020). In the meantime, Human Rights Watch (2021) has reported that the government instrumentalized the pandemic for authoritarianism in Turkey.

Since "press-party parallelism" is the *modus operandi* of Turkey's polarized media system, a given outlet's critical coverage depends on its political party/ socio-political camp affiliation. This is the case for the public broadcaster TRT, as well. Due to their independence from state led financial means and market pressures, we presume that alternative media outlets have the potential to go beyond party/socio-political lines and freely criticize politicians' populist rhetoric. In sum, the increasing polarization during the time of the COVID-19 pandemic in Turkey is likely to follow patterns that are similar to those of earlier events (e.g., elections, the corruption probe, and the coup attempt), which were determined based on previous research (Çarkoğlu et al., 2014; Yıldırım et al., 2020; Panayırcı et al., 2016; İşeri et al., 2019). Therefore, to learn whether the media's sharp polarization regarding national-level conflicts evinces the same patterns during a global health crisis, namely the novel coronavirus pandemic, we propose answering the research question and testing the below hypotheses:

RQ: How do news outlets frame the conflict over the aid campaigns during the COVID-19 pandemic in a polarized media system under a rising competitive authoritarian regime?

H1: There will be a disparity regarding populist framing strategies between the pro-government outlets *Hürriyet*, *Sabah*, and the public broadcasting outlet TRT on the one hand and the opposition *Sözcü* and *Cumhuriyet* on the other hand.

H2: In an increasingly polarized context, the pro-government outlets *Hürriyet*, *Sabah*, and the public broadcasting outlet TRT will heavily rely on official governmental sources, while the opposition *Sözcü* and *Cumhuriyet* will heavily rely on the opposition parties' sources, and Bianet, as an alternative media source, will reflect different perspectives on the issue.

Methodology, Data Collection, and Analysis

To understand how different media outlets operating under a rising competitive authoritarian regime responded to a global crisis such as COVID-19, we adopted a quantitative content analysis method and investigated the framing strategies of the selected media regarding aid campaign coverage during the pandemic. Framing strategies become crucial to determine the way media set the baseline for both the political and public agendas by altering opinions and attitudes (Scheufele & Tewksbury, 2007; Melek & Uluçay, 2019). Therefore, adopting a revised version of Mazzoleni and Bracciale's (2018) populist frames (i.e., appeal to the people, attacking internal/external elite, ostracizing the others; Table 9.1), we developed a coding instrument to conduct a content analysis. The coding instrument also included variables to detect the populism index (zero level, soft, moderate, and bold populism) of the news outlets, the writing style (i.e., reporting or commentary), and the news outlets' preferred sources (i.e., the pro-Islamist incumbent AKP; their coalition partner, the ultra-nationalist MHP; the main opposition secular social democrat CHP; their coalition partner, the secular nationalist İYİP; and the pro-Kurdish HDP or others).

Sampling and Data collection

We used a purposive sampling method, which is a form of non-probability sampling often used to analyze online news (Baxter & Babbie, 2004). In this method, the researchers' judgment and expertise are significant while selecting the site for the study, and "the site should be selected strategically to provide rich opportunities to gather data relevant to the guiding question"

(Baxter & Babbie, 2004, p. 306). Therefore, we chose four news websites from the mainstream media that are affiliated with certain socio-political camps in accordance with the aim of our study: the pro-government hurriyet.com.tr and sabah.com.tr, as well as the pro-opposition media sozcu.com.tr and cumhuriyet.com.tr. Our main criteria for selecting these news outlets were both their ideological perspectives and ownership structures (Table 9.2).

TABLE 9.1 Explanations and Examples of the Populist Frames

Frame	a) Explanation	b) Examples
(1) Appeal to the people	Referring to the people in a manner that presumes or calls upon their consent.	
(1.1) Sovereignty	"The people" is the ultimate democratic sovereign or the "ruler" often betrayed by the elites. While the "outside" is dangerous, the "inside" is a safe space for popular sovereignty.	"Even during our country's fight against the pandemic, the separatist organization didn't stop their activities, which revealed the ugly face of terrorism. We are determined not to let the terrorist organization breathe. … We are working continually and uncompromisingly for Turkey's internal and external security" (President Erdoğan, quoted in *Sözcü*).
(1.2) Class	"'The people' are depicted as a deprived socio-economic class or subset of the population" (Mazzoleni & Bracciale, 2018).	"We struggled with the money-lender lobbies who are accustomed to adding wealth to their wealth without any producing, sweating, or taking any risks" (President Erdoğan, quoted in TRT).
(1.3) Nation/ Ethnic Group	"The people are understood as a national community or ethnic group, with emphasis on belonging to the native population as the main criterion to discriminate who is part or not part of the nation" (Mazzoleni & Bracciale, 2018).	"No illness can prevent the bright future ahead of us. No threat can dissuade us from our goals. Because we are Turkey. Because we are the Turkish Nation" (President Erdoğan, quoted in *Hürriyet*).

(1.4) Cultural	To influence ordinary people by using their cultural values. Shared and common values, religion, history, customs.	"This is the day of the unification against the common enemy, just like in our War of Independence" (President Erdoğan, quoted in *Hürriyet*).
(2) Attacking the elite	Anti-elite, anti-establishment rhetoric and orientation Populists portray the established ruling elites as corrupt, self-interested, arrogant, exploitative, and often treacherous.	"Expressing that this opposition understanding led by the CHP is always based on conflict instead of reconciliation, separatism instead of unity and solidarity, inciting hatred and hatred instead of tolerance" (TRT).
(3) Ostracizing the others	"Implies that protesters and/or supporters of certain political views do not represent the community at large" (İşeri et al., 2019: 1470).	
(3.1) Dangerous others	"Stigmatizing and excluding segments of the people from the specific population" (Mazzoleni & Bracciale, 2018).	For PKK and FETO: "Those who wait for the collapse of the health system due to the pandemic, the weakening of public security... They are trying to sabotage public services" (President Erdoğan, quoted in *Sabah*).
(3.2) Authoritarianism	"When political actors press for severe political measures or illiberal policies against those who threaten the homogeneity of the people" (Mazzoleni & Bracciale, 2018).	"All these campaigns are carried out only by the units announced by our state, namely the Presidency. If our municipalities open such campaigns without the permission of our administration, then this is the logic of being a state within the state, so it will distribute the power" (President Erdoğan, quoted in *Sabah*).

TABLE 9.2 Outlet, Ownership, Coverage Style

Outlet	c) Ownership	d) Coverage Style
Bianet	IPS İletişim Vakfı (IPS Communication Foundation) with the support of the Swedish International Development Agency (SIDA)	Alternative
Cumhuriyet	Cumhuriyet Foundation (Yeni Gün Press Agency and Publishing Inc.)	Secular, opposition
Sözcü	Burak Akbay (Estetik Publishing Joint Stock Company)	Secular, opposition
Hürriyet	Demirören Holding (until March 2018, Doğan Holding)	Moderate (until March 2018); pro-status quo/pro-incumbent AKP government
Sabah	Zirve Holding (Kalyon Group)	Pro-status quo/pro-incumbent AKP government
TRT (Turkish Radio and Television Corporation)	Republic of Turkey	Public broadcasting

Source: Media Ownership Monitor (MOM) Turkey website; Günay et al. (2018); Ersoy and İşeri (2020).

In Turkey, online news and social media are now broadly popular sources for urban individuals to obtain alternative and critical perspectives, and analyzing them is a common practice in the literature (Newman et al., 2020; Melek, 2017; Günay et al., 2018; Ersoy & İşeri, 2020). This is why we also included an alternative media source in our sample, again in accordance with our research goal, as they are on the rise and may provide an alternative perspective within a polarized media system. We selected Bianet's website (bianet.org) as an alternative media outlet in line with previous studies (Günay et al., 2018; Ersoy & İşeri 2020) for two main reasons: (1) its financial structure and the fact that, as an online-only publication, Bianet would likely be less exposed to governmental and corporate pressures than the mainstream media in its editorial policies; (2) Bianet is one of the oldest online news platforms and has more than 330,000 followers on Twitter. Finally, we included the public broadcasting outlet TRT's news website (trthaber.com) in our sample to detect whether there is a difference between the coverage of polarized commercial media and public broadcasting.[3]

We collected all the news content related to COVID-19 aid campaigns in seven months, starting from the announcement of the campaigns in March 2020 through the end of September 2020. Two assistants archived the news stories via Google advanced search using keywords,[4] and in total this procedure resulted in 1,143 news stories from Bianet ($n = 42$), *Cumhuriyet* ($n = 306$), *Hürriyet* ($n = 273$), *Sabah* ($n = 257$), *Sözcü* ($n = 129$), and TRT ($n = 136$).

Coding

The codebook consisted of three parts. The first included the seven populist frames and the populism index. The unit of analysis was a news story, and the presence of each frame was coded as a dummy variable. The populism index variables were only coded into one of the four categories. Therefore, if a story utilized none of the populist frames, it was coded under "zero-level populism." If at least one of the populist meta-frames was used in the story, it was coded under "soft populism." The stories were coded under "moderate populism" if they utilized at least two populist meta-frames, and lastly, if all three meta-frames were available, those stories were coded under "bold populism."

The second part consisted of variables to detect whether the coverage was predominantly factual reporting or largely commentary and stories coded into only one or the other variable. The last part concerned the news outlets' preferred sources and consisted of six variables, including five political parties (the pro-Islamist incumbent AKP, their coalition partner the ultra-nationalist MHP, the main opposition secular social democrat CHP, their coalition partner the secular nationalist İYİP, and the pro-Kurdish HDP) and an "other" category for any other individuals, institutions, businesses, etc. The coders coded every political party, individual, and/or institution used as a source in the news story.

The training period for the coding instrument lasted several weeks, and the agreement between the two coders was very high. Using Krippendorff's Alpha for calculating intercoder reliability, we obtained $\alpha = 0.95$. The agreement

---

3 According to Konda's (2019) media report, the majority of the TRT's audience has consisted of AKP supporters for the last decade. However, the people who stated they had modern lifestyle have moved away from TRT over the last decade (with a ratio down to 10% from 17%), and the ratio of religious conservatives has increased from 30% to 37%, while the ratio of traditional conservatives remained the same (Konda, 2019). As of 2019, 90% of the audience consists of conservatives (either religious or traditional).
4 We tracked each news outlet's content between March and September 2020. Using the keywords "aid campaign" and "fundraiser campaign," we collected every story regarding the aid campaign issue over the period.

ranged around 0.92 for the source variables, 0.95 for the writing style variables, and 0.98 for the populist frame variables.

Results

In line with our hypotheses, we find that the Turkish mainstream media outlets, including the public broadcasting (i.e., *Cumhuriyet*, *Sözcü*, *Hürriyet*, *Sabah*, and TRT), covered the COVID-19 aid campaigns in a partisan way and therefore further polarized the political dispute regarding those campaigns. More concretely, our hypotheses proposed that media outlets would adopt differing (populist) framing strategies and source adoptions to propagate their affiliated political actor/socio-political camp's discourses in their coverage of the issue at stake. The populist frames are most frequently featured in pro-government news outlets, whereas pro-opposition and alternative news outlets have a relatively low populist frame utilization which is mainly the result of reproducing entire speeches of the ruling AKP politicians. At the same time, in other instances, only opposition and alternative media critically covered the ruling AKP's actions and statements with their commentary style. While the public broadcasting outlet TRT would not serve as an exception in this partisan media landscape, the alternative media outlet Bianet adopted a balanced stance in terms of its source utilization.

According to our findings, indeed, different media outlets have utilized differing framing strategies to cover the political discord of the COVID-19 campaigns, reflecting their stances in the polarized political context of Turkey. This divergence is most evident in the way the media outlets affiliated with the incumbent pro-Islamist AKP and the ultra-nationalist MHP governmental coalition have adopted populist frames of "attacking the elite," "nation/ethnic group," and "culture." With a combined share of 70.2% in total, *Sabah* (29.8%) and *Hürriyet* (27.4%), and to a lesser extent public broadcasting outlet TRT (13%), adopted "attacking the elite" to denigrate the main opposition party and thus their pandemic campaigns. By the same token, the pro-government news outlets widely adopted "dangerous others" (71.3%) and "authoritarianism" (62.9%) frames, targeting those with dissident views. In addition, the pro-government outlets reproduced the incumbent coalition government's discourses with their wide adoption of "culture" (religious discourses such as *umma*) and "nation-ethnic group" with respective shares of 86.1% and 74.9% in total.

This "press-party parallelism" is also discernible in news outlets' varying degrees of populist meta-frame ("appeal to the people," "attacking the elite," and "ostracizing the others") adoptions in their coverage of the COVID-19 aid campaigns (see Figure 9.1). The findings reveal that the pro-government outlets and the public broadcasting outlet TRT recorded the lion's share of populist frame utilizations to various degrees: 86.4% in soft populism, 70.5% in moderate populism, and 69.1% in bold populism.

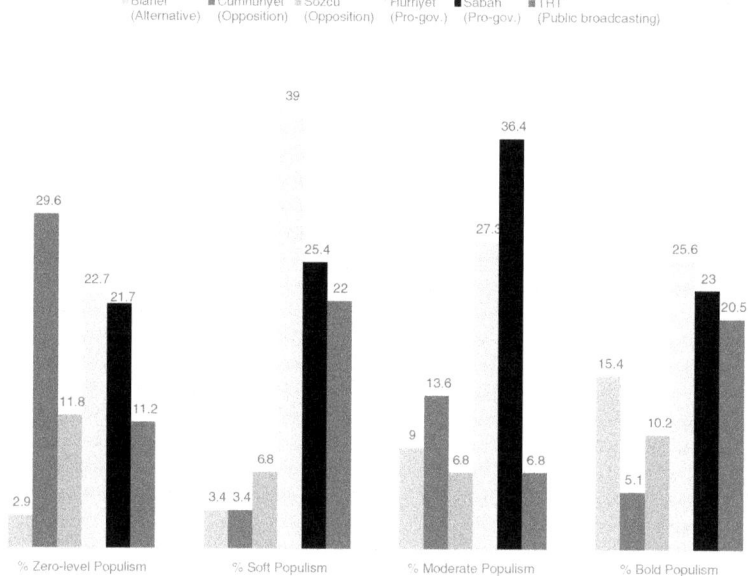

FIGURE 9.1 Populism index score for different outlets.

According to Figure 9.2, the writing styles of the Turkish news outlets on the pandemic aid campaign conflict differ between commentary and reporting styles. Commentary-based journalism is a feature that is more common in polarized media systems (Hallin & Mancini, 2004, p. 62). However, in the case of news outlets that lean toward a commentary style, such as *Cumhuriyet* (56.5%), *Sabah* (52.1%), and *Sözcü* (55%), the share of the factual reporting style was also somewhat high. In the case of the public broadcasting outlet TRT, the share of commentary and reporting was almost equal. However, the alternative online news outlet Bianet and the pro-government *Hürriyet* used a significantly lower amount of commentary (Bianet: 16.7%, *Hürriyet*: 23.1%); instead, they mainly used a factual reporting style (Bianet: 83.3%, *Hürriyet*: 76.9%) in their coverage. In other words, the opposition *Sözcü* and *Cumhuriyet* and the pro-government *Sabah* news outlets used subjective evaluations in more than half of their aid campaign coverage, whereas the public broadcasting outlet TRT used the subjective style in half of its coverage.

Here, it is also worth explaining that a closer look at the framing strategies of the opposition (*Cumhuriyet* and *Sözcü*) and alternative media (Bianet) outlets reveals that their populist frame usage is usually a result of directly quoted statements from the President and other AKP politicians (e.g., the interior minister, MPs, the head of religious affairs, pro-businessmen) and are covered with a factual reporting style. However, their subjective commentary style coverage tends to be journalists critically covering the AKP's actions. For instance,

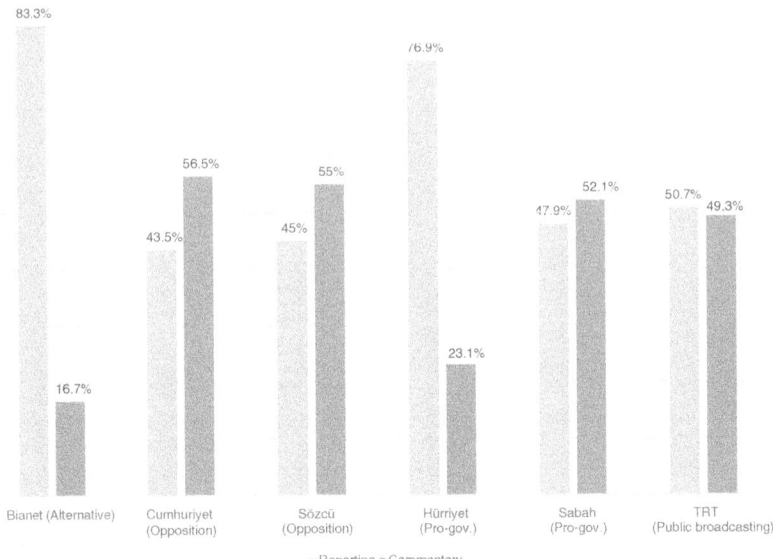

FIGURE 9.2 Writing style of different outlets.

"A decision worse than the virus: State blocks the CHP municipalities' aid!" titled news coverage of opposition *Cumhuriyet* on 1 April 2020 should be noted.

The pro-government news outlets' (*Hürriyet*, *Sabah*, and TRT) populist frame utilization occurred with both politicians and journalists themselves. These news outlets used direct quotations from the government, but in some instances they also utilized a commentary writing style to attack the opposition block. Accordingly, the pro-government *Sabah*'s news coverage titled "CHP's aid game has failed" on 2 April 2020 can be given as an example.

As Table 9.3 indicates, the selected media outlets gave more space to their affiliated political actors in the direct source utilization in their coverage of this polarizing issue. While pro-government outlets (i.e., *Sabah* and *Hürriyet*) and the public broadcasting outlet TRT covered the governing political party (AKP) and its coalition partner (MHP) representatives distinctly more than others, the opposing media (i.e., *Cumhuriyet* and *Sözcü*) preferred to directly quote politicians of opposition parties, mostly CHP and İYİP. The different use of sources is also clear concerning the pro-Kurdish HDP; only *Cumhuriyet* and Bianet covered what the politicians of HDP had to say. Moreover, the alternative media outlet Bianet gave almost equal space to both the ruling AKP ($n = 17$) and the main opposition CHP ($n = 15$). Apart from political actors, the media outlets quoted others (e.g., celebrities, civil society, academics, and ordinary people on the street), as well. In the first instance, this could be interpreted as a positive signal of their intention to reflect the diversity of opinions in their coverage.

However, those in the "others" category were primarily cherry-picked to propagate partisan views. More concretely, pro-government outlets (*Hürriyet* and *Sabah*) and the public broadcasting outlet TRT gave space mostly to ministers (e.g., of religious affairs), business associations (e.g., MÜSİAD), chambers of commerce (e.g., TOBB), companies (e.g., LİMAK), governing coalition-affiliated municipal leaders, governors of provincial districts, rectors appointed by the President, and celebrities with favorable views of the government's stance on the polarizing COVID-19 aid campaign issue. Conversely, the few "other" voices in Bianet reflected different perspectives on the issue.

When we take a closer look at the distribution of the selected media's usage of governing political actors' populist discourses on the COVID-19 aid campaign coverage, the findings suggest that the populist frames were most frequently featured in pro-government news outlets. Those pro-government media outlets' populist frame utilization is 27% (*Sabah*) and 30% (*Hürriyet*). If we were to include public broadcasting outlet TRT (17.2%) in this calculation, their combined share would be 74.2% of the total populist frame adoptions. However, opposing news outlets' populist frame utilization share is only 7.8% (*Cumhuriyet*) and 9% (*Sözcü*). The alternative media Bianet's populist frame usage portion is 9%.

Against this backdrop, our hypotheses (H1–H2) anticipating the media outlets' adoption of differing (populist) framing strategies and source utilizations in line with their socio-political camp affiliations have been verified. Nevertheless, the alternative media outlet Bianet adopted a balanced approach by giving almost equal space to both ruling and opposition parties and relatively low utilization of the governing elite-induced populist frames in its coverage. However, in some cases, Bianet provided Erdoğan's full speeches, which resulted in higher shares of moderate and bold populism indexes than expected, as shown in Figure 9.1. Last, as H2 proposes, the pro-government outlets *Hürriyet*, *Sabah*,

TABLE 9.3 Relative Presence of the News Outlets

	e) AKP	f) CHP	g) MHP	h) İYİP	i) HDP	j) Other
	%	%	%	%	%	%
Bianet (Alternative)	6.9	4.7	0	0	50	2.6
Cumhuriyet (Opposition)	9.8	59.9	8.3	52.6	50	29.4
Sözcü (Opposition)	6.9	21.7	16.6	36.8	0	10.5
Hürriyet (Pro-gov.)	31	11.5	16.6	10.5	0	25.4
Sabah (Pro-gov.)	25.3	1.5	33.3	0	0	19.6
TRT (Public broadcasting)	20	0.6	25	0	0	12.4
Totals (N)	245	322	12	19	6	428

and the public broadcasting outlet TRT heavily drew on the ruling AKP and cherry-picked sources under in the "other" category. The opposition *Sözcü* and *Cumhuriyet* heavily relied on the sources of the opposition parties, whereas the alternative media outlet Bianet provided a more balanced source utilization nevertheless reflected different perspectives on the issue.

Conclusion

The main goal of this research was to determine how different outlets in a competitive authoritarian regime responded to political discord during a global health crisis. As an exemplary case, Turkey is a significantly under-studied media system in the literature, and it has a high level of press-party parallelism and a predominant-party system (Çarkoğlu et al., 2014) in the newly established executive presidency. In parallel with recent research highlighting that news outlets in Turkey use different framing strategies during elections (Çarkoğlu et al., 2014; Yıldırım et al., 2020), corruption probes (Panayırcı et al., 2016), and the coup attempt (İşeri et al., 2019) at the national level, the gap between them deepens. Therefore, the specific issue of the political conflict between the incumbent AKP and the main opposition CHP over the pandemic aid campaigns provided a valuable opportunity to examine the "politicization of media" at the global level crisis. Our results revealed that the semi-authoritarian regime's interaction with the polarized media system determined the contours of media outlets' framing strategies in their coverage of a global health crisis. In other words, the news coverage of the COVID-19 aid campaigns was in line with political party ideologies and the polarization of the media during the pandemic tracks the earlier patterns of political dissensions in Turkey. In that sense there was, in contrast with many other countries, no sign of a rally round the flag effect where all media were temporarily less critical for the government and its leader (see Chapter 1).

Engaging with the relevant literature on the role of media in populism and the nexus of polarized media systems and crisis (e.g., coups, terror, and environmental disasters), our results have revealed the role of media in public debates and democratic consolidation at a time of populist resurgence around the globe. The results reveal that the interaction between the situational factor (i.e., polarizing aid campaigns) and the structural factors (i.e., the competitive authoritarian regime and polarized media system) determines (populist) framing strategies and coverage styles of different media outlets (both mainstream commercial outlets and public broadcasting). In that sense, the one alternative media outlet (i.e., Bianet) we studied proved to be an interesting exception to that rule in the Turkish context. Further studies should be conducted in different/similar regime types and media systems to comparatively discern the media's role in the resurgence of populism in times of crisis (cf., İşeri and Ersoy, 2021).

Acknowledgments

This work was supported by the Project Evaluation Commission of Yaşar University under the project (BAP094) "When Polarized Media System Meets Pandemic: Mediated Pandemic Populism over COVID-19 Fundraising Campaigns in Turkey." We would like to thank the editors, Peter Van Aelst and Jay Blumler, for their valuable feedback; and our coders, Ecem Evrensel and Ezgi Su Mete, for their contribution.

References

Aalberg, T., Esser, F., Reinemann, C., Strömbäck, J., & de Vreese, C. H. (2017). *Populist Political Communication in Europe*. New York: Routledge.

Akman, A. C., & Akçalı, P. (2017). Changing the system through instrumentalizing weak political institutions: the quest for a presidential system in Turkey in historical and comparative perspective. *Turkish Studies*, *18*(4), 577–600. doi:10.1080/14683849.2017.1347508

Akser, M. (2018). News media consolidation and censorship in Turkey: From liberal ideals to corporatist realities. *Mediterranean Quarterly*, *29*(3), 78–97. doi:10.1215/10474552-7003180

Aydın-Düzgit, S. (2020, April 28). Turkey: Deepening discord and illiberalism amid the pandemic. *Carnegie Endowment for International Peace*. https://carnegieendowment.org/2020/04/28/turkey-deepening-discord-and-illiberalism-amid-pandemic-pub-81650

Baxter, L. A., and Babbie, E., (2004). *The basics of communication research*. Belmont: Thomson Wadsworth.

Bogaards, M. (2009). How to classify hybrid regimes? Defective democracy and electoral authoritarianism. *Democratization*, *16*(2), 399–423. doi:10.1080/13510340902777800

Carothers, T., & O'Donohue, A. (2020, April 28). Polarization and the pandemic. *Carnegie Endowment for International Peace*. https://bit.ly/3eCYyhO

Chakravartty, P., & Roy, S. (2015). Mr. Modi goes to Delhi: Mediated populism and the 2014 Indian elections. *Television & New Media*, *16*(4), 311–322. doi:10.1177/1527476415573957

Çalışkan, K. (2018). Toward a new political regime in Turkey: From competitive toward full authoritarianism. *New Perspectives on Turkey*, *58*, 5–33. doi:10.1017/npt.2018.10

Çarkoğlu, A., Baruh, L., & Yıldırım, K. (2014). Press-party parallelism and polarization of news media during an election campaign: The case of the 2011 Turkish elections. *The International Journal of Press/Politics*, *19*(3), 295–317. doi:10.1177/1940161214528994

Erdoğan, E., & Erçetin, T. (2019). Popülist Liderlerinin Başarısına Medya Sistemleri Perspektifinden Bir Bakış: Birleşik Krallık, Hollanda ve Türkiye Karşılaştırması [Looking to the success of populist leaders from the perspective of the media systems: A comparison on the United Kingdom, the Netherlands and Turkey]. *Moment Dergi*, *6*(1), 38–74. doi:10.17572//mj2019.1.3874

Ersoy, M., & İşeri, E. (2020). Framing environmental debates over nuclear energy in Turkey's polarized media system. *Turkish Studies*, 1–27. doi:10.1080/14683849.2020.1746908

Esen, B., & Yardımcı-Geyikçi, Ş. (2019). An alternative account of the populist backlash in the United States: A perspective from Turkey. *PS-Political Science and Politics*, *52*(3), 445–450. doi:10.1017/S1049096519000180

Esser, F., & Strömbäck, J. (2014). A paradigm in the making: Lessons for the future of mediatization research. In F. Esser & J. Strömbäck (Eds.), *Mediatization of Politics. Understanding the Transformation of Western Democracies* (pp. 223–242). Basingstoke: Palgrave Macmillan.

Günay, D., İşeri, E., & Ersoy, M. (2018). Alternative media and the securitization of climate change in Turkey. *Alternatives*, *43*(2), 96–114. doi:10.1177/0304375418820384

Gürhanlı, H. (2020). Turkey. In G. Katsambekis & Y. Stavrakakis (Eds.), *Populism and the Pandemic: A Collaborative Report. POPULISMUS Interventions No. 7* (special edition), Thessaloniki (pp. 46–52). https://repository.lboro.ac.uk/articles/report/Populism_and_the_pandemic_A_collaborative_report/12546284

Hallin, D. C., & Mancini, P. (2004). *Comparing media systems: Three models of media and politics*. Cambridge: Cambridge University Press.

Human Rights Watch. (2021). *World Report 2021 Turkey Events of 2020*. https://www.hrw.org/world-report/2021/country-chapters/turkey

İşeri, E., & Ersoy, M. (2021). Framing the Syrian Operations: Populism in Foreign Policy and the Polarized News Media of Turkey. *International Journal of Communication*, *15*, 2870–2893.

İşeri, E., Şekercioğlu, E., & Panayırcı, U. C. (2019). The sphere of consensus in a polarized media system: The case of Turkey during the catastrophic coup attempt. *International Journal of Communication*, *13*, 1462–1486.

Kaltwasser, C. R. (2012). The ambivalence of populism: Threat and corrective for democracy. *Democratization*, *19*(2), 184–208. doi:10.1080/13510347.2011.572619

Kaya, R., & Çakmur, B. (2010). Politics and the mass media in Turkey. *Turkish Studies*, *11*(4), 521–537. doi:10.1080/14683849.2010.540112

Kendall-Taylor, A., Frantz, E., & Wright, J. (2017). The global rise of personalized politics: It's not just dictators anymore. *The Washington Quarterly*, *40*(1), 7–19. doi:10.1080/0163660X.2017.1302735

Konda. (2019). *Media Report*. https://konda.com.tr/wp-content/uploads/2020/01/KONDA_MediaReport_LS2018.pdf

Korkmaz, S. S. (2020, May 11). Could Turkey's opposition provide a model for the defeat of populist authoritarian rule? *Open Democracy*. https://www.opendemocracy.net/en/can-europe-make-it/could-turkeys-opposition-provide-a-model-for-the-defeat-of-populist-authoritarian-rule/

Krämer, B. (2014). Media populism: A conceptual clarification and some theses on its effects. *Communication Theory*, *24*(1), 42–60. doi:10.1111/comt.12029

Levitsky, S., & Way, L. A. (2010). *Competitive authoritarianism: Hybrid regimes after the Cold War*. New York: Cambridge University Press.

Manucci, L. (2017). Populism and the media. In C. R. Kaltwasser, P. Taggart, P. O. Espejo, & P. Ostiguy (Eds.), *The Oxford handbook of populism* (pp.467–488). United Kingdom: Oxford University Press.

Mazzoleni G. (2008) Mediated Populism. *The International Encyclopedia of Communication*. doi:10.1002/9781405186407.wbiecm057

Mazzoleni, G., & Bracciale, R. (2018). Socially mediated populism: the communicative strategies of political leaders on Facebook. *Palgrave Communications*, *4*(1), 1–10. doi:10.1057/s41599-018-0104-x

Mazzoleni, G., & Schulz, W. (1999). "Mediatization" of politics: A challenge for democracy?. *Political communication*, *16*(3), 247–261. doi:10.1080/105846099198613

Mazzoleni, G., Stewart, J., & Horsfield, B. (Eds.). (2003). *The media and neo-populism: A contemporary comparative analysis*. Westport, CT: Praeger.

Melek, G. (2017). A Study on Hürriyet and Twitter within the Framework of Intermedia Agenda-Setting. *İletişim Kuram ve Araştırma Dergisi*, *44*, 17–41.

Melek, G., & Uluçay, D. M. (2019). Media attributes and attitude change: Experiments on the impact of second-level agenda-setting on attitudes towards Syrian refugees. *Estudios Sobre El Mensaje Periodístico*, *25*(1), 381–392. doi:10.5209/ESMP.63735

Meyen, M., Thieroff, M., & Strenger, S. (2014) Mass Media Logic and The Mediatization of Politics. *Journalism Studies*, *15*(3), 271–288. doi:10.1080/1461670X.2014.889459

Mounk Y. (2018). *The People Vs. Democracy: Why Our Freedom Is in Danger and How to Save It*. Cambridge, MA: Harvard University Press.

Mudde, C. (2020, March 27) Will the coronavirus 'kill populism'? Don't count on it. *The Guardian*. https://www.theguardian.com/commentisfree/2020/mar/27/coronavirus-populism-trump-politics-response

Mudde, C., & Kaltwasser, C. R. (Eds.). (2012). *Populism in Europe and the Americas: Threat or Corrective for Democracy?* Cambridge: Cambridge University Press. doi:10.1017/CBO9781139152365

Müller, J. W. (2020, April 16) Populists are likely to benefit from the coronavirus pandemic. *IWM*. https://www.iwm.at/always-active/corona-focus/jan-werner-mullerhow-populists-will-leverage-the-coronavirus-pandemic/

Newman, N., Fletcher, R., Schulz, A., Andı, S., & Nielsen, R. K. (2020). Digital news report 2020. *Reuters Institute*. https://reutersinstitute.politics.ox.ac.uk/sites/default/files/2020-06/DNR_2020_FINAL.pdf

Norris, P., & Inglehart, R. (2019). *Cultural Backlash: Trump, Brexit, and Authoritarian Populism*. Cambridge: Cambridge University Press.

O'Donohue, A., Hoffman M., & Makovsky, A. (2020, June 10). Turkey's Changing Media Landscape. *Center for American Progress*. https://www.americanprogress.org/issues/security/reports/2020/06/10/485976/turkeys-changing-media-landscape/

Panayırcı, U. C., İşeri, E., & Şekercioğlu, E. (2016). Political agency of news outlets in a polarized media system: Framing the corruption probe in Turkey. *European Journal of Communication*, *31*(5), 551–567. doi:10.1177/0267323116669455

Sade, G. (2020, April 17). İçişleri Bakanlığı Yavaş ve İmamoğlu hakkında soruşturma başlattı. [The Ministry of Interior launched an investigation against Yavaş and İmamoğlu]. *Euronews Turkish*. https://tr.euronews.com/2020/04/17/icisleri-bakanligi-mansur-yavas-imamoglu-hakkinda-sorusturma-baslatti-koronavirus-belediye

Sartori, G. (1976). *Parties and Party Systems: A Framework for Analysis*. Cambridge: Cambridge University Press.

Sayın, A. (2020, April 1). Koronavirüs: Belediyelerin yardım kampanyaları neden tartışma yarattı, iktidar ve muhalefet ne diyor? [Coronavirus: Why did municipalities' aid campaigns spark debate, what does the government and opposition say?] *BBC Turkish*. https://www.bbc.com/turkce/haberler-turkiye-52127212

Scheufele, D. A., & Tewksbury, D. (2007). Framing, Agenda Setting, and Priming: The Evolution of Three Media Effects Models. *Journal of Communication*, *57(1)*, 9–20. doi:10.1111/j.0021-9916.2007.00326.x

Seymour-Ure, C. (1974). *The Political Impact of Mass Media*. London: SAGE.

Uluçay, D. M., Melek, G., & Özyurda-Ergen, D. (2020). Public perception of data visuals in media coverage during COVID-19 pandemic: The risk perception model revisited. *Tripodos, 1*(47), 135–153.

Yeşil, B. (2018). Authoritarian turn or continuity? Governance of media through capture and discipline in the AKP era. *South European Society and Politics, 23*(2), 239–257. doi:10.1080/13608746.2018.1487137

Yıldırım, K., Baruh, L., & Çarkoğlu, A. (2020). Dynamics of campaign reporting and press-party parallelism: Rise of competitive authoritarianism and the media system in Turkey. *Political Communication*. doi:10.1080/10584609.2020.1765913

PART 3
Public Opinion

10
DIVIDED WE TRUST?

The Role of Polarization on Rally-around-the-Flag Effects during the COVID-19 Crisis

Ana S. Cardenal, Laia Castro, Christian Schemer, Jesper Strömbäck, Agnieszka Stępińska, Claes de Vreese, and Peter Van Aelst

Introduction

The COVID-19 pandemic and its rapid unfolding took many leaders by surprise. The spread of the virus, and the harsh consequences for public health and the economy made political leaders vulnerable to public and media criticism. However, the health crisis also provided political actors with an opportunity to show strength and determination in fighting the crisis and its consequences. Furthermore, the COVID-19 crisis is in some respects comparable with war time, as it is an exogenous shock which involves several nations and has severe health effects and economic consequences. During this kind of events, research has found that the usual mode of opinion formation is suspended (Brody, 1991), that people tend to "rally around the flag", and that support for and trust in leaders is often increased (Mueller, 1970).

Since politicians have reacted differently and the media landscapes in which they operate strongly vary across countries, we argue that the COVID-19 crisis may have had different effects on the trust citizens have in their political institutions. In this chapter, we investigate whether the level of political division and media polarization shaped changes in trust in governmental officials differently across countries. In contexts where political and media polarization are weak, we expect that public assessment of the government's management of the crisis will not be guided by partisan considerations. Therefore, in these contexts, we hypothesize increases in governmental trust as a result of incumbents' management of the crisis, and a clear "rally-around-the-flag" effect. In contrast, where political and media divisions are high, we expect that partisan considerations will guide citizens' evaluations of the government's management of the crisis. Hence, for these contexts, we hypothesize small or no changes at all in trust toward incumbents as a result of their handling of the crisis, i.e., lower or no rally-around-the-flag effect at all.

To test these expectations, we rely on a comparative research design, which explores changes in trust in government before (t1) and after (t2) the outbreak of the pandemic, and the moderating role of political and media polarization. We built on a two-wave panel survey data collected in December 2019 and May–June 2020 in 17 European countries (Sweden, Denmark, Norway, Belgium, the Netherlands, Germany, Switzerland, Britain, Spain, Israel, Romania, France, Austria, Italy, Poland, Hungary, and Greece). In each country, approximately 800 respondents participated in both waves of the survey. The data allow for a compelling test, both at the country and the individual level, of changing patterns in political trust in response to the pandemic, controlling for a large number of covariates. The comparative approach furthermore allows us to explore the moderating role of political and media polarization in an unprecedented number of countries.

The analyses show that changes in political polarization before and after the outbreak of the pandemic strongly influence rally effects: where polarization decreases overtime, rally effects increase, while where polarization increases, rally effects tend to disappear. We also find that where the media is less polarized, governments are more able to capitalize on the crisis to increase their popular support, while the reverse is true – i.e., where media is more polarized, governments are less capable to exploit the pandemic to increase their public support.

A Rally-around-the-Flag Effect? Political Trust in Times of COVID-19

The rally-around-the-flag effect suggests that popular support for incumbents increases in times of international crises and external threats to a nation (Mueller, 1970). Accordingly, confronted with abrupt exogenous shocks and threats to a whole country "the public is thought to suspend its usual mode of opinion formation and form ranks behind the president and the flag" (Brody, 1991, p. 46). Follow-up research demonstrates that this rally effect is observable not only for presidential or government approval, but also for incumbent voting shares (Healy & Malhotra, 2009), trust in government (Hetherington & Nelson, 2003), and support for democratic institutions at large (Parker, 1995).

There are several explanations for this effect. They range from elicited patriotic feelings, nationalism, and social cohesion around country representatives to more "rational retrospective evaluations" of needed-to-be-taken policy measures (Bechtel & Hainmueller, 2011; Brody, 1991; Lian & Oneal, 1993). There is also research positing that a tendency for political opponents to set aside political differences and media granting higher visibility and "incumbency bonuses" to government officials favors a rally effect (Baker & Oneal,

2001; Hopmann et al., 2010; see also Chapter 1). Overall, there is hence little doubt that this phenomenon exists.

What is unclear, however, are the criteria that events must fulfill to elicit a rally effect. To date, most studies have focused on events related to the use of military force or military operations (Baker & Oneal, 2001; Lian & Oneal, 1993; Parker, 1995), such as bombings or invasions. However, there is also evidence of increases in government support and trust amidst terrorist attacks (Hetherington & Nelson, 2003), economic downturns, and natural disasters (Bechtel & Hainmueller, 2011; Healy & Malhotra, 2009). In his seminal article, Mueller (1970) presented three criteria that events should fulfill to elicit a rallying effect in the United States. Accordingly, a rally effect is more likely for an event that (1) is international and (2) involves the United States and the President directly, and is (3) specific, dramatic, and sharply focused. Later research has demonstrated that these criteria are applicable not only in the United States but also in Western Europe (Kuijpers, 2019).

Against this backdrop, we argue also that the COVID-19 pandemic outbreak potentially represents a rallying event. The outbreak is an international event, involves entire nations, is quite specific, and has dramatic ramifications. Thus, the pandemic fulfills the criteria of rally events and offers a unique opportunity to test rally effects for non-military topics and even across different nations that are all affected by the pandemic. Arguably, the pandemic is an opportunity for those in power to show strength and determination in fighting the crisis and its consequences. We argue that unlike citizens' support of parties or, more diffusely, the democratic regime, the direct responsibility of incumbents in dealing with the crisis was easily identifiable by the public and made public officials particularly liable to citizens' accountability and also susceptible to be rewarded for fighting the crisis "on the front line".

Indeed, recent research on trust dynamics amidst the COVID-19 pandemic shows average increases in trust in government and satisfaction with democracy after the pandemic outbreak in several countries. Bol et al. (2020) demonstrated that lockdowns increased vote intentions for the incumbent party or Prime Minister, trust in government, and satisfaction with democracy in seven European countries. By contrast, Amat et al. (2020) found greater approval of resorting to exceptional government powers at the expense of democratic freedom and documented increases in citizens' support for autocratic and technocratic governance in Spain. Most relevant for this study, Merkley et al. (2020) used social media data to show increased government support in Canada, while Leininger and Shaub (2020) revealed greater support for the dominant party in Germany in response to the pandemic. Therefore, we start from the basic *Rally-around-the-flag hypothesis (H1):* COVID-19 boosted trust in the national government.

However, the quick spread of the virus and the lack of preparation and readiness to face a health crisis of such magnitude made leaders of advanced democracies vulnerable to public scrutiny and media criticism. In many countries, anchormen or political rivals publicly vituperated incumbents, blaming them for wrong policy approaches and rushed and unjustified political decisions. Heated discussions among politicians with differing ideological leanings on the trade-offs between economic and public health interests also proliferated, if more so in some than in other countries. As the number of cases skyrocketed and the death toll increased dramatically, many felt the urge to raise their voice and denounce the (in)appropriateness of severe lockdowns, mandatory face masks, or business disruptions (or the lack of such measures, in countries such as Sweden). This public outrage resonates with past studies showing incumbent punishments, increased political distrust and so-called "blind retrospection" due to health crises, economic shocks, or even happenings that were clearly beyond governmental control (such as massive shark attacks) (Achen & Bartels, 2003; Amat et al., 2020; Margalit, 2019).

Thus, on the one hand, the COVID-19 crisis offered the opportunity for political leaders to show determination and effective government action, which could boost their image in the media and among the public. On the other hand, incumbents expose themselves to the risk of criticism from oppositional parties, the media, and civil society actors. The crucial question that the present chapter examines is what factors shaped public opinion toward the government during the first phase of the COVID-19 pandemic. We argue that political polarization and media polarization are two important conditions that shape the ebb and flow of a rally-around-the-flag effect in times of crisis. In the following, we further explore the impact of these moderators.

How Political and Media Polarization Can Undermine a Rally-around-the-Flag Effect

One important premise of the rally-around-the-flag effect is that the usual mode of opinion formation is suspended (Brody, 1991). This holds true for the political elite, the media, and the public. Specifically, incumbents are more likely to benefit from mastering a crisis when political opposition parties close ranks behind the incumbent government (Groeling & Baum, 2008). This, in turn, means that elite actors put party loyalties aside. In the absence of elite criticism, the president or an incumbent government is more likely to become a symbol of unity in the eye of the public, which is then unlikely to use partisan heuristics to judge governmental action (Groeling & Baum, 2008). In such a context, the public perceives the political elite as unified behind the government and is more likely to approve of its course of action, resulting in a rallying effect.

If, however, political elites are less unanimous and government action during a crisis is contested, this tenor of the elite debate is likely to affect public opinion since party cues are now at play and can affect people's opinion about the government (Baker & Oneal, 2001; Brody, 1991). Indeed, political polarization may underlie contemporary crisis in trust by lowering trust in government among individuals whose favored party is not in office (Hetherington & Rudolf, 2015; Gidron, Adams, & Horne, 2018). Thus, when there is a partisanship-motivated opposition to the government's course of action, rally effects can be expected to be less likely or less pronounced, since people in favor of oppositional parties are then unlikely to show stronger support of the government.

Relatedly, in situations where people perceive that they are losing control over the world surrounding them (such as in a global pandemic), individuals may resort to others they perceive as thinking and being alike to make sense of it, as the "uncertainty reduction theory" and the "uncertainty-identity theory" posit (Berger and Calabrese, 1975; Hogg & Belavadi, 2017). Hence, in-group dynamics might be exacerbated and political compromise and support for governmental responses to the crisis might in turn be undermined when partisan cues are salient in the debate and people rely on such party heuristic to judge the government (Rahn, 1993). In such situations, supporters of governing parties are more likely to support the incumbent government, while partisans of the opposition are more likely to disapprove of it (Baker & Oneal, 2001; Groeling & Baum, 2008).

We hence posit that in settings where standpoints are extreme and there is little common ground among political elites – namely, where political polarization is high – rally effects will be weaker. Elite polarization increases the salience of partisanship in the public debate in a crisis, and therefore the tendency for people to rely on partisanship for governmental approval. This rationale motivates the *Political polarization hypothesis (H2): the higher the level of political polarization, the lower the rally-around-the-flag effect.*

Similarly, we argue that the media can be a particular important catalyzer of public discontent with governments and their management of the COVID-19 by entrenching people along lines of political difference and inducing hostility toward political adversaries.

Since it is still primarily through the mass media that citizens can learn about governments' policy measures in times of crisis, media reporting is an important condition of rally effects (Baum, 2013; Lian & Oneal, 1993). In order for a rally-around-the-flag effect to be at play, the media need to "play along" and present incumbents as effective leaders in times of crisis (Brody, 1991). Specifically, when media coverage unanimously refrains from attacking the incumbent government during a crisis, the media audience is more likely to approve of the course of governmental action since there is no signal to react otherwise. If, however, media criticism is salient and news coverage of governmental crisis policies becomes more controversial, the audience of such news may be more reluctant to give incumbents the benefit of the doubt. Furthermore, elite criticism in the media is more likely the more polarized the media are. Media polarization can structure media audiences along partisan or ideological lines since partisans of a given political camp are more likely to follow news with the corresponding political slant than news of the oppositional camp (Coe et al., 2008; Stroud, 2011).

In essence, countries where media are more polarized provide better opportunity structures for partisan-selective exposure (Skovsgaard, Shehata, & Strömbäck, 2016). We hence expect that, in more polarized media environments, people will have more opportunities to assess governmental action and handling of the crisis according to partisan lines. In particular, in contexts where the media are more polarized, we expect people will be less willing to rally around incumbent politicians whom they dislike and distrust. This, in turn, may offset rally effects. Based on this, we formulate a *Media polarization hypothesis (H3)*: the higher the level of media polarization, the weaker the rally-around-the-flag effect.

Data and Methods

Data and Measurements

To investigate our hypotheses we relied on data collected from a two-wave panel survey fielded in 17 democracies (Austria, Belgium, Denmark, France, Germany, Greece, Hungary, Israel, Italy, the Netherlands, Norway, Poland, Romania, Spain, Sweden, Switzerland, and the UK). The first wave was conducted in December 2019 (before the outbreak of the COVID-19), and the second wave, in May and June 2020 (after the outbreak of the COVID-19). This was the period in which most countries under study were no longer in lockdown, but still had stringent measures limiting social life and public interaction. In light of the COVID-19 pandemic, we repeated several measures in the second wave to investigate change. The fieldwork was conducted by Dynata and quotas were used for age, gender, and metropolitan region. A total of 28,317 respondents completed the online survey in wave 1, and 14,218, completed the online survey in wave 2. The retention rate ranged from 40% to 61%. The sample in each country is relatively representative of the population at large, although lower-educated and older citizens are slightly underrepresented. As for changes in sample composition between the two waves, the distribution of respondents by education and gender group barely changed, while the sample surveyed in the second wave is slightly older than the initial sample in wave 1 (see Castro et al., 2020 for more information).

Main Dependent and Independent Variables

Change in Government Trust

To investigate rally-around-the-flag effects, we focused on how trust in government changed from w1 to w2. We used the following question: "How much of the time do you think you can trust the government to do what is right?" The response alternatives were: "Just about always" (1), "Most of the time" (2),

"Only some of the time" (3), and "Almost never" (4). Respondents were also allowed to answer "Don't know/Depends". Those selecting this option were excluded from the analyses. Our main dependent variable was computed subtracting trust in wave 2 from trust in wave 1 for each respondent. Before doing this, we inverted the scale, so that 1 stood for "Almost never", and 4, for "Just about always".

$$\text{Change in government trust}_j = \text{Trust in government w2}_i - \text{Trust in government w1}_i$$

Table A1 in the Online Appendix[1], summarizes the main statistics for all the variables in the study, including those measuring trust in government in waves 1 and 2 (Trust Gov. w1, Trust Gov. w2) and our main dependent variable: change in government trust (Gov. Trust change).

Political Polarization

Political polarization is based on an aggregate measure of affective polarization designed for comparative research across multiparty democracies (see Gidron et al., 2019).

To construct political polarization, we used the probability to vote for the eight most important political parties in each country. We asked respondents how probable it would be that they will ever vote for a list of eight political parties in national elections in their country. To answer, they were provided a scale ranging from 0 ("not at all probable") to 10 ("very probable"). The list of parties included the main incumbent and opposition parties in all countries as well as radical right and radical left parties for some countries.

The measure of political polarization was created by computing the absolute distance between the probability of voting for the main incumbent party and the probability of voting for the main opposition party for each respondent.

$$\text{Political polarization}_i = |\text{Prob. voting incubent}_i - \text{Prob. voting opposition}_i|$$

Political polarization at the country level is simply the mean of this difference considering only incumbent and opposition party supporters.[2] As Table A1 shows, the mean of political polarization for wave 1 is 5.89, and for wave 2, 5.85.

---

1 The Online Appendix can be found here: https://www.dropbox.com/s/81v3tgsdatbnbnk/Chapter10_Supplementary_Material.docx?dl=0.
2 To identify incumbent and opposition supporters we used two rules: (1) the incumbent or the opposition party had to be assigned the maximum probability across all parties and (2) this probability had to be > 0.5. Twenty-nine percent of respondents supported the incumbent and 22% of respondents supported the opposition party in w1. This means that more than 50% of the sample supported either the incumbent or the opposition party.

Media Polarization

To construct the measure of media polarization we use online media. Although there are differences across countries, news consumption in many countries increasingly takes place online and the pandemic has been reported to accelerate this trend (Newman et al., 2020). Additionally, the online domain offers the audience maximum choice and the best opportunity structure for selective exposure, and it is where most partisan consumption of media likely takes place (Bennett & Iyengar, 2008; Iyengar & Hahn, 2009; Skovsgaard et al., 2016; but see Fletcher & Nielsen, 2017).

We used a question that asked panelists to report visits to a list of 15 news sites. This list included the most visited news sites in each country according to the Reuters Institute (see Newman et al., 2019). The question was formulated as follows: "Which of these news outlets have you visited or used in the past 30 days, if any?" Following this question, respondents were presented with the list of the news sites, from which they had to select all the outlets they remembered having visited. This list included most of the traditional media platforms, which are among the most visited news sites online.

To compute the measure of media polarization, we first had to assign a slant to each outlet in our lists of 15 outlets per country. To do this, we used the conservative share (see, e.g., Gentzkow & Shapiro, 2010). This measure uses the number of conservative individuals (those located between 6 and 10 on the left-right scale) reporting having visited an outlet (j). It is computed by subtracting from this number the number of liberals (individuals located between 0 and 4 on the same scale) reporting visiting that same outlet j. This number is then divided by the total number of conservatives and liberals reporting having visited outlet j.

$$\text{Conservative share}_j = \left(\text{cons}_j - \text{lib}_j\right) / \left(\text{cons}_j + \text{lib}_j\right)$$

We used the following rule to assign a slant to a given outlet: when the conservative share of an outlet was more than 55%, that outlet was classified as "conservative"; when the conservative share of a given outlet was less than 45%, that outlet was classified as "liberal". Note that this is an audience-based measure of slant, not a content-based measure, which is more commonly used in media studies.

Finally, we used net partisan skew (NPS) to compute online media polarization. This measure subtracts from the number of reported visits to conservative outlets the number of reported visits to liberal media for each individual i (An et al., 2013; Cardenal et al., 2019). High negative values in this index indicate a liberal skew in media consumption while high positive values indicate a conservative skew in media consumption. Media polarization at the country level was calculated subtracting the mean of net partisan skew for self-defined liberals from the mean of net partisan skew for self-defined conservatives in country j.

$$\text{Online media polarization}_j = \text{mean(NPS)}_{\text{cons}\,j} - \text{mean(NPS)}_{\text{lib}\,j}$$

As shown in Table A1, the mean of media polarization for wave 1 is 1.26 (SD = 1.15, min = 0.03, max = 4.25); for wave 2, this mean is 1.21 (SD = 1.16), and the minimum and maximum values are 0.125 and 4.16, respectively. Table A4 in the Online Appendix shows the values of political and media polarization break down by country.

Controls

As controls we included first a set of key political behavior variables – the probability of voting for the incumbent, for the opposition and for extreme right and extreme left parties. The probability of voting for the incumbent and the opposition as well as of voting for extreme parties (right and left) is expected to influence both rally effects and political polarization. These, as most of the controls we include in our models, are measured in wave 1, before the outbreak of the pandemic.

As a second set of controls we included media-related variables. We used frequency of use of several media, all measured in wave 1. Use of public broadcasting service is expected to increase trust in government and it might also be negatively related to partisan consumption of media online. The same can be said about broadsheet use. Trust in media might be positively related to trust in government and negatively related to use of partisan media online (for an overview of research on media trust, see Strömbäck et al., 2020).

Third, we used COVID-19-related variables which might be related to trust in government and polarization. In particular, we used two questions, asking respondents to state how worried they were about being infected and whether they knew someone who had been infected with COVID-19. Exposure and anxiety toward the COVID-19, we believe, might affect both trust in government and polarization.

Finally, we included left-right self-placement, which is expected to be related to trust in government and polarization. Extreme right positions have been shown to reduce trust in government and are related to polarization. We also included the following basic socio-demographics: age, gender, and education, all of them important predictors of political attitudes and behavior.

Analytical Strategy

For the analysis, we used multilevel mixed-effects linear regressions with varying intercepts for the 17 countries on almost all models. The main models (in Table A2 in the Online Appendix) use change in trust in government between wave 1 and wave 2 as dependent variable. To make effects comparable, all input variables in these models (except for dichotomous variables) were centered and re-scaled. For each variable, this transformation is the result of subtracting the mean and dividing the result by two standard deviations (for details on the advantages of this transformation, see Gelman & Hill, 2007). Hence, for all input variables except for dichotomous ones, which were not transformed, coefficients have to be interpreted as the effect on y of moving in x from one standard deviation below the mean to one standard deviation above the mean. Using this transformation, interaction effects do not change but the terms' coefficients do: these coefficients now have to be interpreted as the effect of that term when the other variable is set to its mean.

Results[3]

Turning to the results, we will begin by an overview of levels of trust in government across countries. In line with recent studies and an extensive number of surveys, the results show that trust levels in general are low. Before the outbreak of the COVID-19, the mean was somewhat less than 2 on the 4-point scale (i.e., it ranged from "almost never" (1) to "only some of the time" (2), without reaching 2 on the scale). Low levels of political trust are even more apparent if we compute the percentage of those who say that they almost never trust the government. Figure 10.1 plots these percentages for wave 1. As we can see, those who almost never trust the government are well above 40% in France, Spain, Greece, Hungary, and Poland.

Turning to changes across time, the results show that trust in government increased from an average of 1.9 in wave 1 to an average of 2.1 in wave 2, which is an average increase of 0.13. Although modest, this increase is statistically

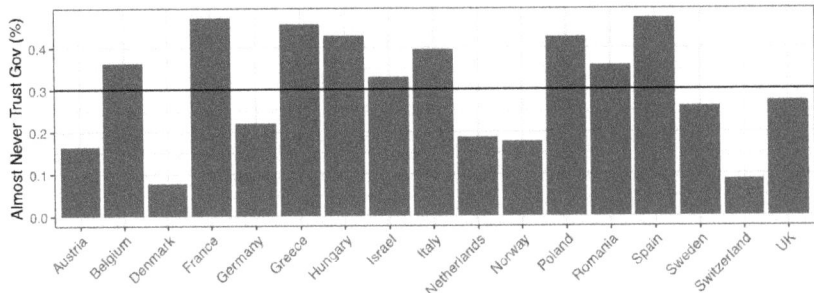

FIGURE 10.1 Percentage reporting that they (almost) never trust the government (w1) by country.

---

3 All the models upon which the results reported here have been estimated can be found here: https://www.dropbox.com/s/81v3tgsdatbnbnk/Chapter10_Supplementary_Material.docx?dl=0.

significant ($t = 20.829$, $p < 0.000$), so our data are in line with an overall rally-around-the-flag hypothesis.

However, this mild rally-around-the-flag effect at the aggregate level masks variation across countries. Figure 10.2 reflects some of this variation showing trust change by country. As can be seen, in almost all countries except Israel and Poland, change in trust was positive. Yet, in France and Romania, positive changes were not statistically significant. The most extreme differences can be found between the Netherlands and Israel. Taking the mean as the reference, trust in government changed to a positive 0.12 in the Netherlands, while it changed to a negative −0.19 in Israel.

Turning to the individual predictors of trust change, Figure 10.3 shows the estimates of these individual predictors. Predictors are ordered, so that at the top we find the predictors with the strongest positive effects, and, at the bottom, those with the strongest negative effects. We should also mention that since all predictors have been centered and re-scaled, the coefficients and size of the effects are comparable. Finally, estimates should be interpreted as the effect on government trust change (y) of moving in x from one standard deviation below the mean to one standard deviation above the mean.

The results show that worry of being infected has the strongest effect on positive changes in trust, followed by the probability of voting to the radical

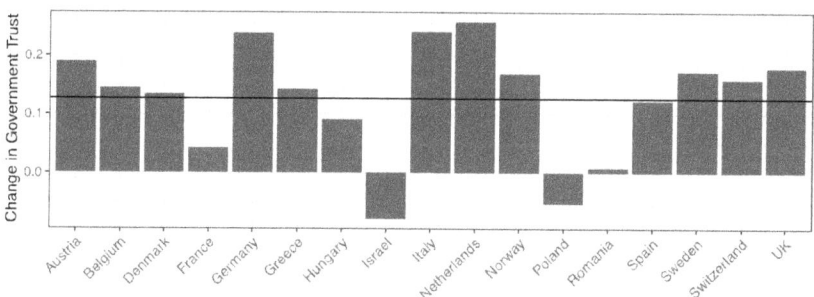

FIGURE 10.2 Trust change by country (mean in black line).

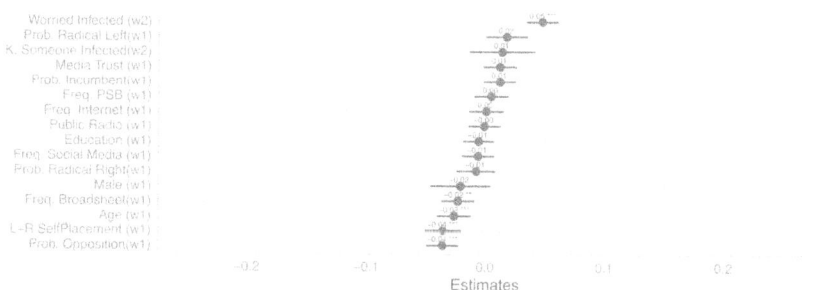

FIGURE 10.3 Individual predictors of positive changes in trust.

left. In contrast, greater probability of voting for the opposition in wave 1 has the strongest negative effect on trust change, followed by being conservative, and aged. Of note here is the null effect of frequency of media use on trust change, or even the negative effect found for broadsheet readership. Trust in the media neither has an effect on trust change. However, when we consider change, all the media variables have a positive effect on rally effects. In other words, increasing exposure to public service broadcasting and broadsheets between w1 and w2 enhances trust in government. The same happens with media trust. Positive changes in media trust from w1 to w2 produces increase in government trust.

To test H2 and H3, we ran several models with trust change as the dependent variable and political and media polarization as contextual predictors as well as some interactions.

We start by reporting the results concerning H3. As hypothesized, media polarization measured before the outbreak of the pandemic has a direct negative effect on trust change. Panel A of Figure 10.4 plots this effect, which is estimated from Model 2 in Table A2. As this Figure shows, when holding all variables at their means, moving one standard deviation below and above the mean of media polarization (from 0.11 to 2.41) decreases change in government trust from 0.17 to 0.05. At high levels of media polarization (i.e., two standard deviations above the mean), predicted levels of trust change are 0.

In contrast, political polarization measured before the outbreak of the pandemic has no effect on changes in government trust (see Panel B in Figure 10.4). In other words, our data do not support H2. However, this result shifts when we consider changes in polarization between t1 and t2. We estimated that a one standard deviation in polarization change reduced average change in government trust by 0.13 (see Table A3 in the Online Appendix). To put it more graphically, moving from a country (UK) with a sharp decrease in polarization (−0.64) to a country (Spain) with a sharp increase (0.49) between w1 and w2, changes in government trust went from 0.19 to 0.05 (see Figure A1 in the Online Appendix).

Moreover, political polarization strongly moderates the relationship between supporting the opposition at time t1 and change in government trust.

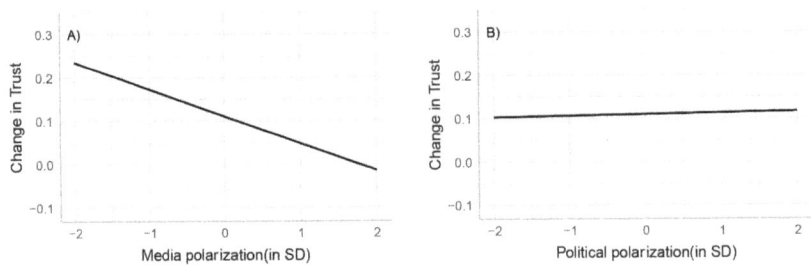

FIGURE 10.4 Effects of media and political polarization in change in trust.

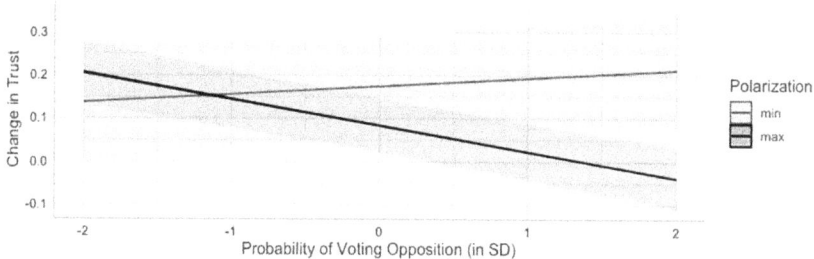

FIGURE 10.5 Interaction effects of political polarization and probability of voting the opposition on trust changes.

Figure 10.5 plots these interaction effects. As this figure shows, in countries where political polarization achieves maximum levels (e.g., Israel, Poland, Spain), supporting the opposition at time t1 strongly reduces positive changes in trust. In particular, in highly polarized countries, a move in the probability to vote the opposition from 1 to 8 (one standard deviation below and above the mean) reduces trust change from 0.14 to 0.02. In contrast, in countries where polarization is at minimum levels (e.g., the Netherlands, Switzerland, Norway), supporting the opposition before the crisis can even slightly increase trust in government overtime. In particular, in low polarized countries, a move in the probability to vote the opposition from 1 to 8 increases trust change from 0.16 to 0.18.

Discussion

In this chapter we have provided evidence that, in times of crisis, citizens tend to unite behind their political leaders and to increase their trust in government. Relying on an original comparative panel survey dataset, we show that the COVID-19 activated rally-around-the-flag effects across most European countries (H1). However, we should also note that this effect was modest and subject to country variation. According to our data, trust in government increased an average of 0.13 before and after the outbreak of COVID-19. Or, put differently, an average of 11% of respondents increased their trust in government before and after the crisis. In addition, in some countries trust increased substantially above the mean (e.g., the Netherlands, Austria, Switzerland), while in others, it decreased substantially below the mean (e.g., France, Poland, Romania, Israel).

More interestingly, we examined the moderating role of political and media polarization. We hypothesized that greater political polarization would depress rally-around-the-flag effects by bringing in partisan motivations to assess the government's management of the crisis and by activating criticism from the opposition (H2). Similarly, we expected that media polarization would reduce rally-around-the-flag effects by emphasizing negative aspects of government action and by increasing the likelihood of partisan selective exposure to media information (H3).

We found that levels of political polarization before the outbreak of the crisis did not affect changes in trust. However, changes in political polarization between t1 and t2 proved to have a significant effect on rally effects. In other words, what seemed to matter for rally effects during the COVID-19 crisis was not initial levels of polarization but changes in polarization, which we presume largely depended on the strategy of the opposition parties. Where opposition parties decided to cooperate with the government, polarization very likely decreased, enhancing potential rally effects. In contrast, where they chose to attack the government for its way of handling the pandemic, polarization probably increased, eroding potential rally effects.

This logic is well illustrated by Spain and the UK, two countries with very similar initial levels of polarization which followed a very different path after the outbreak of the pandemic. In Spain, the opposition party attacked the government for its handling of the crisis, whereas in the UK the opposition party (initially) sided silently with the government while it handled the crisis. As a result, between t1 and t2, trust in government in the UK increased well above the mean ($0.18 > 0.13$) while in Spain it grew below the mean ($0.12 < 0.13$).

This result is consistent with the logic of our argument, which highlights the strategies of the opposition as the mechanism bridging polarization and rally effects. It is also consistent with the finding that polarization moderates change in trust in government through the probability of voting for the opposition. The positive interaction between polarization and support for the opposition suggests that opposition voters are particularly sensitive to the strategies of their party. When polarization is high, opposition voters tend to be less trustful of the government during national emergencies; when it is low, they are more likely to trust the government during critical times.

Concerning the role of media, we found that polarization depressed rally-around-the-flag effects. In countries where media consumption was more polarized before the crisis, there was less change in trust in government as a result of the pandemic. In contrast, where media consumption was less polarized, governments were more much more successful in capitalizing on the crisis to widen their public support.

Overall, our results suggest a different logic for the effect of media and political polarization on rally-around-the-flag effects. Media polarization would affect rally effects depending on initial levels, implying that once audiences cluster around media on partisan lines the effects of polarization set off. This suggests a less contingent and more persistent impact of media polarization on rally effects. In contrast, the role of political polarization on rally effects seems more contingent on the strategy decided by the opposition in response to the crisis.

Future studies should explore more deeply the logic and consequences of polarization on changes in trust in government during times of crisis.

As democratic societies grow more divided, understanding the impact of polarization on government capacity becomes of the utmost importance. Polarization not only complicates the day-to-day running of our democracies but could arguably compromise the success of democratically elected governments managing future crises, especially if – as in this crisis – this depends on the cooperative behavior of citizens.

Although this study makes some important contributions, it also has some limitations. First, our research design does not allow us to claim causality. Even if we relied on panel data and used wave 1 as the baseline to explain change, we cannot rule out selection effects. For example, we cannot rule out that baseline trust levels influence both polarization and rally effects. It might well be that both political and media polarization are more prevalent in countries with low levels of trust in government. Second, our main findings are based on context-level variables, and thus on a small-N design $(N = 17)$. This means that single countries have a lot of influence on these results, and that excluding one or two might substantially change the results. Third, our aggregate measures of political and media polarization are not exogenous, but were generated from the survey data. This might limit the comparability and reproducibility of our findings across these same contexts.

Despite these limitations, our study makes a significant contribution to the-rally-around-the-flag effect literature by testing this effect cross-nationally in an unprecedented health crisis and offering evidence of the potential consequences of polarization for rally effects and political trust. Finally, the measures used can be seen as a contribution to the extant body of research on political and media polarization and the rally-around-the-flag effect.

References

Achen, C. H., & Bartels, L. M. (2003, April). Party systems, credible opposition, and democratic stability: 1992 and 1932. In *Annual Meeting of the Midwest Political Science Association, Chicago, IL*, pp. 3–6.

Amat, F., Arenas, A., Falcó-Gimeno, A., & Muñoz, J. (2020). Pandemics meet democracy. Experimental evidence from the COVID-19 crisis in Spain. *SocArXiv*. doi:10.31235/osf.io/dkusw

An, J., Quercia, D., & Crowcroft, J. (2013). Fragmented social media: A look into selective exposure to political news. In *Proceedings of the 22nd International Conference on World Wide Web*, pp. 51–52.

Baum, M. A. (2013). The Iraq coalition of the willing and (politically) able: Party systems, the press, and public influence on foreign policy. *American Journal of Political Science, 57*(2), 442–458.

Baker, W. D., & Oneal, J. R. (2001). Patriotism or opinion leadership? The nature and origins of the "rally'round the flag" effect. *Journal of Conflict Resolution, 45*(5), 661–687.

Bechtel, M. M., & Hainmueller, J. (2011). How lasting is voter gratitude? An analysis of the short-and long-term electoral returns to beneficial policy. *American Journal of Political Science, 55*(4), 852–868.

Bennett, W. L., & Iyengar, S. (2008). A new era of minimal effects? The changing foundations of political communication. *Journal of Communication, 58*(4), 707–731.

Berger, C. R., & Calabrese, R. J. (1975). Some explorations in initial interaction and beyond: Toward a developmental theory of interpersonal communication. *Human Communication Research, 1*(2), 99–112.

Bol, D., Giani, M., Blais, A., & Loewen, P. J. (2020). The effect of COVID-19 lockdowns on political support: Some good news for democracy? *European Journal of Political Research, 60*(2), 497–505.

Brody, R. M. (1991). *Assessing the president. The media, elite opinion, and public support.* Stanford, CA: Stanford University Press.

Cardenal, A. S., Aguilar-Paredes, C., Cristancho, C., & Majó-Vázquez, S. (2019). Echo-chambers in online news consumption: Evidence from survey and navigation data in Spain. *European Journal of Communication, 34*(4): 360–376.

Castro, L., Strömbäck, J., Esser, F., Van Aelst, P., de Vreese, C., Aalberg, T., ... & Theocharis, Y. (2021). Navigating high-choice European political information environments: A comparative analysis of news user profiles and political knowledge. *The International Journal of Press/Politics*. doi: 10.1177/19401612211012572

Coe, K., Tewksbury, D., Bond, B. J., Drogos, K. L., Porter, R. W., Yahn, A., & Zhang, Y. (2008). Hostile news: Partisan use and perceptions of cable news programming. *Journal of communication, 58*(2), 201–219.

Fletcher, R., & Nielsen, R. K. (2017). Are news audiences increasingly fragmented? A cross-national comparative analysis of cross-platform news audience fragmentation and duplication. *Journal of Communication, 67*(4), 476–498.

Gelman, A., & Hill, J. (2007). *Data analysis using regression and multilevel hierarchical models* (Vol. 1). New York: Cambridge University Press.

Gentzkow, M., & Shapiro, J. M. (2010). *Ideological segregation online and offline.* National Bureau of Economic Research. http://www.nber.org/papers/w15916

Gidron, N., Adams, J., & Horne, W. (2018). How ideology, economics and institutions shape affective polarization in democratic polities. In *Annual Conference of the American Political Science Association, Washington, DC.*

Gidron, N., Adams, J., & Horne, W. (2019). Toward a comparative research agenda on affective polarization in mass publics. *APSA Comparative Politics Newsletter, 29*, 30–36.

Groeling, T., & Baum, M. A. (2008). Crossing the water's edge: Elite rhetoric, media coverage, and the rally-round-the-flag phenomenon. *The Journal of Politics, 70*(4), 1065–1085.

Healy, A., & Malhotra, N. (2009). Myopic voters and natural disaster policy. *American Political Science Review*, 387–406.

Hetherington, M. J., & Nelson, M. (2003). Anatomy of a rally effect: George W. Bush and the war on terrorism. *PS: Political Science and Politics, 36*(1), 37–42.

Hetherington, M. J., & Rudolph, T. J. (2015). *Why Washington won't work: Polarization, political trust, and the governing crisis.* Chicago, IL: University of Chicago Press.

Hogg, M. A., & Belavadi, S. (2017). Uncertainty management theories. In Nussbaum, J. F. (Ed.) *Oxford research encyclopedia of communication.* Oxford: Oxford University Press.

Hopmann, D. N., Vliegenthart, R., De Vreese, C., & Albæk, E. (2010). Effects of election news coverage: How visibility and tone influence party choice. *Political Communication, 27*(4), 389–405.

Iyengar, S., & Hahn, K. S. (2009). Red media, blue media: Evidence of ideological selectivity in media use. *Journal of Communication, 59*(1), 19–39.

Kuijpers, D. (2019). Rally around All the Flags: The Effect of Military Casualties on Incumbent Popularity in Ten Countries 1990–2014. *Foreign Policy Analysis, 15*(3), 392–412.

Leininger, A., & Schaub, M. (2020). Voting at the dawn of a global pandemic. *SocArXiv.* doi: 10.31235/osf.io/a32r7

Lian, B., & Oneal, J. R. (1993). Presidents, the use of military force, and public opinion. *Journal of Conflict Resolution, 37*(2), 277–300.

Margalit, Y. (2019). Political responses to economic shocks. *Annual Review of Political Science. 22,* 277–295.

Merkley, E., Bridgman, A., Loewen, P. J., Owen, T., Ruths, D., & Zhilin, O. (2020). A rare moment of cross-partisan consensus: Elite and public response to the COVID-19 Pandemic in Canada. *Canadian Journal of Political Science/Revue canadienne de science politique, 53*(2), 311–318.

Parker, A. N. (1995). *Decentralization: The way forward for rural development?* Policy research working paper no. 1475, Agriculture and Natural Resources Department, World Bank, Washington, DC.

Mueller, J. E. (1970). Presidential popularity from Truman to Johnson. *American Political Science Review, 64*(1), 18–34. doi:10.2307/1955610

Newman N., Fletcher R., Kalogeropoulos A., & Nielsen, R.N. (2019). Reuters institute digital news report 2019. *Report of the Reuters Institute for the Study of Journalism.*

Newman N., Fletcher R., Shultz A., Andi, S., & Nielsen, R.N. (2020). Reuters institute digital news report 2020. *Report of the Reuters Institute for the Study of Journalism.*

Rahn, W. M. (1993). The role of partisan stereotypes in information processing about political candidates. *American Journal of Political Science, 37*(2) 472–496.

Skovsgaard, M., Shehata, A., & Strömbäck, J. (2016). Opportunity structures for selective exposure: Investigating selective exposure and learning in Swedish election campaigns using panel survey data. *The International Journal of Press/Politics, 21*(4), 527–546.

Strömbäck, J., Tsfati, Y., Boomgaarden, H., Damstra, A., Lindgren, E., Vliegenthart, R., & Lindholm, T. (2020). News media trust and its impact on media use: toward a framework for future research. *Annals of the International Communication Association, 44*(2), 139–156.

Stroud, N. J. (2011). *Niche news: The politics of news choice.* Oxford: Oxford University Press on Demand.

11
THE ROLE OF POLITICAL POLARIZATION ON AMERICAN AND AUSTRALIAN TRUST AND MEDIA USE DURING THE COVID-19 PANDEMIC

Andrea Carson, Shaun Ratcliff and Leah Ruppanner

Introduction

The COVID-19 pandemic has tested the relationship between politics and media in a time of low trust in democratic institutions. Prior to the global health crisis, in many countries, public trust in news media was lower than trust in other democratic institutions (van Dalen, 2020). This is troubling, as democratic media theorists posit that news media play a central role in providing citizens with reliable information in the public sphere in order to make informed choices, a precondition of a well-functioning democracy (McNair, 2017).

While research finds media trust is conditional upon news audiences' political ideologies, demographic features and news choices (Tsfati & Ariely, 2014; Fletcher & Park, 2017), there is less evidence about how much media trust matters for citizens' uses of different media types and under what conditions (Strömbäck et al., 2020). Put simply, what are citizens' news choices and levels of media trust under conditions of a crisis, and do they matter?

The pandemic offers the opportunity to look at a critical juncture in the public's use and trust in media, during a time when news engagement is at a peak. Studies of media use during past crises such as the 2003 SARS pandemic, 9/11 terrorist attacks and the global financial crisis find greater public engagement with news, with television and newspapers being the most relied upon sources (Brug et al., 2004; Carey 2002; Knowles & Schifferes, 2020, p. 64). Other crisis communication studies suggest that mainstream media play a lead role in promoting health knowledge during a health crisis (van Velsen et al., 2012); while social media fulfils a secondary, complementary role for people to share information about the situation with friends and family (van Velsen et al., 2012; Carey 2002; Westlund & Ghersetti, 2015). Westlund and Ghersetti find that

DOI: 10.4324/9781003170051-14

people generally rely on habitual media during a crisis, but may add in sources of breaking news (2015, p. 147).The effects of a crisis on media trust are less understood. Notable exceptions include Knowles and Schifferes' finding that the global financial crisis worsened low levels of trust in the news media (2020, p. 66). In contrast, in April 2020, in the early stages of the COVID-19 pandemic, the Reuters Institute for the Study of Journalism Digital News Report 2020 found trust in news organizations' coverage of COVID-19 was relatively high (59%) in the six countries surveyed, including the USA but not Australia (Newman et al., 2020, p. 12). Yet, just prior to the pandemic in January 2020, only 38% of respondents in the six countries said they had trust in news most of the time (Newman et al., 2020, p. 14). The two surveys show a significant upswing for trust in established media during the crisis, more than double trust in COVID-19 information on social media (Newman et al., 2020, p. 12).

The aim of this chapter is to understand how audiences in two comparable liberal democracies, the USA and Australia, use and trust news related to the COVID-19 global health crisis. In doing so, we examine the role of political partisanship in the use and trust of different types of news sources (journalists, friends and family on social media) as well as trust in medical experts. We also measure citizens' concerns about the health risks posed by coronavirus, and their levels of support for government interventions to stem its spread.

This chapter proceeds as follows. We outline key literature on media trust, theories on media use and political polarization, and provide background information on the unfolding of the pandemic in the two studied nations. We briefly outline our method and then detail our findings about citizens' trust in media during the pandemic and support for government measures to tackle it. Finally, we discuss findings in relation to the state of the public sphere in both countries, and implications for managing the public health crisis.

Media Trust and Political Partisanship

Pre-Pandemic

While studies vary in their operationalization of media trust (Strömbäck et al. 2020), Australia and the USA consistently rank poorly on public trust in the media as a democratic institution (Edelman, 2019; Newman et al., 2019). In the USA, trust in media fell to a historic low of 32% in 2016 (Swift 2016). Similarly, public trust in Australian media is typically under 50% (Fisher, 2019).

Scholars have attributed falling levels of media trust in democracies to a range of factors including structural change resulting in mass media job losses (Fletcher & Park, 2017), political polarization (Hetherington & Rudolph, 2015), and the rise in misinformation and disinformation. More pointedly, scholars argue critics of the press – notably US President Donald Trump and some conservative Australian politicians – erode media trust by labelling journalists and their outlets as 'fake news' (Van Duyn & Collier, 2019; Farhall et al., 2019). Further, many citizens get their news online in an environment in which credible news exists alongside falsehoods, causing concern that consumers have difficulty discerning fact from fiction (Barthel et al., 2016, Fisher et al., 2019).

However, Edelman (2019) and others have shown that the largest media trust gap in the USA is partisan. Democrats are likely to be twice as trusting of mainstream media than Republicans (69% vs 33% respectively). Mourão and colleagues (2018, p. 1953) show that one of the strongest predictors of media trust was a citizen's perceptions of US President Donald Trump. They argued that citizens do 'pick sides' when these two institutions (the media and the presidency) clash, with Trump supporters trusting the press significantly less than other voters (Mourão et al., 2018, p. 1953). This is consistent with Zaller's (1992) 'political elite cue' theory that posits citizens use party identification as a heuristic to form political attitudes, and that partisans media trust levels will reflect the viewpoint of the political elite from which citizens take cues. While research in Australia on media polarization is limited, Jackman and Ratcliff (2018) show partisan differences in trust are generally smaller in Australia compared to the USA.

Media Use and Political Selective Exposure Theory

The twenty-first century has engendered high-choice media environments (Van Aelst et al., 2017). According to some theorists, diverse media choices can serve to increase public news exposure and deepen understanding of civic affairs thereby creating 'a virtuous circle' for public engagement and democratic participation (Norris, 2000, p. 317). This theory is predicated on the idea that media choice and diversity allow for a pluralism of views in the public sphere and greater public engagement with the contest of ideas. It provides one perspective for considering the consequences of media attention, political partisanship and policy responsiveness during the COVID-19 pandemic.

A contrasting view is that of proponents of the political selective exposure (PSE) theory. PSE is when a sizable proportion of citizens select news and information congruent with their existing political preferences. This selectiveness is thought to lead to an increase in political and media polarization in the USA in the digital age. In their seminal study, Iyengar and Hahn (2009) conclude that high-choice news environments would result in further polarization of news audiences, effectively creating media echo-chambers.

This chapter examines the role of political partisanship in media use and trust in two similar liberal democracies during the pandemic. However, it should be noted that an important difference between the Australian and US news ecosystems is the long-standing influence of the Australian Broadcasting Corporation, a national public broadcaster. Bos and colleagues find that public broadcasting can have a mitigating effect against polarization by offering a unifying, and nation-binding role in otherwise fragmented media environments (2016, p. 10). This makes the comparison of Australia to the USA during the pandemic particularly meaningful.

Background: US and Australian Political Communications about COVID-19

During the Pandemic

In May 2020, during the first wave of the COVID-19 pandemic, Australia had no major political figures downplaying the threat of coronavirus or contradicting medical advice about its treatment. Australian political elites provided citizens with mostly unified cues about the threat posed by and response required to limit disease spread. For example, Prime Minister Scott Morrison (from the centre-right Liberal-National Coalition) established a unique National Cabinet consisting of the state Premiers and territory First Ministers (irrespective of political party) to jointly respond to the pandemic, which principally relied on advice from federal and state chief medical officers (Duckett, 2020). Mainstream media generally reported the Cabinet's decisions and expert medical advice with little contestation. Of course, there was some heterogeneity in coverage. Some broadcasters on the News Corporation-owned TV station Sky News Australia downplayed the threat. Like some hosts on its US sister station, Fox News, Sky broadcaster Alan Jones adopted a polemic approach to coronavirus, telling viewers: 'I've sought to dismantle coronavirus hysteria by sticking to the facts' (Sky News, 2020). However, unlike its US equivalent, Sky has a niche audience share compared to Australia's free-to-air networks and its public broadcaster, the ABC. Also, unlike the USA, public rallies against lockdown measures were attended by small crowds of a few hundred Australians who typically bore signs condemning 5G technologies and vaccinations, reflecting broad themes from misinformation sites on social media. Thus, the level of push-back on measures to manage the virus existed in Australia but had little elite or public support.

In contrast, the political messaging about COVID-19 and subsequent government responses in the USA were heavily contested. President Trump regularly contradicted medical advice and National Institute of Allergy and Infectious Diseases (NIAID) director Anthony Fauci. He downplayed the need for harm minimization measures such as mask wearing and described social distancing and lockdown measures on social media as 'too tough'. At one point, he spread misinformation when he suggested that injecting the body with disinfectant might be a treatment for COVID-19, despite medical evidence it could result in serious harm (BBC, 2020). Even when diagnosed with COVID-19 himself in October 2020, he refused to adequately quarantine and mocked the lethalness of the disease that had killed more than 210,000 Americans at that time

(Miller et al., 2020). Trump's responses to coronavirus were highly political. At the beginning of the crisis in South Carolina, he denounced the Democrats, describing coronavirus as their 'new hoax' (Baker & Karni, 2020).

In the next section, we compare news use and public attitudes to different sources of COVID-19 information – from professional journalists, medical experts, and friends and family on social media – to examine if news trust varies by political ideology. From the literature and background outlined above, we expect that US and Australian publics will diverge on issues of trust and satisfaction with government measures to contain COVID-19. We expect polarization is likely amplified in the USA by the lack of bipartisan agreement between its state and federal governments on managing the pandemic.

Data and Methods

To test the relationships between citizens' trust in professional journalists (and others) alongside people's media use and public attitudes to government measures to limit COVID-19 infections, we ran surveys of more than 1,000 respondents in both the USA and Australia over two waves, using the YouGov online representative panels.[1] The first wave (2–3 May 2020) involved 1,050 Americans and 1,005 Australians. The second wave (31 August to 9 September 2020) involved contacting 1,060 American and 1,375 Australian respondents, including 677 Australian and 733 American recontacts. The first wave was fielded during a heightened period of social distancing and restrictions in movements and gatherings in both countries. During the second wave much of the USA was subject to growing numbers of confirmed cases and varying degrees of restrictions while, in Australia, only the state of Victoria was experiencing community transmission of the virus and enforced social distancing measures during this period.

These surveys contained identical questions, with variations in wording used where necessary to account for national differences (e.g. different options on political identification, media choice). It included questions on vote intention and demographic items. Media choice questions were used to measure the left or right political slant of respondents' daily news diets (described below). The survey recorded citizens' levels of trust in COVID-19 information from professional journalists, medical experts, and friends and family on social media. On a 5-point Likert scale, citizens recorded their attitudes to government measures to limit disease spread, such as whether restrictions on movement had gone 'too far' or 'not far enough'.

---

1 Australian data were weighted by age, gender and region; US data by age, race, gender and education.

Weighted Media Ideology Score

We asked participants to rank order their top five most important media outlets for daily news in each country.[2] The ideological leaning [liberal (left-leaning), neither, conservative (right-leaning)] of media outlets was coded using third-party assessments,[3] with this score determining ideology k of the media outlet. A left/liberal outlet was coded −1, a conservative outlet +1 and an outlet that was balanced or had a mixed ideology was coded 0. Using these codes, each respondent was given a score based on the weighted sum of the five media outlets they rated as their most important sources of news and information, using the formula:

$$\sum_{i=1}^{n} x_i \star w_i$$

with each outlet x scored according to its ideology k, and weighted by the rank w given to it by respondent i. A left/liberal newspaper that was listed first by a respondent contributes to the ideology of a respondent with -1 ★ 1, while a conservative newspaper as their third most important outlet is +1 ★ 0.33.

This enabled us to aggregate the rankings to visualize the relationship between media consumption and partisanship with higher scores indicating more conservative media consumption (see Figure 11.1).

This differs from some other measures of media use which tend to ask respondents to recall all the news media that they have consumed over a period. While these approaches have value, they may exaggerate the level of shared media consumption across political divides by not weighting the results according to heavy or casual use. We wished to focus on outlets that respondents considered were their most important news sources and therefore likely to be the most influential on their perception of the world and current events.

Results

Australian and US News Selectivity

When the political leanings of respondents' top five media outlets were aggregated and weighted according to the formula above, we find the median daily news diet tilted slightly left in both countries. The median score of US respondents

---

2 The question asked in both countries: 'Which of the following are your five most important sources of news and information?' Respondents were required to select five outlets from the lists provided (19 in Australia, including state-level variants of daily tabloid papers, 16 in the USA).
3 Third-party assessment tool used for the USA was www.AllSides.com; for Australia, https://mediabiasfactcheck.com/ was referenced.

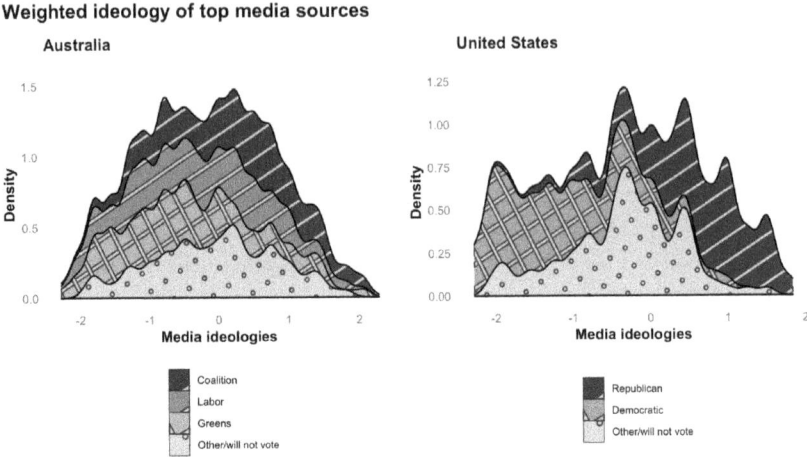

FIGURE 11.1 Distribution of political partisans' media choices in Australia and the USA.

was −0.58, where zero is a diet of mixed or centrist media. In Australia – largely due to the high concentration of media ownership and vast audience reach of Murdoch-owned News Corp newspapers – total news consumption was slightly more centrist, with a median of −0.05 (shown in Figure 11.1).

However, daily media choices are more homogenous among individual partisans in the USA than Australia. This is visualized in Figure 11.1 where US partisans are shown to be less likely to overlap in their news choices with voters from the other side of politics to their own. For example, more than half of Trump supporters (56%) relied on conservative media or mostly conservative news sources.[4] Similarly, almost 65% of Democrat supporters relied almost entirely on liberal media outlets. Just 4% of Democrats consumed mostly or entirely conservative news. This is consistent with earlier studies that find evidence of PSE in the USA, whereby individuals select media outlets that provide information sympathetic to their existing beliefs (Iyengar & Hahn, 2009, p. 35).

In Australia, we find a greater proportion of media consumers had a mixed news diet, selecting media outlets with both left and right political leanings in their daily habit. A partisanship pattern is evident but it is much weaker than the pattern in the USA. Less than half of centre-right Liberal National party

---

4 Here, we have divided respondents into five categories based on the ideologies of the give outlets they reported replying on the most. Those whose weighted media ideology scores below (above) −1 (+1) were coded as relying almost exclusively on liberal (conservative) media. Those with scores between −1 and −0.5 (+0.5 and +1) were coded as relying primarily but not entirely on liberal (conservative) outlets. Those with scores between −0.5 and 0.5 were coded as using mostly moderate, or a relatively even balance between conservative and liberal media.

(henceforth the Coalition) voters (42%) relied entirely or mostly on conservative media. Equally a minority (42%) of centre-left Australian Labor Party (ALP) voters relied entirely or mostly on left-leaning media. To understand the reverse of this pattern, 20% of Labor supporters mostly relied upon conservative media for news, while nearly 27% of Coalition voters consumed mostly left-leaning media. This broader news selection with overlap in top five news choices by supporters of the two major parties may be a product of a lower choice media environment in Australia. Or, as scholars have argued, the presence of popular public-owned news services (Australia's Australian Broadcasting Corporation and Special Broadcasting Service) may mitigate against media polarization (Bos et al., 2016, p. 10). The ABC has national coverage and a statutory duty to ensure factual accuracy 'according to the recognized standards of objective journalism' (ABC, 2013, p. 4).

Frequency of News Use and Media Type

Consistent with past studies that find news use increases during a crisis (Carey, 2002; Knowles & Schifferes, 2020), we find news consumption was up in both countries during the pandemic. Fifty-four per cent of Australians reported that their news consumption during the pandemic had increased (a little or a lot) compared to 36% of Americans who said the same. We also find Americans and Australians rely on a mix of traditional (newspapers, television and radio) and new digital media sources (e.g. Facebook) for pandemic news. Consistent with past studies, both nation's citizens prioritize television and newspapers, but Facebook also features in people's top five list (Brug et al., 2004; Carey, 2002; Knowles & Schifferes, 2020). In other words, and as earlier studies have found, social media do not replace, but complement legacy media use during this crisis period (van Velsen et al., 2012; Carey, 2002; Westlund & Ghersetti, 2015, p. 134).

The overall top five most relied upon news sources in the USA (in rank order) were (1) Fox News, (2) network television, (3) daily newspapers, (4) CNN and (5) Facebook. In Australia, the top five were (1) free-to-air commercial television, (2) ABC TV, (3) NewsCorp's free online website news.com.au, (4) Facebook and (5) NewsCorp's state-based daily tabloids. The next section reveals significant partisan differences in these news selections in the USA compared to Australia, and that trust in professional journalists is contingent on partisanship and news choices.

Trust in Journalists and Other Sources during the Pandemic

In both countries, the first survey in May shows greater overall trust in medical experts as a source of news and information about COVID-19 than other sources, including professional journalists or friends and family on social media

Trust in different sources of news and information

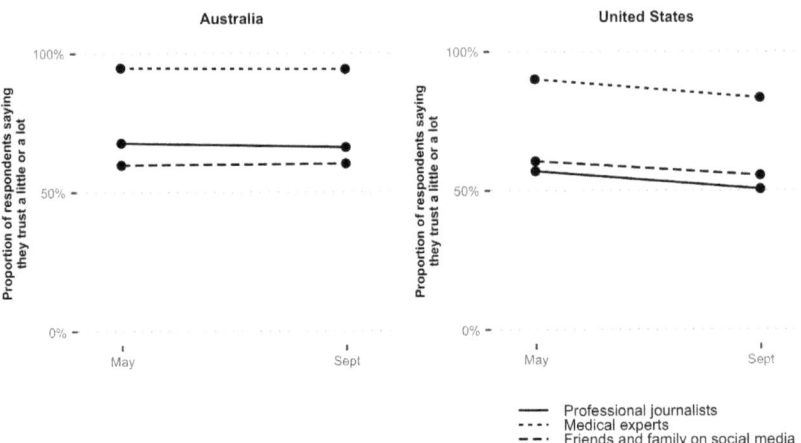

FIGURE 11.2 Trust in different sources of news and information by country for May and September 2020. A line graph showing how trust in three sources – professional journalists, medical experts, and friends and family on social media – about COVID-19 information has changed from May to September 2020.

(Figure 11.2). Worth noting is that trust in professional journalists was above 50% in both countries, and while not a perfect comparator with media trust, it is higher than most media trust measures in the USA and Australia outside pandemic conditions, where it sits below 50% (Edelman 2019). In May, Australians compared to Americans were generally more trusting of professional journalists (68% vs 57% respectively).[5] Unlike Americans, Australians ranked their trust in COVID-19 information from journalists as higher than information obtained from friends and family on social media; however, both countries had about the same level of trust in social media as a source (61% vs 60% respectively).

By September, trust had shifted downwards in the USA for all three sources of COVID-19 information; whereas, in Australia, it remained steady (see Figure 11.2). Trust in both medical experts and journalists fell by 7% in the USA down to 83% and 50% respectively. It fell 6% for social media sources to 55%. To understand this decline, some contextual factors about the pandemic stand out. The first is the severity of impact of the novel coronavirus on the

---

5 The question asked was: when accessing information about the coronavirus, how much do you generally trust the following sources? Professional journalists, friends and family on social media, and medical experts. The answer was a 4-point Likert scale consisting of 'do not trust at all', 'do not trust much', 'trust a little', 'trust a lot'.

two populations between May and September when the national surveys were fielded. Disease spread in the USA was far greater, with a relative change of 450%, from a cumulative 1.13 million to 6.08 million COVID-19 cases. In Australia, the relative change was 282%, from 6,767 to 25,818 cumulative cases, with the overwhelming majority in the state of Victoria (Our World in Data, 2020). While Americans might have had a perception that the health crisis was deepening in the USA, lessening trust in medical experts, Australians were likely to have the opposite perception as the virus rescinded in all states except Victoria, the only Australian state to experience a second wave, and accounting for 74% of Australian cases. Second, in the USA, medical advice was publicly challenged by political elites, most notably President Trump and sections of the (mostly conservative) news media. In Australia, support for medical expertise remained largely bipartisan with no major political figures challenging advice.

Also notable is the partisan gap in media choices and trust in professional journalists between the two nations. The US data reveal substantial differences in trust of journalists as a source of information – again revealing polarization. A minority (22%) of Republicans expressed some trust for journalists in May, which fell to a lowly 15% in September. While a majority (86%) of Democrats expressed trust for journalists in May, which fell slightly to 83% in September. People who trust journalists were most likely to rely on established mainstream brands such as the *New York Times*, MSNBC, *Washington Post* and CNN for their news. This reliance on television and newspapers for trusted news during a crisis is consistent with past findings in crisis communication literature, as discussed earlier. Those with little trust in journalists tended to select polemic outlets like Breitbart News, AM radio and Fox News. In Australia, there is not this degree of media polarization. Most Australians (regardless of partisanship) trusted journalists during the pandemic and relied on a mix of news sources including the public broadcaster and Murdoch's daily tabloids.

Partisan Differences

Overall, the US data show COVID-19 information from journalists is less trusted than information from close contacts on social media. The reverse is true in Australia. There is a partisan story here. Trump supporters were approximately three times more likely to trust COVID-19 news from friends and family on social media than reports by professional journalists. The difference between partisans and their trust in journalists is stark. In May, as noted earlier, about a fifth (22%) of Trump voters trusted professional journalists, compared with more than four-fifths (86%) of Biden supporters. Republicans were also less likely than other Americans to trust medical experts: 81% of Republicans said they trusted medical experts a lot or a little, compared to 99% of Democrats. These gaps between Democrats and Republicans widened by September, largely due to declining trust among Republicans. For example, Republican trust for medical experts fell by nine points to 72% compared to a 4% decline for Democrats to 95%, thus widening the gap between Republicans and Democrats by 5%.

While partisan differences in trust in news exist in Australia, they were significantly smaller. Most Labor supporters (77%) said they had a little or a lot of trust in journalists, while two-thirds of Coalition supporters (66%) agreed. Trust in medical experts was very high with unexceptional partisan difference (96% Coalition and 98% Labor). Unlike the USA, these patterns changed very little in Australia between May and September. Coalition support for all three sources remained exactly the same. Labor trust was stable for medical experts and social media sources, but dipped 6% for journalists, although still high at 71%.

Meanwhile, trust in friends and family on social media for COVID-19 information reflected very similar partisan patterns in Australia and the USA: conservatives in both countries are more trusting in this online communicative space. Republicans were more trusting of friends and family online than Democrats (62% vs. 57% in May respectively); while Australia's conservative Coalition supporters were also more trusting of personal associates online, three points ahead of Australia's Labor party (61% vs 58% respectively). These percentages remained stable in September.

Consistent with Zaller's political elite cue theory, and Mourão and colleagues' (2018) findings on the relationship between media trust and partisan allegiance, it appears that when it comes to a trust contest between Trump and journalists (which he decries as 'fake news'), conservative partisans follow elite cues and choose Trump. In Australia, mainstream media messaging and political cues about the health risks of COVID-19 were largely unified during the first survey thus providing no reason for partisan division. By the second survey, tension was building between the Coalition Prime Minister and the Labor Victorian Premier about the strictness of the lockdown, but not about the broader principle that social distancing was necessary. The daily televised press conferences also revealed the critical questioning of the Victorian Premier by the media, earning the media some public criticism, which may account for the drop in support for journalists among Labor voters (Simons, 2020). Meanwhile, Trump and some Democrat governors had opposing views about the first principle of applying lockdown measures. President Trump tweeted his opposition to lockdowns describing them as 'too tough' and targeting his message to states with Democrat governors via Twitter (e.g. 'LIBERATE MINNESOTA' , 'LIBERATE MICHIGAN') (BBC, 2020).

Consistent with PSE theory, we find Americans who consumed more conservative media expressed much lower trust in both professional journalists and medical experts than Democrats. However, as noted above, as the crisis deepens in the USA, we witness a loss of overall trust in all actors, but this trust deficit is greater for Republicans than Democrats regarding journalists and medical experts. Republican trust also begins at a much lower starting point than

Democrats and falls sharply, widening the gap between the two parties. In Australia, trust overall is largely unchanged across the three sources. A broader question, then, is: does it matter if citizens distrust these messengers during a health crisis? The findings below suggest it does.

Media Use, Partisanship and Concern about Catching COVID-19

Partisan differences in journalistic trust about COVID-19 and regard for medical experts' advice appear to have consequences for how individuals evaluate their personal risk of catching the virus (see Figure 11.3). In the USA, these differences are stark and grow wider (in our September data), as the pandemic deepened. Very few Republicans (19%) felt 'extremely' or 'very worried' about catching the disease; with Republicans becoming even less concerned in September (11%) despite the widening contagion. In contrast, Democrats, who generally trust journalists, and have very high regard for medical expertise, became more concerned. Almost half (48%) reported feeling 'extremely' or 'very worried' about catching the novel virus in May, and this figure increased by September (50%). Conversely, in Australia where media, political and medical messaging were mostly unified, we see little partisan difference in concern about catching COVID-19 and it remains constant from May to September (see Figure 11.3). Of those who were worried, Coalition supporters (26%) were slightly less worried than Labor voters (29%).

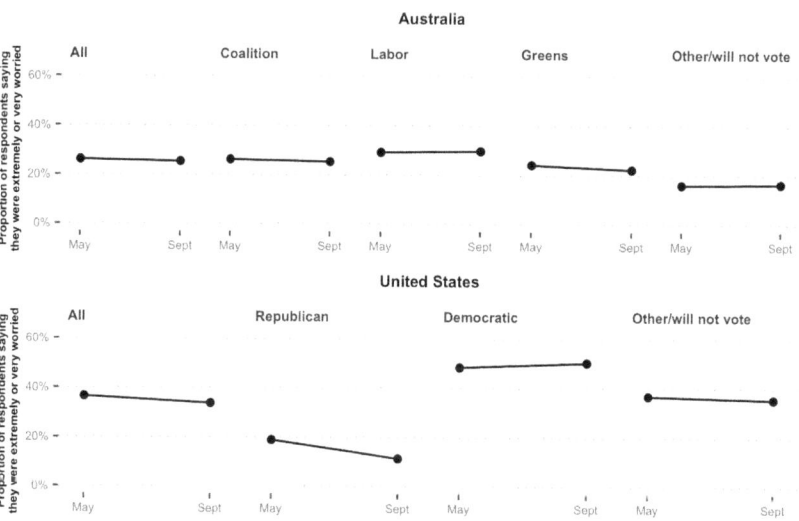

FIGURE 11.3 Change in proportion of respondents being very or extremely worried about COVID-19, as a function of vote intention.

Public Satisfaction with COVID-Safe Policy Measures

Given Republicans feel least concern about catching COVID-19, it is unsurprising then that a majority are more opposed to government interventions such as lockdowns (see Figure 11.4). In contrast, only a minority of Australians opposed government restrictions with much smaller partisan differences. Conservatives (22%) were more likely to say that the measures had 'gone too far' compared to Labor voters (10%). We find that American attitudes about government restrictions correlate with partisanship, and the gulf widens as the pandemic endures. By September, as the contagion continues and trust in experts and journalists falls, a whopping 71% of Trump supporters felt that lockdown measures had gone 'too far' or 'much too far' compared to just 5% of Biden supporters, notwithstanding the rising COVID-19 death toll in the country.

The data also show that public attitudes about how governments best deal with the pandemic are linked to citizens' media choices for COVID-19 information (see Figure 11.5). Those whose news diet was mostly conservative were most likely to oppose lockdowns. This proportion increased between May and September in both countries. However, US news audiences who consumed mostly left-leaning media (the outlets most likely to report the messages of medical experts) were wanting governments to do more to restrict movements

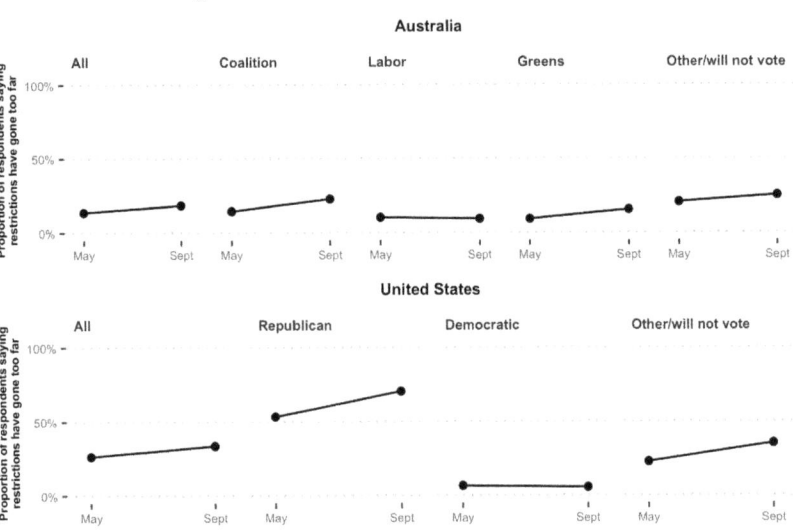

FIGURE 11.4 Change in proportion of respondents saying restrictions in movement and public gatherings had gone (much) too far, as a function of vote intention.

**Changing support for restrictions
by ideology of top media sources**

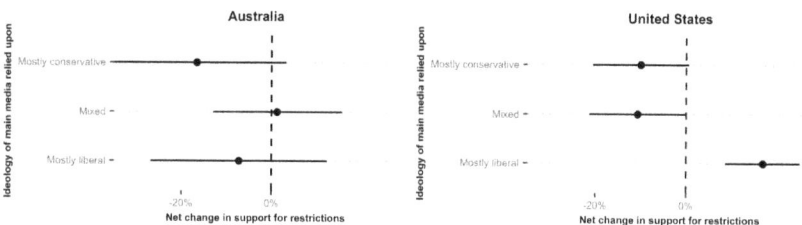

FIGURE 11.5 Change in within-respondent support for restrictions, by ideology of main media sources.

as the pandemic worsened. This divergent trend was not evident in Australia. Instead, support for lockdowns actually fell among both right- and left-leaning media consumers. However, confidence intervals are large in the Australian data meaning less certainty in this finding. A factor that might be linked to falling, yet still majority support, for government restrictions in Australia is the much-reduced threat of the virus across the nation by the time of the second survey. In September, there was no community transmission except in the state of Victoria, thus deeming restrictions in movement largely redundant everywhere but Victoria.

Conclusion

In this chapter, we have shown that political partisanship is more strongly tied to trust in journalists and news use in the USA than Australia. Republicans were highly unlikely to trust information on COVID-19 from professional journalists, and were somewhat less trusting of medical experts, compared to Democrats. In Australia, there were only minor differences in trust of professional journalists between partisans, and very strong bipartisan trust in medical experts. The findings reflect a stark difference in overall public satisfaction with COVID-19 lockdown measures and health outcomes between the two democracies during the first wave of infection. In the USA, a minority (one-third) of Americans were satisfied with lockdown measures to restrict disease spread. Drilling down further, most Trump supporters (71%) thought lockdowns went too far compared to 5% of Democrats. In contrast, Australia exhibited largely bipartisan support with two-thirds of Australians agreeing that government restrictions were 'about right'.

The data gathered and analysed during the unfolding health crisis assist with understanding the roles of media trust and political polarization on policy effectiveness during a global health emergency. The combination of political polarization and journalistic distrust reflects mostly ideologically homogenous news diets for US citizens. This is problematic as it hinders the formation of a common public sphere with consistent messaging about the threat of COVID-19. Such polarization has an impact on people's level of concern (low for conservatives) that further impedes a bipartisan government approach (with coordinated state-federal relations) to enact policies to limit disease spread to save lives.

We also observe increased use of news media during the pandemic. Citizens in both countries rely on a combination of established and new media sources in their news diets. But in the USA, there is little ideological diversity in individuals' news choices. Rather, we see evidence of political selective exposure theory to explain US citizens' media use. News selectivity and trust in journalists are linked to political partisanship in the USA. In Australia, these partisan patterns are weaker. Generally, Australians engage with more diverse news sources and have higher trust in professional journalists. These stark country differences are unsurprising given the use of elite cues and concerted efforts by President Trump to delegitimize the credibility of the mainstream media in the USA through the weaponization of fake news language since coming to office in 2016. Studies show this phenomenon erodes trust in the media, and that it is less advanced in Australian political communications (Farhall et al., 2019). An area of further research is to examine the role Australia's public broadcaster might play in mitigating against PSE.

Overall, in both countries, trust in journalists and use of established news brands for COVID-19 information are strong (above pre-pandemic levels), a finding consistent with other studies of media trust during the pandemic (Newman et al., 2020). Yet, as we have shown, a different picture emerges in the USA when partisanship is considered. Trust in journalists and use of diverse news outlets for COVID-19 news are very low among US conservatives and this gap widens as the pandemic endures. Trust in medical experts also falls, which may reflect a degree of dismay with its management and experts as the pandemic deepens.

This creates a dissensual public sphere in the USA characterized by sharp partisan divisions not only in political communication, but in audiences' media choices, trust in journalists and medical experts. This fragmentation affects public perceptions of risk and compliance with health measures thus impeding governments' capacity to manage the pandemic. In Australia, trust in journalists and medical experts, bipartisan political agreement and federal-state support for COVID-safe policies have led to a more consensual public sphere about measures to contain COVID-19. Even when community transmission is non-existent in most Australian states in September, support for government restrictions eases but still has overall majority support. We conclude that cleavages in trust in mainstream information sources, combined with disparate concerns about COVID-19's health impacts, have dire consequences for achieving unified government actions to combat the disease spread. Unified political and medical messaging combined with media trust and news preferences appear to matter in a time of a crisis.

References

ABC [Australian Broadcasting Corporation]. (2013). *ABC code of practice*, http://about.abc.net.au/wp-content/uploads/2012/12/CodeofPractice2013.pdf

Baker, P., & Karni, A. (2020, February 28). Trump accuses media and democrats of exaggerating coronavirus threat. *New York Times*. https://www.nytimes.com/2020/02/28/us/politics/trump-accuses-media-democrats-coronavirus.html

Barthel, M., Mitchell, A., & Holcomb, J. (2016, December 15). Many Americans believe fakes news is sowing confusion. *Pew Research Centre: Journalism & Media*. https://www.journalism.org/2016/12/15/many-americans-believe-fake-news-is-sowing-confusion/

BBC [British Broadcasting Company]. (2020, April 18). Coronavirus: President Trump defends tweets against US states' lockdowns. *BBC*. https://www.bbc.com/news/world-us-canada-52330531

Bos, L., Kruikemeier, S., & de Vreese, C. (2016). Nation binding: How public service broadcasting mitigates political selective exposure. *PloS One*, *11*(5), p.e0155112.

Brug J., Aro, A. R., Oenema, A., de Zwart, O., Richardus, J. H., & Bishop, G. D. (2004). SARS risk perception, knowledge, precautions, and information sources, the Netherlands. *Emerging Infectious Diseases*, *10*(8), 1486–1489.

Carey, J. (2002). Media use during a crisis. *Prometheus*, *20*(3), 201–207.

CNN. (2020, May 10). How the New York Times is weathering the pandemic. *CNN Business*. https://edition.cnn.com/videos/business/2020/05/10/nyt-ceo-pandemic-proves-value-of-trustworthy-news.cnn

Duckett, S. (2020). Coming out of COVID-19 lockdown: The next steps for Australian health care. *The Grattan Institute*, pp. 1–15. https://grattan.edu.au/wp-content/uploads/2020/06/Coming-out-of-COVID-lockdown-the-next-steps-for-Australian-health-care.pdf

Edelman, D. (2019). *2019 Edelman Trust Barometer: Global Report* https://www.edelman.com/sites/g/files/aatuss191/files/2019/02/2019_Edelman_Trust_Barometer_Global_Report.pdf

Farhall, K., Carson, A., Wright, S., Gibbons, A., & Lukamto, W. (2019). Political elites' use of fake news discourse across communications platforms. *International Journal of Communication*, *13*(0), 4353–4375.

Fisher, C. (2019). Australia. In N. Newman, R. Fletcher, A. Kalogeropoulos, & R. K. Nielsen (Eds.), *Reuters Institute Digital News Report 2019* (pp. 132–133). Oxford: Reuters Institute for the Study of Journalism. https://reutersinstitute.politics.ox.ac.uk/sites/default/files/inline-files/DNR_2019_FINAL.pdf

Fletcher, R., & Park, S. (2017). The impact of trust in the news media on online news consumption and participation. *Digital Journalism*, *5*(10), 1281–1299.

Hetherington, M. J., & Rudolph, T. J. (2015). *Why Washington won't work: Polarization, political trust, and the governing crisis*. Chicago: University of Chicago Press.

Iyengar, S., & Hahn, K.S. (2009). Red media, blue media: Evidence of ideological selectivity in media use. *Journal of Communication*, *59*(1), 19–39.

Jackman, S., & Ratcliff, S. (2018, February 18). America's trust deficit. *United States Studies Centre*. https://www.ussc.edu.au/analysis/americas-trust-deficit

Knowles, S., & Schifferes, S. (2020). Financial capability, the financial crisis and trust in news media. *Journal of Applied Journalism & Media Studies, 9*(1), 61–83.
McNair, B. (2017). *An introduction to political communication* (6th edn.), Oxon: Routledge.
Miller, Z., Colvin, J., & Madhani. A. (2020, October 5). Trump, still infectious, back at White House—without mask. *GBH News*. https://www.wgbh.org/news/national-news/2020/10/05/trump-aims-for-monday-release-after-outside-drive-by
Mourão, R. R., Thorson, E., Chen, W., & Tham, S. M. (2018). Media repertoires and news trust during the early Trump administration. *Journalism Studies, 19*(13), 1945–56.
Newman, N., Fletcher, R., Kalogeropoulos, A., & Nielsen, R. K. (2019). *Reuters Institute Digital News Report 2019*. Oxford: Reuters Institute for the Study of Journalism. https://reutersinstitute.politics.ox.ac.uk/sites/default/files/inline-files/DNR_2019_FINAL.pdf
Newman, N., Fletcher, R., Schulz, A., Andi, S., & Nielsen, K. (2020) *Reuters institute digital news report 2020*. Oxford: Reuters Institute for the Study of Journalism. https://reutersinstitute.politics.ox.ac.uk/sites/default/files/2020-06/DNR_2020_FINAL.pdf
Norris, P. (2000). *A virtuous circle: Political communication in post-industrial societies*. Cambridge: Cambridge University Press.
Our World in Data. (2020). United States vs Australia: Coronavirus pandemic country profile, 2 May–2 Sept. https://ourworldindata.org/coronavirus/country/united-states?country=USA~AUS#cumulative-confirmed-cases-how-rapidly-have-they-increased-compared-to-other-countries
Simons, M. (2020, October 11). One hundred days of Andrews' press conferences: What do they tell us about journalism? *The Age*. https://www.theage.com.au/national/victoria/one-hundred-days-of-andrews-press-conferences-what-do-they-tell-us-about-journalism-20201009-p563lt.html
Sky News. (2020, March 18). I've sought to dismantle coronavirus hysteria by sticking to the facts': Alan Jones. *Sky News*. https://www.skynews.com.au/details/_6142500065001
Strömbäck, J., Tsfati, Y., Boomgaarden, H., Damstra, A., Lindgren, E., Vliegenthart, R., & Lindholm, T. (2020). News media trust and its impact on media use: Toward a framework for future research. *Annals of the International Communication Association, 44*(2), 139–156. doi:10.1080/23808985.2020.1755338
Swift, A. (2016, September 14). American's trust in mass media sinks to new low. *Gallup*. http://news.gallup.com/poll/195542/americans-trust-mass-media-sinks-new-low.aspx
Tsfati, Y., & Ariely, G. (2014). Individual and contextual correlates of trust in media across 44 countries. *Communication Research, 41*(6), 760–782. doi:10.1177/0093650213485972
Van Aelst, P., Strömbäck, J. Aalberg, T., Esser, F., de Vreese, C., Matthes, J., … Stanyer, J. (2017). Political communication in a high-choice media environment: a challenge for democracy? *Annals of the International Communication Association, 41*(1), 3–27. doi: 10.1080/23808985.2017.1288551
Van Dalen, A. (2020). Journalism, trust, and credibility. In K. Wahl-Jorgensen, & T. Hanitzsch, (Eds.), *Handbook of journalism studies* (pp. 356–371). London: Routledge.

Van Duyn, E., & Collier, J. (2019). Priming and fake news: The effects of elite discourse on evaluations of news media. *Mass Communication and Society*, *22*(1), 29–48. doi:10.1080/15205436.2018.1511807

Van Velsen, L., van Gemert-Pijnen, J. E., Beaujean, D. J., Wentzel, J., & van Steenbergen, J. E. (2012). Should health organizations use web 2.0 media in times of an infectious disease crisis? An in-depth qualitative study of citizens' information behavior during an EHEC outbreak. *Journal of medical Internet research*, *14*(6), e181. https://doi.org/10.2196/jmir.2123

Westlund, O., & Ghersetti, M. (2015). Modelling news media use. *Journalism Studies*, *16*(2), 133–151.

Zaller, J. R. (1992). *The nature and origins of mass opinion*. Cambridge: Cambridge University Press.

12

"I DON'T VOTE BECAUSE I DON'T WANT TO GET INFECTED"

Pandemic, Polarization, and Public Trust during the 2020 Presidential Election in Poland

Damian Guzek, Sabina Mihelj, and Václav Štětka

Introduction

Akin to other crisis situations, the COVID-19 pandemic has dramatically changed the course and dynamics of political communication in the countries affected by the rapid spread of the virus in 2020. In normal, politically routine times, communication from the government to the citizens usually faces competition from and critical scrutiny by the opposition, news media, and other actors within the democratic political and media system. In contrast, in times of national emergency government communication becomes prioritized by the media, and a truce is often called between the government and the opposition in order to jointly work toward the solution to protect the country and its citizens (Barnett & Roselle, 2008; Giorgi & Moury, 2015; Reynolds & Barnett, 2003). In addition, people's support of the government might temporarily increase, as people put aside their partisanship and "rally-around-the-flag" when they feel there is an imminent danger to their safety or well-being (Hetherington & Nelson, 2003).

In many countries around the globe, we have seen this rally-around-the-flag phenomenon during the first wave of the COVID-19 pandemic, as evidenced by the increase in political trust and/or support for the government's measures to tackle the pandemic (Bol et al., 2020; Schraff, 2020; see also Chapter 1). In the UK, notably, the approval ratings of Prime Minister Boris Johnson jumped by 30% in March 2020, and 94% of the British public expressed support for the government's lockdown measures at the beginning of April 2020 (Wiseman, 2020). However, in some countries – including the USA (Green et al., 2020; Sides et al., 2020) – the pandemic appears to have had an opposite effect – deepening political and social divides, and intensifying ongoing political battles.

DOI: 10.4324/9781003170051-15

While the factors that play a part in steering the country toward such scenario might be manifold, the level of existing political and media polarization might be among the key ones. According to Hart et al. (2020), polarization is holding back the implementation and coordination of official measures, amplifying partisan differences in perceptions of the pandemic; other authors remind us that this can in effect "lead different segments of the population to arrive at different conclusions about the threat in the situation and appropriate actions" (Bavel et al., 2020, p. 464). This risk is further exacerbated by the "infodemic" of misinformation and conspiracy theories circulating on social media (WHO, 2020), which is sowing confusion and distrust in measures adopted to tackle the disease (Edelman, 2020; Roozenbeek et al., 2020). Existing research on the link between media consumption and attitudes to public health measures during the first wave of the COVID-19 pandemic in the USA supports these arguments; greater reliance on Fox News was associated with greater likelihood of endorsing misinformation and believing that the authorities exaggerated the risks (Motta et al., 2020) as well as lower likelihood of compliance with public health measures (Simonov et al., 2020). One such country where one might expect polarization to have interfered with the government's response to the COVID-19 crisis was Poland. Since the 2015 parliamentary elections, Poland has been embroiled in bitter political clashes between the conservative, right-wing nationalist government and the liberal opposition, which has been accusing the government of authoritarian tendencies and stirring culture wars (Ágh, 2016; Przybylski, 2018; Sadurski, 2018). One of the most recent examples of the political and ideological polarization in the country were the clashes and mass protests arising in response to the new anti-abortion law adopted in October 2020 (Daniels, 2020). The COVID-19 pandemic has arrived to Poland at the time of preparations for the 2020 Presidential Election which were foreseen to be a tight race between the incumbent, government-backed President Andrzej Duda, and his liberal opponent, Mayor of Warsaw Rafał Trzaskowski. The overlap between the time of the election campaign and the first wave of the pandemic further complicated the already entangled political situation, and created a challenge for government communication, especially from the point of view of gaining citizens' trust in a climate already infested with heavily polarized opinions, promoted and amplified via mutually opposing media channels.

Our chapter seeks to explore how this existing polarization and the ongoing election campaign affected audience engagement with government communication during the first wave of the COVID-19 pandemic in the spring 2020. We draw on data from our field research, which involved 29 in-depth interviews and media diaries detailing news consumption habits, political attitudes and opinions on the pandemic. By adopting a qualitative approach and focusing on the meaning-making practices of media consumption, rather than on the sheer amount and type of news sources that people have been exposed to (e.g.,

Nielsen et al., 2020), we want to fill a gap in the growing number of studies on the character and role of information-seeking behavior during the pandemic, as well as to add to general debate on the role of communication during public health crises (Briggs & Hallin, 2017).

Poland's Political and Media Context: In the Shadow of Democratic Backsliding

A "specimen of the crisis of democracy and constitutionalism," according to Wojciech Sadurski (2019, p. vii), Poland has been experiencing arguably the most tumultuous period of its post-1989 history in the last several years. Following the 2015 Presidential and then Parliamentary Elections which brought to power the right-wing populist party Law and Justice (Prawo i Sprawiedliwość, PiS), the country has been characterized by significant democratic backsliding, manifested by government's attacks on key democratic institutions, as well as by decline of media freedom and public trust.

Headed by its co-founder Jarosław Kaczyński, the Law and Justice party has been gradually remolding the separation of the three branches of government and the system of democratic checks and balances. In a process labeled "anti-constitutional populist backsliding" (Sadurski, 2018), the PiS-led government has strived to capture the Constitutional Court, to introduce indirect control over the Ministry of Justice, and to make prosecutors once again directly dependent on the Minister of Justice as their superior (Tworzecki, 2019). The efforts at assuming control over the judiciary have been complemented by sustained government's attacks on minorities and other "social enemies," particularly the refugees, "gender ideology," and LGBT community (Krzyżanowska & Krzyżanowski, 2018), which were among the main reasons why Freedom House's 2020 Nations in Transit report has downgraded Poland to "semi-consolidated democracy" (Csaky, 2020).

Another notable aspect of the illiberal shift after 2015 has been related to the changing relationship between the Polish media and politics, characterized by growing political parallelism and increasing attempts by the government to stifle media freedom. Shortly after the 2015 elections, the Parliament has enacted a new regulatory framework for public service broadcasters which brought them under direct government control (Surowiec et al., 2020). PSB's managing boards have been subordinated to the government-dependent Council of National Media, which in practice doubled the independent Constitutional Media Authority (Grzesiok-Horosz, 2019), and the management and editorial rooms of both TVP and Polskie Radio have seen a string of departures and political appointments, resulting in a tight alignment of the editorial content with the government's preferences and ideological agenda (Krzyżanowski, 2018). Apart from effectively turning the PSB into an instrument of government propaganda (Żuk, 2020), the government has been putting increasing pressure on independent commercial media, particularly those that have been seen as siding with the parliamentary opposition, like the Discovery-owned *TVN* broadcaster, the leading quality newspaper *Gazeta Wyborcza*, or the newspapers belonging to the Swiss-German publishing house Ringier Axel Springer. Outlets like these have been regularly threatened with government lawsuits, intimidation of their journalists, calls for "re-polonization," or denied advertising by state-controlled companies (Glenny et al., 2020; Selva, 2020; Szabó, 2020).

The process of politicization of state institutions and the media has gone hand in hand with the decline of public trust. As documented by recent surveys, Poland has recorded one of Europe's weakest levels of social trust (CBOS, 2018; Edelman, 2018). Sadurski (2019, p. 9) has suggested that trust in political institutions and elites has been systematically weakened by the populist rhetoric of the PiS party, particularly with regard to the 2010 Smolensk tragedy (the air crash that killed President Lech Kaczynski, together with dozens of prominent political figures) that the PiS politicians and aligned media exploited to spread conspiracy theories. The political scene has lost its credibility while proceeding with rapid changes in the law due to PiS followers taking over the Constitutional Tribunal. The authority of the judiciary community has been significantly weakened during the reforms carried out by PiS, accompanied by verbal attacks on the judges, called by the derogatory term "caste" (RMF FM, 2020). Such an aggressive and antagonizing political communication has been covered by the heavily polarized media outlets, amplifying both pro- and anti-government positions but clearly speaking to ever more polarized audiences, as indicated by gradually decreasing average trust in media, monitored by the Reuters Institute's Digital News Survey – between 2016 and 2020, trust in news has dropped by 10% (from 55% to 45%), while trust in brands that people use has declined more slowly (from 60% to 55%) during the same time (Newman et al., 2016, 2020). The government-controlled TVP, while still one of the most important players on the Polish news market (Newman et al., 2020), however seems to have been hit by the loss of trust more than other brands, being the least trusted of the 15 most important news media brands that the respondents were asked about, and also one that was the most polarizing, with 43% expressing trust and 39% distrust in TVP (Newman et al., 2020). The low credibility of the Polish state television in comparison to other countries was also notable during the pandemic – as confirmed by an international survey of 17 European countries (Van Aelst et al., 2021), Poland was one of the few countries where the use of public TV has declined during the first wave of the pandemic in the spring 2020; Poland has also recorded a considerable decline of trust in public media outlets.

The 2020 Presidential Election

Having comfortably won the 2018 municipality elections and the 2019 Parliamentary Elections (with 43.6% of popular vote), the Law and Justice party was initially on the course to win the 2020 Presidential Elections – originally scheduled on 10 May – as well. However, the preparations for the elections were disrupted by the COVID-19 pandemic. On 6 April, the PiS-controlled Parliament passed a bill (at an express pace) stating that the election was to be held by postal voting. In response to this last-minute change, highly criticized by oppositional candidates as unconstitutional, Małgorzata Kidawa-Błońska, the candidate of the largest oppositional party Civil Platform (PO), threatened to boycott the all-postal elections (Vashchanka, 2020).

The subsequent part of the election campaign saw three distinct types of candidate strategies, reacting to this unexpected turn. The PO's candidate spoke with the media about the boycott, suspended her campaign, and then suddenly resumed it again (Radio Zet, 2020). The other opposition candidates became active mostly on the Internet and demanded opening the public sphere to make the race fair. Meanwhile, the incumbent President Duda focused on television, benefiting from favorable state TV coverage by fulfilling his duties in the regions struggling with COVID-19 restrictions, something that the other candidates could not compete with (Vashchanka, 2020). Knowing that the National Electoral Commission (NEC, 2020) – the authority supervising over the electoral process – would not allow the election to proceed with postal-only voting, PiS forced a series of chaotic provisions which resulted in printing the ballots for voting, mandating the Polish Post to accommodate the demands by the NEC, and finally postponing the election until June 28 with a hybrid version which also guaranteed postal voting (Vashchanka, 2020). Moreover, the disruption and confusion in the main opposition party (PO) forced its leaders to withdraw Kidawa-Błońska and make Rafał Trzaskowski, the Major of Warsaw, its new candidate. The first round of election saw the highest-ever voter turnout since 1995 (64.4%), and the incumbent President Duda won it with 43.5% of votes, 13% ahead of his challenger Trzaskowski. The campaign culminated in the second round in rather bizarre circumstances, as there was no direct debate between the candidates who refused to meet on the same stage. The close race was ultimately won by President Duda with 51.03% of the votes (NEC, 2020); a tight victory that underlined, and arguably further exacerbated, the deep polarization of the contemporary Polish society.

Methodology

While research on COVID-19 in Poland has been growing quickly (Jarynowski et al., 2020; Krzysztofik et al., 2020), issues of communication and media within these works are mostly discussed with regard to minorities (Sorokowski et al., 2020), mental anxiety (Moroń & Biolik-Moroń, 2021), or the practice of law-making (Serowaniec & Witkowski, 2020). Little is known about how the existing societal polarization – as outlined above – affects audience engagement with, and trust in, government communication during the pandemic. The analysis that follows seeks to answer the following two questions:

RQ1: How did participants engage with different channels of government communication during the first wave of the pandemic?
RQ2: How was audience engagement with government communication affected by existing political and media polarization in Poland?

To answer these questions, we draw on a set of semi-structured interviews and media diaries conducted with a total of 29 participants in Poland. Participants were recruited from population surveys, using a combination of purposive and quota sampling. The sample was limited to participants who were at least minimally politically engaged (meaning that they followed politics on a regular basis (minimum weekly). Quota sampling was used to ensure that the purposive sample was sufficiently diverse on key demographic dimensions known to shape media use and political behavior, including age, gender, and location (i.e., urban vs. rural); political preferences were also taken in consideration.

Each participant was asked to participate in two interview sessions, one face-to-face in February/March 2020, and the second one remotely in April 2020, as well as to keep a diary for three weeks from 9 to 29 March 2020. The first interview lasted an hour on average, and covered everyday routines, political engagement, the media environment, and news consumption routines and preferences, as well as served to introduce the diary. The diary period coincided with the most dramatic phase of the pandemic in the country, including the introduction of a national lockdown. In their diaries, participants were asked to include descriptions of all their encounters with information about politics, broadly defined, regardless of whether these encounters involved media or not, or if they included information about the COVID-19 pandemic. The second interview lasted for an average of 40–45 minutes and covered general recollections of news consumption during the first few weeks of the COVID-19 pandemic, participants' views on various issues concerning the COVID-19 pandemic (such as views on measures in their respective countries, views on the EU and China, and conspiracy theories), as well as follow-up questions on selected aspects of a participant's diary.

All interviews were transcribed directly from local languages into English, and paper-based media diaries were digitized. All material was analyzed using NVivo and thematic analysis (Braun & Clarke, 2006). Coding the first interviews focused on one's news consumption pattern, reasons for selecting (or avoiding) particular news sources, and attitudes toward various political and social issues. The media diaries and second interviews were coded with a concentration on COVID-19, focusing on reactions to COVID-19 related news, including measures and changes in media use and news consumption patterns.

Engagement with Government Communication

Polish authorities responded to the pandemic by introducing several restrictions on public life, ranging from the cancellation of mass events and closure of the service industry to online education and remote working. At the same time, the Polish government, along with regional and local authorities, intensified its communication with the public, utilizing a variety of channels, from live broadcasts to text messages. The analysis of interviews and diaries confirmed that the first wave of the pandemic and the introduction of restrictions were accompanied by considerable changes in news consumption. Most participants mentioned following the news more often, watching considerably more television, especially public broadcasting channels, and also reported news exhaustion after about a week of intense news consumption – all results that resonate with findings of existing work on news consumption during the pandemic (e.g., Casero-Ripollés, 2020; Nielsen et al., 2020; Van Aelst et al., 2021) including research focused specifically on Eastern Europe (Mihelj et al., 2021).

Looking specifically at audience engagement with government communication, our analysis showed that participants engaged with government communication across a variety of channels, including live broadcasts of government's press conferences (followed either through broadcast media or online), government-sponsored text messages, dedicated COVID-19 webpages, and government-sponsored adverts online and on broadcast media. Participants also tended to perceive government communication on COVID-19 as trustworthy, regardless of their political orientations and misgivings about the government's handling of elections – a subject we return to later in the analysis. However, as shown below, the proportion of participants encountering each of these channels of communication varied considerably, and so did their assessment of their relative effectiveness. Also notable was the reliance on news reports on governments' activities and latest measures; as shown below, such reports were perceived as more accessible and clearer than direct government communication.

One of the most frequently mentioned and best assessed channels of government communication were the live broadcasts of government's press conferences. These were mentioned by 20 participants, all of whom found them to be most effective in providing the necessary information and reducing the tensions and anxieties surrounding the pandemic. The participants reported following live broadcasts of Prime Minister Mateusz Morawiecki and the Minister of Health Łukasz Szumowski over public service and commercial TV channels (*TVP, TVN24, TVN*) and radio channels (*Polskie Radio 1, RMF FM, Radio Zet*), websites (*Wirtualna Polska*), and social media (*Facebook*). The following excerpt from one of our interviews illustrates this perception of the central role played by the live broadcasts of press conferences, and their reverberations in subsequent news reports across a range of media platforms:

> Press conferences. All broadcasters showed it, then there were highlights in the news bulletins. They were writing about them on the Internet as

well. That was the most successful way to reach people. Willingly or not, any media user had to come across some mention of it somewhere.

(Pol-09, male, 30, urban)

Among the different modes of accessing live briefings, watching the briefings via public service television channels (*TVP1* and *TVP2*) was most common, and perceived as most effective even among anti-government participants who otherwise avoided these channels due to their link with the government. The following excerpt, from an interview with one of our anti-government participants, illustrates this tension between the recognition of the effectiveness of live briefings televised over public service channels, and a clear negative perception of public service television as a means of government "propaganda":

> I think the press conferences, because many people watch them on public TV, *TVP1* and *TVP2*, because many people do not have internet access, and this is the source that they use. Especially the elderly, and the propaganda of *TVP* tells them that things are ok, that it's not that bad.
>
> *(Pol-11, female, 63, rural)*

Government-sponsored text messages were another frequently mentioned channel of government communication. Twenty-three participants mentioned receiving one or two text messages, typically including the announcement of the state of emergency, or providing a link to the government website with information on COVID-19. However, in contrast to live briefings, our participants were almost unanimously skeptical of the efficacy of such an approach and found the messages superfluous. Nonetheless, some participants also acknowledged their potential importance in reaching citizens who are otherwise disconnected from news. The following excerpt is illustrative of this:

> I feel that the text messages would be most effective if I wasn't already getting information elsewhere. You wouldn't be able to evade getting the text, so this way, the message would surely reach you. I also think that radio communications are very effective, because the radio is on a lot, at least at my house.
>
> *(Pol-11, female, 63, rural)*

Also common were mentions of the government COVID19 website, recorded in 14 out of 29 interviews. Although most of our participants mentioned receiving a text message with a link to the website, these did not seem effective in directly prompting participants to use the website. Rather, our participants reported either following a link to the website they received through social media (typically via Facebook Messenger) or searched for the website using a search engine. Participants clearly perceived the government website as trustworthy, and used it to obtain reliable information or dispel their doubts with regard to specific measures. The following two excerpts illustrate this well:

> Yes, I did. Just facts, some of which I already knew. Some were new to me. I consulted this website again recently to confirm whether or not you are allowed to visit your city vegetable garden. Whether you can go there or not. And still I don't know, it's not a clear issue.
> *(Pol-04, female, 62, rural)*

> When it comes to following what the government was doing, I consulted the web portal run by the government. I trusted that they would do exactly what they said they will. If someone sent me something via Messenger, I would have a look at it. But I generally used the media I usually use.
> *(Pol-21, female, 67, urban)*

Twelve of our participants also mentioned coming across government-sponsored adverts, with six encountering them only on television, four only online, and two both on television and online. Television adverts were more favorably received, with participants describing them in positive terms, and mentioning seeing several of them. For one participant, the success of television adverts lay in their audio-visual form, which added to their "straightforward" character:

> I think all of them were equally successful. But there was a lot of it on television. A lot of information got to me through television. And television communication was the most straightforward in my opinion.
> *(Pol-06, female, 43, rural)*

Another participant, who was equally positive about government-sponsored TV adverts, also contrasted them favorably with regular, commercial adverts:

> There's a lot of it. And I must say that I don't switch the channel when it's on television, unlike other commercials, when I immediately change the channel. They are not that annoying I must say.
> *(Pol-07, female, 46, rural)*

In contrast, pop-up adverts encountered online were largely dismissed, with participants arguing that they did not really pay attention to them, or felt they repeated information they already had. Nonetheless, it is worth noting that participants appeared to remember the content of these adverts in considerable detail. The following two extracts offer a case in point:

> I don't really pay attention to … Oh you mean this social campaign about the coronavirus. Then yes, I've seen this one short clip online. I think

there were two clips actually. At first, there were written recommendations and later the government made a clip about it and it popped up on my YouTube page. It was about social interactions featuring a father with his son.

(Pol-14, male, 25, urban)

For me personally, the most effective were the ads displayed in between YouTube clips. And some graphics issued by the Health Ministry. But it didn't say anything I hadn't heard before or it said things that seemed too obvious."

(Pol-24, female, 24, urban)

Despite frequent encounters with direct government communication in a range of forms, it is important to highlight the fact that the majority of our participants (20 out of 29) also frequently mentioned relying on news reports, and found these reports to be equally important as live broadcasts of government press conferences. The primary reason for that was that media reports made the information more readily understandable than direct government communication; and provided essential information on new restrictions and recent developments in a concise and easily accessible form. For instance, one participant drew a telling contrast between the official COVID-19 website and news reports:

Yes. I haven't been using the official websites directly. Because they write in a specific manner suitable for the government. I don't understand what they mean sometimes. Today the President of Narodowy Bank Polski said something about the sales of stocks. For an average person to understand, they need to be more straightforward and say things more clearly.

(Pol-15, male, 38, rural)

In sum, although all participants reported coming into contact with at least one form of government communication, and the majority found live broadcasts of government's press conferences particularly effective, news reports remained a vital source of information for the majority as well. Although such news reports were arguably very close to direct government communication, our data suggest that they played an important role in making government messaging more accessible and effective.

Polarization and the Use of Public Service Media

While our participants generally trusted government communication on the pandemic, and also relied on government-controlled public service media channels to access information on the pandemic, their attitudes to these channels nonetheless differed significantly depending on their political orientation, which suggests that polarization did indeed shape audience engagement to a degree. Yet, as we show below, this polarization did not extent to our participants' responses to controversy surrounding elections; interestingly, this controversy led to a deterioration of trust in the government among a significant number of our participants, including some who were otherwise supportive of the government. This indicates that polarization – while present – had its limits.

Over half of our participants (16) mentioned consuming more public service media than prior to the pandemic – a trend clearly noticeable also in some of the diaries. Public service media increased also among some of the anti-government participants, who avoided them prior to the pandemic because they found them politically biased – a change evident from the comparison of news consumption profiles created based comparing the first and second wave of interviews, but also directly acknowledged in interviews. As one of our anti-government participants explained:

> Before I watched *Wiadomości* on *TVP* only sporadically. During the pandemic, we would switch the channel to watch *Wiadomości* intentionally. So we tuned to *TVP* more often and with the intention of watching it.
> *(Pol-07, female, 46 rural)*

Several of our anti-government participants also made it clear that the main reason for greater reliance on public service media during the pandemic was access to government communication, and that their general assessment of the trustworthiness of public service media as a source of other news remained negative. The following excerpt from an anti-government participant illustrates this attitude very clearly:

> *TVP Info* was the easiest to access, it's one of the main channels and that's why I started watching it. At some point, it was all beginning to look the same to me. But I turned to *TVP Info* to get the coronavirus information. When it comes to political news, I turned mainly to the Internet and online discussion boards.
> *(Pol-09 male, 30, urban)*

Some of our anti-government participants also mentioned checking the information received through public service media against information broadcast by commercial broadcasters, which were perceived as more independent. For instance, one of our participants mentioned watching both the daily news bulletin *Dziennik Telewizyjny* broadcast on the public service channel TVP1, and the *Fakty* news bulletin on the commercial channel *TVN*:

> Almost every day I watched *Fakty*, sometimes we watched *Dziennik Telewizyjny* as well, to compare news. Some facts are just facts irrespective

of the political sentiment of the channel broadcasting. Separating the interpretation from the facts is enough to get a picture of what's happening. To be up to speed with what's going on, it's necessary to know the numbers, news on the restrictions implemented. Knowing this was important to me.

(Pol-04, female, 62, rural)

One might perhaps expect that these disparate, polarized attitudes toward government-controlled channels, as presented above, would have provided fertile grounds for equally polarized responses to the government's handling of elections. Yet, our analysis suggests that concerns about the risks posed by conducting elections amidst a pandemic were shared also by most of our pro-government participants, who felt the government was willing to risk the health of citizens in the interest of pursuing its own political interests. Indeed, when it came to responses to the controversy surrounding elections, it was difficult to discern significant differences between views expressed by critical pro-government participants, and those expressed by anti-government participants. For instance, in the extract below, taken from a media diary on 19 March 2020, one of our anti-government participants describes being shocked by the behavior of President Andrzej Duda, who continued to collect signatures from his supporters regardless of risks this posed for public health:

5:00 pm, *TVP1 Teleexpress* – The anti-crisis shield is to help entrepreneurs, assures the President. New border crossings have been opened to increase the flow of traffic. They again discussed research according to which the PiS government has received more and more support by over 9 percent. What a failure! Duda has collected more supporting signatures than required. My husband is shocked because everyone is being called not to leave their homes while Duda collects his supporting signatures.

(Pol-07, female, 46, rural)

Only a minority of pro-government participants supported the government's attempts to continue with the presidential campaign, and had no safety concerns about participating in the elections during a pandemic. To justify their position, these participants tended to repeat the arguments provided via public service media – including the idea that postponing the election may pose a threat for Polish democracy. The following quote provides a good illustration of the attitudes shared by this small group:

There are some voices that the election is a threat to public health. But, I don't think there is any safer way to conduct the election, although I'm not a strong proponent of voting at this time myself. We should go with the lesser evil, but I don't really see any evil in that. I think that election has to take place, because knowing our opposition…. If until 4 August, when the President finishes his term, the election doesn't take place, the opposition will refute everything.

(Pol-05, male, 51, urban)

Conclusion

Although we should be mindful of the small scale and qualitative nature of our data, these results provide important new insights into audience engagement with government communication in Poland. First, they highlight the effectiveness of live coverage of government's press conference as the most effective means of government communication, while also noting the continued reliance on news reports as the more accessible and concise source of information about key developments. Second, our results suggest that existing levels of political and media polarization in the country had only a moderate impact on audience engagement with government communication, which was at the beginning perceived largely positively. This is broadly compatible with the findings by Schraff (2020) or Bol et al. (2020), confirming citizens' increased political support in the initial phase of the pandemic, even if the rally-around-the-flag was perhaps not as visible in the Polish case as in some other countries – certainly not to the extent seen for example in the UK, Germany, or Australia (see also Chapter 1). As we have seen, most participants, regardless of political orientation and regardless of general misgivings about the government and about government-controlled public service media, tended to trust government communication on COVID-19. Furthermore, although the government's handling of the elections provoked contrasting responses among participants, these were only partially aligned with political leanings. The majority of our pro-government participants was critical of the decision to continue with the campaign, and expressed disappointment at the government for putting its political interests over and above the safety of tis citizens.

We can therefore conclude that in the Polish case, the disappearance of the rally-around-the-flag phenomenon in the later phase of the first wave of the pandemic can only partly be explained as a consequence of pre-existing polarization. Rather, it was the government's mishandling of the elections that caused public trust to drop across the political spectrum. The dip in viewing figures for the government-controlled public broadcaster between December 2019 and May 2020 (Van Aelst et al., 2021) can likewise be explained in this context, as a reflection of a general decline in media trust in response to the controversy surrounding elections, and the attempt by the government to politicize and "presidentialize" the pandemic communication, rather than as an indicator of the public broadcasters' lack of perceived credibility on the actual issue of the pandemic. On the contrary, most of our interviewees seemed to have been able to separate factual information from political bias in their use and critical perception of *TVP* broadcasting. To put it differently, despite a notable level of existing political polarization, our results suggest that the Polish public was, to a degree, united in their rejection of the politicization of the pandemic. This lends support for the thesis that polarization, while still playing a role in shaping citizens' news habits, does not necessarily have to completely hinder government communication in times of severe crisis, such as the pandemic. It could be argued that it was rather the chaos around the 2020 Presidential Election that damaged the – already fragile – trust between the government and the Polish citizens during the pandemic, which otherwise Poland managed to cope with relatively successfully during the first wave, being hailed as one of the exemplars of halting the pandemic in the spring (Sirotnikova et al., 2020). Further research should attempt to explore to what extent this damage of trust could have contributed to the dramatically harder impact of the second wave of the pandemic in the autumn 2020, which, sadly, saw Poland among the worst affected countries in Europe (Kość, 2020). In any case, it is clear that the collision of a planned, routine political event with an unexpected public health emergency has thrown democracy and political communication into a largely uncharted territory. Given the disruptive effects of the pandemic on political life, these changes will undoubtedly draw more research attention in the future.

References

Ágh, A. (2016). Cultural war and reinventing the past in Poland and Hungary: The politics of historical memory in east–central Europe. *Polish Political Science Yearbook*, 45(1), 32–44. https://doi.org/10.15804/ppsy2016003
Barnett, B., & Roselle, L. (2008). Patriotism in the news: "Rally round the flag." *Electronic News*, 2(1), 10–30. https://doi.org/10.1080/19312430701807713
Bavel, J. J. V., Baicker, K., Boggio, P. S., Capraro, V., Cichocka, A., Cikara, M … Willer, R. (2020). Using social and behavioural science to support COVID-19 pandemic response. *Nature Human Behaviour*, 4(5), 460–471. https://doi.org/10.1038/s41562-020-0884-z
Bol, D., Giani, M., Blais, A., & Loewen, P. J. (2020). The effect of COVID-19 lockdowns on political support: Some good news for democracy? *European Journal of Political Research*, 60(2), 497–505. https://doi.org/10.1111/1475-6765.12401
Braun, V., & Clarke, V. (2006). Using thematic analysis in psychology. *Qualitative Research in Psychology*, 3(2), 77–101. https://doi.org/10.1191/1478088706qp063oa
Briggs, C. L., & Hallin, D. C. (2017). *Making health public: How news coverage is remaking media, medicine, and contemporary life*. Routledge.
Casero-Ripollés, A. (2020). Impact of Covid-19 on the media system. Communicative and democratic consequences of news consumption during the outbreak. *El Profesional de La Información*, 29(2), 1–11. https://doi.org/10.3145/epi.2020.mar.23
CBOS. (2018). *O nieufności i zaufaniu [On distrust and trust]* (No. 35/2018).
Csaky, Z. (2020). *Nations in transit 2020*. Freedom House. https://freedomhouse.org/report/nations-transit/2020/dropping-democratic-facade

Daniels, N. (2020, November 5). Lesson of the day: 'How Poland's new abortion law became a flash point.' *The New York Times.* https://www.nytimes.com/2020/11/05/learning/lesson-of-the-day-how-polands-new-abortion-law-became-a-flash-point.html

Edelman. (2018). *Trust barometer: Global report.* Edelman.

Edelman. (2020). *Trust barometer: Global report.* Edelman.

Giorgi, E. D., & Moury, C. (2015). Conclusions: Great recession, great cooperation? *The Journal of Legislative Studies, 21*(1), 115–120. https://doi.org/10.1080/13572334.2014.939560

Glenny, M., Borchardt, A., Štětka, V., & Kaczorowski, A. (2020, August 25). *A new threat to press freedom: Lawsuits* [Politico]. https://www.politico.eu/article/a-new-threat-to-press-journalism-freedo

Green, J., Edgerton, J., Naftel, D., Shoub, K., & Cranmer, S. J. (2020). Elusive consensus: Polarization in elite communication on the COVID-19 pandemic. *Science Advances, 6*(28), 1–5. https://doi.org/10.1126/sciadv.abc2717

Grzesiok-Horosz, A. (2019). Krajowa Rada Radiofonii i Telewizji a Rada Mediów Narodowych [The National Council of Radio Broadcasting and Television and the National Media Council]. *Studia Politicae Universitatis Silesiensis, 27,* 103–132. https://doi.org/10.31261/SPUS.2019.27.05

Hart, P. S., Chinn, S., & Soroka, S. (2020). Politicization and polarization in COVID-19 news coverage. *Science Communication, 42*(5), 679–697. https://doi.org/10.1177/1075547020950735

Hetherington, M. J., & Nelson, M. (2003). Anatomy of a rally effect: George W. Bush and the war on terrorism. *PS: Political Science and Politics, 36*(1), 37–42.

Jarynowski, A., Wójta-Kempa, M., Płatek, D., & Czopek, K. (2020). *Attempt to understand public health relevant social dimensions of COVID-19 outbreak in Poland* (SSRN Scholarly Paper ID 3570609). Social Science Research Network. https://doi.org/10.2139/ssrn.3570609

Kość, W. (2020, November 2). *Where did it go wrong for Poland's pandemic response?* [Notes from Poland]. https://notesfrompoland.com/2020/11/02/where-did-it-go-wrong-for-polands-pandemic-response/

Krzysztofik, R., Kantor-Pietraga, I., & Spórna, T. (2020). Spatial and functional dimensions of the COVID-19 epidemic in Poland. *Eurasian Geography and Economics, 61*(4–5), 573–586. https://doi.org/10.1080/15387216.2020.1783337

Krzyżanowska, N., & Krzyżanowski, M. (2018). 'Crisis' and migration in Poland: Discursive shifts, anti-pluralism and the politicisation of exclusion. *Sociology, 52*(3), 612–618. https://doi.org/10.1177/0038038518757952

Krzyżanowski, M. (2018). Discursive shifts in ethno-nationalist politics: On politicization and mediatization of the "refugee crisis" in Poland. *Journal of Immigrant & Refugee Studies, 16*(1–2), 76–96. https://doi.org/10.1080/15562948.2017.1317897

Mihelj, S., Kondor, K., & Štětka, V. (2021). Audience engagement with Covid-19 news: The impact of lockdown, live coverage, and polarization. *Journalism Studies.* https://doi.org/10.1080/1461670X.2021.1931410

Moroń, M., & Biolik-Moroń, M. (2021). Trait emotional intelligence and emotional experiences during the COVID-19 pandemic outbreak in Poland: A daily diary study. *Personality and Individual Differences, 168,* 1–11. https://doi.org/10.1016/j.paid.2020.110348

Motta, M., Stecula, D., & Farhart, C. (2020). How right-leaning media coverage of COVID-19 facilitated the spread of misinformation in the early stages of the pandemic in the U.S. *Canadian Journal of Political Science/Revue Canadienne de Science Politique, 53*(2), 335–342. https://doi.org/10.1017/S0008423920000396

NEC. (2020, March 9). *Informacja Państwowej Komisji Wyborczej z dnia 9 kwietnia 2020 r. [Information from the National Electoral Commission of 9 April 2020]*. National Electoral Commission. https://prezydent20200510.pkw.gov.pl/prezydent20200510/pl/informacje/37191

Newman, N., Fletcher, R., Levy, D. A. L., & Kleis Nielsen, R. (2016). *Reuters institute digital news report 2016*. Reuters Institute for the Study of Journalism.

Newman, N., Fletcher, R., Schulz, A., Andi, S., & Kleis Nielsen, R. (2020). *Reuters Institute Digital News Report 2020*. Reuters Institute for the Study of Journalism.

Nielsen, R. K., Fletcher, R., Newman, N., Brennen, J. S., & Howard, P. N. (2020). *Navigating the 'infodemic': How people in six countries access and rate news and information about coronavirus* (p. 36). Reuters Institute for the Study of Journalism.

Przybylski, W. (2018). Explaining Eastern Europe: Can Poland's backsliding be stopped? *Journal of Democracy, 29*(3), 52–64.

Radio Zet. (2020, April 20). *Wybory prezydenckie 2020. Kidawa-Błońska wznowi kampanię? PO uznało wzywanie do bojkotu za błąd [Presidential Election 2020. Kidawa-Błońska will resume campaign? The PO considered the boycott call to be a mistake]*. https://wiadomosci.radiozet.pl/Polityka/Wybory-prezydenckie-2020/Wybory-prezydenckie-2020.-Kidawa-Blonska-wznowi-kampanie-PO-uznalo-wzywanie-do-bojkotu-za-blad

Reynolds, A., & Barnett, B. (2003). This just in … How national TV news handled the breaking "live" coverage of September 11. *Journalism & Mass Communication Quarterly, 80*(3), 689–703. https://doi.org/10.1177/107769900308000312

RMF FM. (2020, December 19). *Sondaż dla "DGP" i RMF FM: "Tak" dla ustawy dyscyplinującej sędziów [Poll For 'DGP' and RMF FM: 'Yes' For the Law Disciplining Judges]*. https://www.rmf24.pl/raporty/raport-batalia-o-sady/fakty/news-sondaz-dla-dgp-i-rmf-fm-tak-dla-ustawy-dyscyplinujacej-sedzi, nId, 4233584

Roozenbeek, J., Schneider, C. R., Dryhurst, S., Kerr, J., Freeman, A. L. J., Recchia, G., … van der Linden, S. (2020). Susceptibility to misinformation about COVID-19 around the world. *Royal Society Open Science, 7*(10), 1–15. https://doi.org/10.1098/rsos.201199

Sadurski, W. (2018). *How democracy dies (in Poland): A case study of anti-constitutional populist backsliding* (SSRN Scholarly Paper ID 3103491). Social Science Research Network. https://doi.org/10.2139/ssrn.3103491

Sadurski, W. (2019). *Poland's constitutional breakdown*. Oxford University Press.

Schraff, D. (2020). Political trust during the Covid-19 pandemic: Rally around the flag or lockdown effects? *European Journal of Political Research*, 1–11. https://doi.org/10.1111/1475-6765.12425

Selva, M. (2020). *Fighting words: Journalism under assault in Central and Eastern Europe* (p. 32). Reuters Institute for the Study of Journalism.

Serowaniec, M., & Witkowski, Z. (2020). Can legislative standards be subject to 'quarantine'? The functioning of the Tablet Sejm in Poland in the COVID-19 era. *The Theory and Practice of Legislation, 8*(1–2), 155–170. https://doi.org/10.1080/20508840.2020.1805851

Sides, J., Tausanovitch, C., & Vavreck, L. (2020). The politics of COVID-19: Partisan polarization about the pandemic has increased, but support for health care reform hasn't moved at all. *Harvard Data Science Review*, 1–12. https://doi.org/10.1162/99608f92.611350fd

Simonov, A., Sacher, S., Dube, J.-P., & Biswas, S. (2020). The persuasive effect of Fox News: Non-compliance with social distancing during the COVID-19 pandemic. In *Working Papers* (No. 2020–67; Working Papers). Becker Friedman Institute for Research in Economics. https://ideas.repec.org/p/bfi/wpaper/2020-67.html

Sirotnikova, M. G., Inotai, E., Watson, N., & Ciobanu, C. (2020, October 15). Central Europe: From pandemic exemplar to pariah. *Balkan Insight*. https://balkaninsight.com/2020/10/15/central-europe-from-pandemic-exemplar-to-pariah/

Sorokowski, P., Groyecka, A., Kowal, M., Sorokowska, A., Białek, M., Lebuda, I., ... Karwowski, M. (2020). Can information about pandemics increase negative attitudes toward foreign groups? A case of COVID-19 outbreak. *Sustainability*, *12*(12), 1–10.

Surowiec, P., Kania-Lundholm, M., & Winiarska-Brodowska, M. (2020). Towards illiberal conditioning? New politics of media regulations in Poland (2015–2018). *East European Politics*, *36*(1), 27–43. https://doi.org/10.1080/21599165.2019.1608826

Szabó, J. (2020). First as tragedy, then as farce: A comparative study of right-wing populism in Hungary and Poland. *Journal of Comparative Politics*, *13*(2), 24–42.

Tworzecki, H. (2019). Poland: A case of top-down polarization. *The Annals of the American Academy of Political and Social Science*, *681*(1), 97–119. https://doi.org/10.1177/0002716218809322

Van Aelst, P., Toth, F., Castro, L., Štětka, V., de Vreese, C. H., Aalberg, T., ... Theocharis, Y. (2021). Does a crisis change news habits? A comparative study of the effects of COVID-19 on news media use in 17 European countries. *Digital Journalism*, https://doi.org/10.1080/21670811.2021.1943481

Vashchanka, V. (2020). *Political manoeuvres and legal conundrums amid the COVID-19 pandemic: The 2020 presidential election in Poland*. International Institute for Democracy and Electoral Assistance.

WHO. (2020, September 23). *Managing the COVID-19 infodemic: Promoting healthy behaviours and mitigating the harm from misinformation and disinformation*. https://www.who.int/news/item/23-09-2020-managing-the-covid-19-infodemic-promoting-healthy-behaviours-and-mitigating-the-harm-from-misinformation-and-disinformation

Wiseman, O. (2020, April 11). *How coronavirus punctured the Brexit-Trump parallels* [Politico]. https://www.politico.com/news/magazine/2020/04/11/coronavirus-uk-us-brexit-trump-177924

Żuk, P. (2020). One leader, one party, one truth: Public television under the rule of the populist right in Poland in the pre-election period in 2019. *Javnost – The Public*, *27*(3), 287–307. https://doi.org/10.1080/13183222.2020.1794413

13
THE SWEDISH WAY

How Ideology and Media Use Influenced the Formation, Maintenance and Change of Beliefs about the Coronavirus

Adam Shehata, Isabella Glogger and Kim Andersen

Sweden's handling of the COVID-19 pandemic has provoked extensive international attention. Based on voluntary social distancing rather than lockdowns, the strategy contrasted sharply with most other countries in Europe – generating both praise and criticism. With numbers of COVID-19-related deaths surging, however, discussions about "the Swedish way" quickly became polarized in Sweden and abroad.

In addition to being a polarized issue, the COVID-19 pandemic is characterized by widespread uncertainty in all its aspects: uncertainty with respect to the nature of the virus; uncertainty with respect to public and personal health; uncertainty regarding the social, political and economic consequences of the pandemic; uncertainty about how to best contain further spread. This chapter focuses on how citizens make up their minds about a highly pressing issue characterized by uncertainty and polarization, such as the COVID-19 pandemic.

To this end, this chapter examines public opinion formation in Sweden during the first six months of the COVID-19 pandemic. Data come from a unique representative three-wave panel survey among Swedish citizens collected during this period. Three broad questions anchored in the literature on media effects and sociotropic beliefs are addressed. First, we describe how public opinion developed over time in response to media coverage and real-world developments. Second, we turn to the antecedents of beliefs. Based on theories of sociotropic belief formation, the analysis focuses on how citizens' ideology, personal experience, social networks and media use influence their beliefs about the coronavirus disease. Third, we study the importance of initial belief formation for subsequent opinion dynamics – looking specifically at the role of ideology and news media use as factors behind belief maintenance and updating over time.

DOI: 10.4324/9781003170051-16

The Formation of Sociotropic Beliefs

How citizens form perceptions about societal developments and problems has been a key issue in communication and public opinion research for a long time. On the one hand, so-called sociotropic beliefs are fundamental for political accountability and voting behavior. How citizens perceive the major challenges facing the country, their causes and consequences, ultimately shape how governments are held responsible during elections. On the other hand, few people have first-hand experiences or knowledge of most societal issues. As Lippmann succinctly noted almost 100 years ago, the world that we have to deal with politically is "out of reach, out of sight, and out of mind" (Lippmann, 1922, p. 18). Even when citizens do have personal experiences relating to specific problems, it remains unclear how these are generalized into perceptions of broader societal conditions. Thus, judgments about collective experiences constitute a foundation of public opinion – and such inferences are made constantly as part of people's everyday lives and interactions with their social surroundings.

Theories of sociotropic belief formation stress the significance of *media coverage* in shaping perceptions of society (Mutz, 1998; Shehata & Strömbäck, 2014). Media coverage is also believed to be specifically important when people lack alternative sources of information or personal experiences, as highlighted by media system dependency theory (Ball-Rokeach, 2010). More specific theories of media effects, such as agenda setting (McCombs, 2014), cultivation (Morgan, Shanahan, & Signorielli, 2015) and framing (Lecheler & De Vreese, 2018), emphasize particular relationships between media content characteristics, issue characteristics and individual characteristics in shaping perceptions of societal conditions. In all cases, however, cues from the media play a distinct role in terms of influencing beliefs about collective experiences.

Apart from the traditional media, the literature on sociotropic belief formation outlines three other sources that matter: ideological or partisan rationalization, interpersonal communication and personal experiences. First, research shows that citizens' political identities color their perceptions of societal conditions. Political *rationalization* comes into play when people assess issues that are highly politicized and polarized. Research on motivated reasoning (Taber & Lodge, 2006), cultural cognition (Kahan, Jenkins-Smith, & Braman, 2011) and partisan perceptual screening (Bisgaard, 2015) shows that these mechanisms cut across various issue domains. Second, *personal experiences* with everything from unemployment, health care and crime to less tangible issues, such as climate change, have potential to exert a great impact on sociotropic beliefs (Egan & Mullin, 2012; Kinder & Kiewiet, 1981; Kumlin, 2004). Making inferences about societal conditions from personal experiences involves a specific type of generalization from the personal to the political. Third, everyday *interpersonal conversation* with family and friends is a key source of information and opinions as well. Not only do citizens learn about the experience of others from everyday talk, but such discussions also serve a "filtering function" where perceptions and opinions are socially negotiated and validated (Gamson, 1992; Schmitt-Beck, 2003).

These factors potentially played an important role during the COVID-19 pandemic. In just a few weeks of February and March 2020, the collective media agenda quickly shifted in response to real-world developments and actions taken by international organizations and governments around the world. Intense media coverage, extensive public restrictions and lockdowns, massive mobilization of health-care services and profound economic downturn and layoffs have significant repercussions on people's lives. During these times of uncertainty coupled with great personal and societal risks, information (and misinformation) spread rapidly across media and social networking platforms – turning into a war of worldviews, where beliefs about the coronavirus and appropriate regulations were quickly politicized.

The Swedish Case: COVID-19 and the Great Uncertainty

Sweden's handling of the COVID-19 pandemic drew international attention and became a topic of extensive discussions. While neighboring countries, such as Denmark and Norway, quickly implemented major lockdowns and restrictions in March 2020, the Swedish strategy relied on voluntary social distancing. Schools, shops, restaurants and workplaces were kept open – even though large groups of people also worked from home. The Swedish strategy was led by the *Public Health Authority* (PHA) while the government largely followed their advice from a "back-seat" position. This arrangement differed from many other countries and reflects a system of highly autonomous public agencies in Sweden. Thus, the left-wing coalition government led by the Social Democratic Party played a much less prominent role compared to many other countries:

> Already at an early stage of the crisis, it was clear that the core executive, i.e. the Prime Minister and other Cabinet ministers and their staff, would not be operationally involved in the crisis management. Instead, agencies like the PHA and the NBHW were to take the lead by virtue of their expertise on pandemics.
>
> *(Pierre, 2020, p. 483)*

Early discussions concerning the "Swedish way" were triggered by the different approaches taken by neighboring Nordic countries as well as the rest of Europe. In that sense, questions grounded in fundamental uncertainties – How severe is the current pandemic? How does the virus spread? How dangerous is it? Who is vulnerable? What is the best strategy for fighting it? – permeated public discussions and actions from the very beginning. At the same time, however, public support for the Swedish government and the Public Health Authority was widespread initially. As in many other countries, Sweden witnessed a substantial rally-around-the-flag effect following the outbreak of COVID-19 (Johansson, Hopmann, & Shehata, 2021). Government approval increased significantly from 34% to 65% during the initial phase of the pandemic (Andersson & Oscarsson, 2020; see also Esaiasson, Sohlberg, Ghersetti, & Johansson, 2020).

Criticism toward the government and the PHA strategy gradually became more intense, however (Esaiasson et al., 2020). With rapidly increasing numbers of deaths, Sweden contrasted remarkably to the other Nordic countries not only in terms of the overall corona strategy, but with respect to mortality rates as well. These country differences were evident already at an early stage and Swedish mortality rates remained substantively higher throughout the year.

In light of the extraordinary circumstances that characterize the coronavirus as a societal problem, a few aspects may be of particular importance for belief formation and updating. First, COVID-19 quickly emerged as an entirely new issue on the political and media agenda. Most citizens had very little prior knowledge of the virus and its implications at the outset – and would therefore be highly susceptible to early belief formation influences. Second, the salience of the coronavirus on the media agenda during the initial months made it almost impossible for anyone to avoid it. Developments related to the coronavirus crowded out most other issues on the media agenda from mid-March and onward (Esaiasson et al., 2020). The combination of weak (or non-existent) prior beliefs and high salience on the media agenda is precisely the condition that should promote belief change rather than stability over time (Druckman & Leeper, 2012). Third, while COVID-19 dominated the media agenda for months, real-world developments also had profound impact on people's everyday lives. From a media effects perspective, we are dealing with an obtrusive issue, where people's personal experiences may either resonate or contrast with news coverage (McCombs, 2014; Mutz, 1998).

How citizens' perceptions are shaped in such exceptional and uncertain times is not very well-known. In this chapter, we therefore look specifically at the development of public beliefs about the coronavirus as a societal problem during the first six months of the pandemic. In doing so, we return to some basic questions in the public opinion literature. More specifically, three research questions will be addressed:

RQ1: How stable or sensitive are citizens' sociotropic COVID-19 beliefs over time?

RQ2: How does ideology, personal experiences, interpersonal communication and media use influence sociotropic COVID-19 beliefs?

RQ3: How do these factors influence stability and change of COVID-19 beliefs over time?

We rely on data from a unique three-wave panel survey conducted in Sweden between April and September 2020. The survey was conducted by the Laboratory of Opinion Research (LORE) at the University of Gothenburg, using a probability-based sample of web survey participants. A sample of 4,000 respondents, stratified on gender, age and education, was drawn from LORE's pool of probability-recruited participants. Wave 1 was fielded in late April (April 14–May 8), wave 2 in June 2018 (June 9–July 1) and wave 3 in August (August 17–September 9). In terms of respondents, 2,347 participated in wave 1 (58%), 2,229 in wave 2 (55%) and 1,985 in wave 3 (52%). A total of 1,716 respondents participated in all three waves.

Change and Stability of Sociotropic COVID-19 Beliefs in Sweden

One of the most fundamental issues in public opinion research concerns the stability and mutability of citizens' beliefs and attitudes. This question goes to the heart of the nature and characteristics of mass beliefs. Do people have "real", elaborated and strongly anchored opinions on various societal matters – or are beliefs on policy issues expressed in different social settings highly sensitive to contextual cues and what comes to people's mind at the moment (Slater, 2015; Zaller, 1992)?

Attitudes and beliefs are of course two separate concepts that may display distinct processes of stability and change. While beliefs refer to perceptions of social reality, attitudes are evaluations (positive or negative) toward objects (Potter, 2012). Perceptions are sometimes considered more sensitive and mutable – and thereby open for influence – than attitudes (McCombs, Holbert, Kiousis & Wanta, 2012). This is, however, a position that can be questioned on several grounds. First, if we think of beliefs not as isolated perceptual elements, but rather as anchored in citizens' cognitive schemas, the stability of beliefs may be much greater than commonly assumed. Cognitive schemas are typically considered highly stable over time – and human consistency mechanisms operate in ways that maintain and reinforce established schemas rather than change them (Matthes, 2008; Fiske & Taylor, 2017). Approaching beliefs from a schema perspective highlights a number of specific schema characteristics that condition belief stability, including level of schema development and abstraction (Shehata et al., 2021). Second, many beliefs are not pure perceptions but rather anchored in political values and attitudes. Whenever specific perceptions are strongly tied to political and social identities, they become more resistant to change (Slater, 2015).

Levels of belief stability and change depend on both individual and environmental factors. Looking specifically at opinion dynamics, Druckman and Leeper (2012) argue that attitude change/stability is a function of attitude strength and exposure to attitude-relevant stimuli. More specifically, change is most likely when individuals hold weak attitudes and are exposed to intense communication (see also Zaller, 1992). In contrast, while strong attitudes are always resistant, weakly held attitudes remain intact in the absence of stimuli. In a similar vein, Wilson and Hodges (1992) note that "stable attitudes are those with stable contexts" (p. 53). But the context was definitely not stable during the first months of the COVID-19 pandemic. Media coverage was massive. Events and developments were characterized by great uncertainties. And compared to most other issues that citizens are confronted with, people had no long-standing established beliefs or attitudes toward COVID-19 before these dramatic developments played out. As such, we could expect a substantial amount of belief volatility during the first months of the pandemic.

Figure 13.1 shows how beliefs about the coronavirus among Swedish citizens developed from April to September. Respondents were asked a series of survey questions on the impact of COVID-19 on Swedish society. More specifically, the sample was presented with a number of factual statements about the coronavirus. Response scale ranges from 1 to 7 and capture the extent to which they disagree ("Not true at all") or agree ("Completely true") with each statement. To also get a first glimpse of whether there are ideological gaps in perceptions about the coronavirus, Figure 13.1 displays trends among left-wing and right-wing citizens separately. The top row of the figure presents findings on what could be considered a first dimension of corona beliefs, perceptions about the scale of the coronavirus as a societal problem, while the bottom row focuses on a second dimension, perceptions of how Sweden has managed the coronavirus.

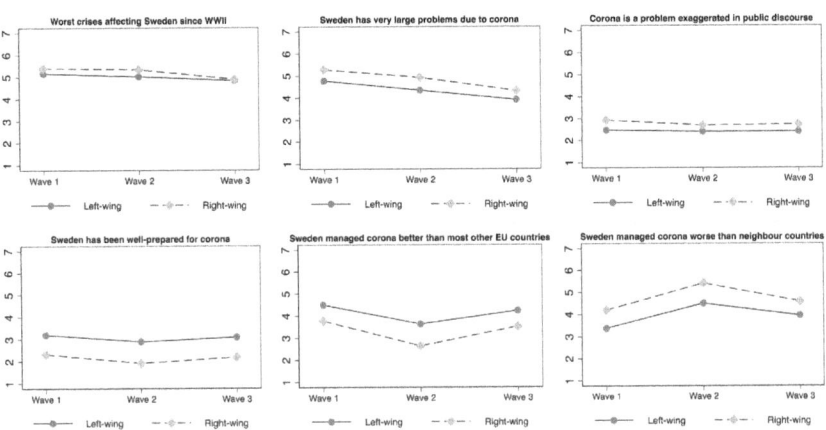

FIGURE 13.1 The development of beliefs about the coronavirus over time (mean values).

Note: Each graph presents mean values on the 1–7 belief scales, where 1 represents "Not true at all" and 7 "Completely true". Political ideology is measured in the first panel wave based on an 11-point left-right ideological placement scale. "Left-wing" represents respondents with a strong left-leaning position on the original scale (0–2) while "Right-wing" represents respondents with a strong right-leaning position (8–9).

Overall, there are indeed significant shifts over time with respect to some of the beliefs. For instance, agreement to the belief statement "Sweden has managed the coronavirus *better* than most other EU countries" decreases by an entire scale point from wave 1 ($M = 4.21$, $SD = 1.49$) to wave 2 ($M = 3.20$, $SD = 1.53$), in order to increase again in wave 3 ($M = 3.92$, $SD = 1.62$). A very similar non-linear trend characterizes the belief statement "Sweden managed the coronavirus *worse* than our neighboring countries". In wave 1, respondents tended to disagree with this statement ($M = 3.69$, $SD = 1.84$), but this changed significantly in the following wave ($M = 4.84$, $SD = 1.86$), in order to partly regress toward a baseline in wave 3 ($M = 4.19$, $SD = 1.90$). These changes are statistically significant. Thus, Swedish citizens responded by continuously updating their beliefs following real-world developments and media coverage. The statistical significance has already been noted.

Other beliefs displayed significant changes over time as well. Overall, there is strong agreement that "The coronavirus is the worst crisis affecting Sweden since World War II", but agreement fell gradually from wave 1 ($M = 5.33$, $SD=1.76$) to wave 3 ($M = 4.89$, $SD = 1.81$). There is, however, much less agreement on the belief that "Sweden has been well-prepared to handle the coronavirus". These numbers were low already in the initial phase ($M = 2.89$, $SD = 1.55$), but decreased further in wave 2 ($M = 2.47$, $SD = 1.41$) before increasing somewhat again in wave 3 ($M = 2.67$, $SD = 1.50$). The belief that "Sweden has very large problems today due to corona" is prevalent among Swedish citizens, but also decreased significantly over time – from wave 1 ($M = 4.97$, $SD = 1.61$) through wave 2 ($M = 4.62$, $SD = 1.59$) to wave 3 ($M = 4.07$, $SD = 1.58$). Few believe, however, that "The coronavirus is a problem exaggerated in public discourse" and mean values remain highly stable across wave 1 ($M = 2.65$, $SD = 1.63$), wave 2 ($M = 2.54$, $SD = 1.55$) and wave 3 ($M = 2.61$, $SD = 1.57$).

Speaking to ideological belief gaps, Figure 13.1 shows how beliefs differ between left-wing and right-wing citizens – but these gaps are more pronounced with respect to perceptions of how Sweden has managed the coronavirus (bottom part of the figure) than perceptions about the magnitude of the problem (upper part). Right-wing citizens have consistently more negative perceptions of how Sweden managed the coronavirus than left-wing citizens. These ideological gaps are evident already in the initial phase – and remain consistent over time. Thus, although substantial belief changes took place over time in response to real-world developments and media coverage, there are few indications of increasing belief polarization.

Factors Influencing Beliefs about the Coronavirus in Sweden

Theories of sociotropic belief formation suggest that societal perceptions are shaped by a combination of ideological predispositions, personal experiences, interpersonal communication and media use. Figure 13.2 focuses particularly on these factors. In addition, we include corona-specific Facebook use as a source of information. Facebook is by far the most widely used social media platform for news in Sweden. Looking at each belief statement about the COVID-19 pandemic in Sweden separately, the graphs display findings from six cross-sectional regression models based on data from the first panel wave.

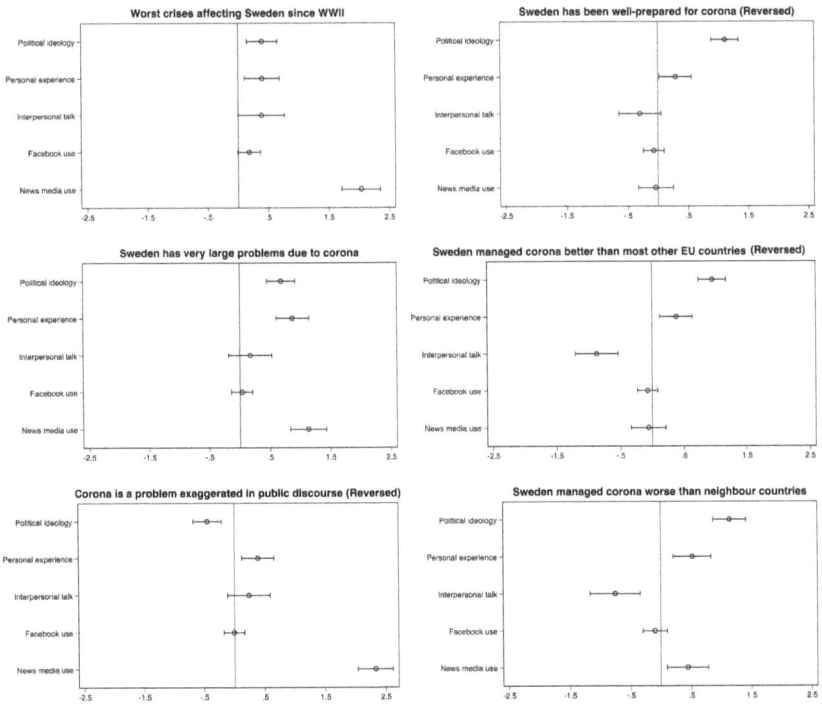

FIGURE 13.2 Factors behind beliefs about the coronavirus (unstandardized b-values).
Note: Estimates are based on six separate OLS regression models, with all predictors rescaled to range between 0 and 1. Dots represent unstandardized b-values with 95% confidence intervals. *Political ideology* is measured using a standard single-item survey question on left-right placement. *Personal experience* with COVID-19 is based on a three-item index focusing on the extent to which the coronavirus has affected respondents' (1) everyday life, (2) economic situation and (3) work situation. Corona-specific *interpersonal talk* is measured using three items on the frequency of discussions about the coronavirus with (1) family members, (2) friends or acquaintances and (3) people you don't know. *Facebook use* is measured using a single item tapping the extent to which respondents were exposed to news, information or discussions via Facebook. News media use is based on a four-item battery tapping the extent to which respondents (1) are uninterested in news about the coronavirus, (2) follow news about the coronavirus every day, (3) try to avoid news about the coronavirus and (4) try to follow news about the coronavirus as much as possible. When relevant, specific items were reversed before added into an index.

All variables are recoded to range between 0 and 1 in order to allow a comparison of maximum possible effects (see figure note for survey measures). Again, we present findings for the two dimensions of corona beliefs separately, with perceptions of the scale of the problem in the left column of the figure, and perceptions of how Sweden has managed the crisis in the right column.

A number of findings emerge from Figure 13.2. To begin with, there is a relatively consistent pattern of effects across the six belief statements. A right-wing political leaning, personal experiences and news media use tend to be related to having more negative perceptions about how the coronavirus has affected Sweden. The effect of interpersonal talk is mostly non-significant, apart from two instances where more frequent discussions about the coronavirus are related to a less negative view of how the coronavirus influences Swedish society. Using Facebook as a source of news and information about the coronavirus is, however, unrelated to corona-specific beliefs.

Furthermore, political ideology and news media use appear differently related to beliefs about the coronavirus. Where ideology matters more, news media appears as less important. For instance, ideology appears to have the strongest effect on the three belief items where the specific Swedish experience and coronavirus management is explicitly evaluated – i.e., "Sweden managed the coronavirus better than most other EU countries" ($b = 0.95$, $p < 0.001$), "Sweden managed the coronavirus worse than neighboring countries" ($b = 1.14$, $p < 0.001$) and "Sweden has been well-prepared for the coronavirus" ($b = 1.11$, $p < 0.001$). In these cases, news media use has a non-significant or marginal impact. This is in contrast to belief items focusing on the magnitude of the coronavirus crisis as a societal problem, where news media use has a substantially stronger effect than ideology – such as "the Corona virus is the worst crisis affecting Sweden since World War II" ($b = 2.03$, $p < 0.001$), "Sweden has very large problems due to the coronavirus" ($b = 1.13$, $p < 0.001$) and "Corona is a problem exaggerated in public discourse" ($b = 2.33$, $p < 0.001$). Thus, ideology and news media use appear to have clearly distinct influences on beliefs. With respect to overall perceptions of the coronavirus as a societal problem, news media use is the key factor. When it comes to assessing how Sweden managed the crisis, ideological predispositions become more important

The findings presented in Figure 13.2 are based on cross-sectional data. In Table 13.1, we turn to longitudinal analyses to estimate how different factors are related to *changes* in beliefs over time. The regression models presented include the lagged dependent variable from the previous wave of the panel, and findings are reported separately for each of the two time periods of the study.

Overall, these autoregressive models confirm the picture of an effect hierarchy noted above. Political ideology and news media use stand out as the key variables behind coronavirus beliefs, while personal experience, interpersonal communication and Facebook use turn out as less important or irrelevant.

TABLE 13.1 Effects on Sociotropic Corona Beliefs (Unstandardized b-Values)

	i) Beliefs about the Magnitude of the Problem			ii) Beliefs about How Sweden Has Managed the Virus			
	World War II	Large Problems	Problems Exaggerated[a]	iii) Well Prepared for Corona[a]	iv) Other EU Countries[a]	v) Neighboring Countries	
Wave 1–Wave 2							
Lagged DV	0.46*** (0.02)	0.34*** (0.02)	0.44*** (0.02)	0.44*** (0.02)	0.47*** (0.02)	0.46*** (0.02)	
Ideology	0.24 (0.13)	0.60*** (0.12)	0.03 (0.11)	0.80*** (0.10)	0.86*** (0.11)	0.79*** (0.14)	
Experience	0.26 (0.15)	0.73*** (0.15)	0.42*** (0.13)	0.09 (0.12)	−0.09 (0.13)	−0.10 (0.16)	
Discussions	0.17 (0.19)	−0.34 (0.19)	−0.21 (0.17)	−0.23 (0.15)	−0.11 (0.17)	−0.20 (0.21)	
Facebook	−0.13 (0.09)	−0.19* (0.09)	0.01 (0.08)	0.02 (0.07)	0.08 (0.08)	−0.11 (0.10)	
News media	0.79*** (0.17)	0.24 (0.16)	1.03*** (0.15)	0.33** (0.13)	0.61*** (0.14)	0.69*** (0.17)	
R^2 adjusted	0.26	0.16	0.28	0.29	0.26	0.25	
N	1,898	1,902	1,901	1,906	1,894	1,900	
Wave 2–Wave 3							
Lagged DV	0.50*** (0.02)	0.34*** (0.02)	0.48*** (0.02)	0.59*** (0.02)	0.55*** (0.02)	0.57*** (0.02)	
Ideology	−0.08 (0.14)	0.34* (0.13)	−0.23* (0.12)	0.36*** (0.11)	0.29* (0.12)	0.35* (0.14)	
Experience	0.26 (0.16)	0.55*** (0.15)	0.26 (0.14)	0.16 (0.12)	0.25 (0.14)	0.20 (0.16)	
Discussions	0.24 (0.20)	0.33 (0.19)	0.06 (0.17)	0.01 (0.16)	0.08 (0.18)	0.01 (0.20)	
Facebook	0.06 (0.11)	0.10 (0.10)	−0.05 (0.09)	−0.17* (0.08)	−0.02 (0.10)	−0.12 (0.11)	
News media	0.74*** (0.17)	0.03 (0.15)	0.68*** (0.15)	−0.06 (0.13)	0.19 (0.15)	0.44** (0.17)	
R^2 adjusted	0.28	0.15	0.29	0.33	0.28	0.33	
N	1,763	1,766	1,699	1,766	1,762	1,765	

Note: Estimates are unstandardized b-values with standard errors in parentheses.

*p < 0.05, **p < 0.01, ***p < 0.001.
[a] Item reversed.

For instance, ideology has an effect on changes in beliefs in nine tests out of 12. News media use has a significant effect in eight tests.

The effects of ideology and news media use are also consistent. Citizens with a right-wing ideology tend to develop a more negative view on how the coronavirus affects the Swedish society over time. The same is true for news media use. Higher level of corona-related news media use is associated with increasing negative perceptions in the subsequent panel wave. The differential effects of ideology and news media use across different types of beliefs are evident here as well, but not as crystalized as in the cross-sectional situation.

The Importance of Initial Belief Formation

Our findings so far suggest that there were some significant belief changes at the aggregate level during the first six months of the COVID-19 pandemic – and that political ideology as well as news media use had a significant impact on coronavirus beliefs.

How citizens form and update sociotropic beliefs in times of great uncertainty may, however, vary significantly at the individual level. Aggregate-level trends say little about individual-level dynamics. If we, for instance, look at each belief item separately and rely on a very conservative understanding of what counts as individual-level belief stability, approximately one-third of all respondents remain on the exact same position on the 1–7 scale between wave 1 and wave 3. The mean value is 32% across the six belief items, ranging from 22% ("Sweden has very large problems due to the coronavirus") to 37% ("The coronavirus is a problem exaggerated in public discourse"). This means that approximately 68% move between positions between wave 1 and wave 3.

These numbers are, however, likely to underestimate the amount of belief stability. Substantively, citizens' movements usually take place within a narrower latitude of belief acceptance. Very few respondents move from one extreme to the other. Methodologically, random measurement error is likely to generate illusory change in the sense that movements between two adjacent scale points do not necessarily mean real change.

Another way of looking at this focuses on the number of citizens who remain within a somewhat wider range of belief positions formed initially, compared to those who convert from one side of the scale to the other. By collapsing the original 7-point scale into a 3-level variable which distinguishes respondents who believe a specific statement is *not true* (value 1–2 on the original scale), *neither true nor false* (3–5) from those who think it is *true* (6–7), individual-level stability increases substantially. Doing so increases belief stability between wave 1 and wave 3 to approximately 59% across the six items. This means that about 40% of the sample moves between positions over time. In total, only 4% represents conversions – i.e., respondents moving from one endpoint of the scale

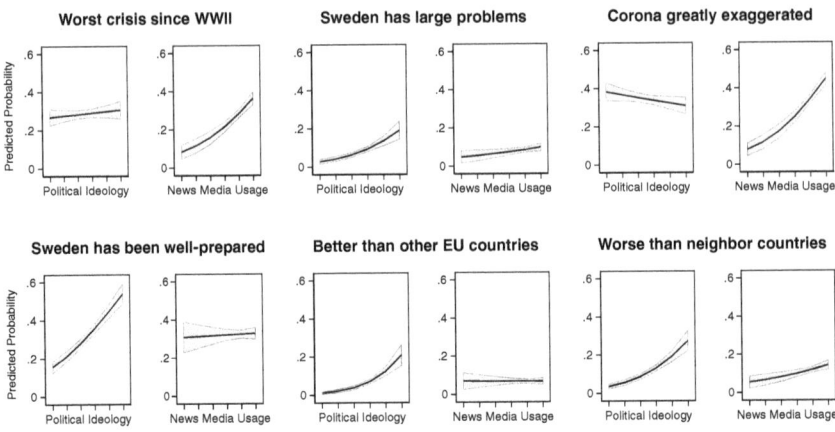

FIGURE 13.3 The effect of ideology and news media use on belief maintenance (predicted probabilities).

Note: Predicted probabilities from six logit models controlling for personal experience, interpersonal talk and Facebook use.

to the other (from *not true* to *true*, or vice versa). Thus, changes are certainly within a latitude of acceptance.

Figure 13.3 focuses on how the two most important factors from the previous analyses – ideology and news media use – influence belief maintenance over time. More specifically, the figure displays the probability that citizens initially form and consistently hold on to a negative belief on how the coronavirus has affected the Swedish society, throughout the three panel waves. Findings come from six logit models controlling for personal experience, interpersonal talk and Facebook use. Again, the top row of the figure shows findings for perceptions about the magnitude of the coronavirus as a societal problem, while the bottom section focuses on perceptions about how Sweden has managed the virus.

Taken together, both ideology and news media use are related to holding on to a negative belief formed in the initial phase of the COVID-19 pandemic. The strength of the effects varies across items, however. In some cases, the impact of ideology is substantial. The probability of holding on to the belief that Sweden has not been well prepared to handle the coronavirus increases approximately from 0.2 to 0.6 along the left-right ideology scale. Correspondingly, news media use increases the probability of consistently seeing the coronavirus as the worst crisis affecting Sweden since World War II from about 0.1 to 0.4.

Taken together, Figure 13.3 largely supports previous findings that ideology and news media usage have somewhat distinct effects on corona beliefs. While news media use is more clearly related to negative beliefs of the magnitude of the problem, ideology matters more with regard to how Sweden has managed the crisis. However, ideology and news media use matter not only for what beliefs people have about the coronavirus, but also for the likelihood of holding on to these beliefs.

Conclusion and Discussion

This chapter has focused on sociotropic belief formation in times of crisis and great societal uncertainty. How do citizens form and update perceptions of the "world outside" under such unusual and turbulent circumstances as the first months of the COVID-19 pandemic? Moreover, the chapter focused specifically on the Swedish case, which gained significant attention world-wide following the Swedish way of handling the coronavirus. When most countries imposed large-scale lockdowns and heavy restrictions, the Swedish strategy led by the *Swedish Health Authority* (PHA) relied much more on voluntary social distancing. At the same time, Sweden was severely hit by the coronavirus. The virus spread rapidly and mortality rates became exceptionally high compared to many other comparable countries – not least Denmark, Finland and Norway. How citizens make sense of a pressing societal issue under these extraordinary conditions has been the key question of this chapter. Let us therefore briefly highlight the main findings presented here.

First, in response to the dramatic real-world developments and intense media coverage of the COVID-19 pandemic, most citizens formed and updated their sociotropic perceptions continuously. Beliefs about how the coronavirus affected Swedish society formed early, but displayed substantial aggregate-level changes over time. While ideological belief gaps were distinct, left-wing and right-wing groups tended to update their perceptions in similar ways in response to real-world events and developments. At the individual level, however, it is clear that belief changes took place within a narrower latitude of acceptance. Very few citizens converted from one belief position to another.

Second, two individual-level factors stand out as particularly relevant for understanding sociotropic coronavirus beliefs: ideology and news media use. Neither corona-specific personal experiences, interpersonal talk nor Facebook's use appears to have any consistent impact on societal-level coronavirus perceptions. Rather, sociotropic perceptions were driven by citizens' political identities and news media use. To some extent, these two factors appear to have differential impacts on beliefs: while news media use was more clearly related to perceptions about the magnitude of the coronavirus as a societal problem, ideology played a larger role for perceptions about how Sweden had managed the virus. These effects were evident not only in the cross-sectional case, as ideology and news media use also influenced changes in beliefs over time.

Third, although belief changes took place over time, most citizens held on to perceptions formed in the early phase of the pandemic. As such, overall impressions of how Sweden was affected by the coronavirus were formed at the outset and remained within a narrow latitude of acceptance over several months. Ideology and news media use also influenced such belief maintenance. The more right-wing a person and the more he/she closely follows news coverage of the pandemic, the higher the likelihood of forming and holding on to more pessimistic coronavirus perceptions.

In sum, the main take-away of this chapter concerns the role played by political ideology and news media use in the formation and updating of societal beliefs – especially in comparison to other sources of information highlighted by the sociotropic belief formation literature. Real-world perceptions about societal problems and collective experiences tend to be shaped by fundamental political identities and/or cues from the news media first and foremost. When issues are salient and media coverage is intense, these factors are particularly important not only in the belief formation process but also for maintaining and updating these beliefs over time.

Acknowledgment

This project has received funding from the European Research Council (ERC) under the European Union's Horizon 2020 research and innovation program (grant agreement no. 804662).

References

Andersson, U., & Oscarsson, H. (2020). *Institutionsförtroendet inte lika politiserat under pandemin*. Göteborgs universitet: SOM-institutet.

Ball-Rokeach, S. J. (2010). Media system dependency theory. In W. Donsbach (Ed.), *The international encyclopedia of communication*. https://doi.org/10.1002/9781405186407.wbiecm051

Bisgaard, M. (2015). Bias will find a way: Economic perceptions, attributions of blame, and partisan-motivated reasoning during crisis. *The Journal of Politics*, 77(3), 849–860. https://doi.org/10.1086/681591

Druckman, J., & Leeper, T. (2012). Is public opinion stable? Resolving the micro/macro disconnect in studies of public opinion. *Daedalus*, 141, 50–68.

Egan, P., & Mullin, M. (2012). Turning personal experience into political attitudes: The effect of local weather on Americans' perceptions about global warming. *The Journal of Politics*, 73(4), 796–809. https://doi.org/10.1017/S0022381612000448.

Esaiasson, P., Sohlberg, J., Ghersetti, M., & Johansson, B. (2020). How the coronavirus crisis affects citizen trust in institutions and in unknown others: Evidence from 'the Swedish experiment'. *European Journal of Political Research*, Online Early. https://doi.org/10.1111/1475-6765.12419

Fiske, S. & Taylor, S. (2017). *Social cognition: From brains to culture*. Thousand Oaks: Sage.

Gamson, W. 1992. *Talking Politics*. Cambridge: Cambridge University Press.

Johansson, B., Hopmann, D-N., & Shehata, A. (2021). When the rally-around-the-flag effect disappears, or: when the COVID-19 pandemic becomes "normalized". *Journal of Elections Public Opinion and Parties*, 31(sup 1), 321–334. https://doi.org/10.1080/17457289.2021.1924742

Kahan, D. M., Jenkins-Smith, H., & Braman, D. (2011). Cultural cognition of scientific consensus. *Journal of Risk Research*, *14*(2), 147–174. http://dx.doi.org/10.1080/13669877.2010.511246

Kinder, D., & Kiewiet, R. (1981). Sociotropic politics: The American case. *British Journal of Political Science*, *11*(2), 129–161.

Kumlin, S. (2004). *The personal and the political: How personal welfare state experiences affect political trust and ideology*. New York: Palgrave.

Lecheler, S., & de Vreese, C. (2018). *News framing effects*. New York: Routledge.

Lippmann, W. (1922/1997). *Public opinion*. New York: Free Press Paperbacks.

Matthes, J. (2008). Schemas and media effects. In W. Donsbach (Ed.), *The international encyclopedia of communication* (pp. 4502–4508). Oxford: Blackwell.

McCombs, M. (2014). *Setting the agenda: The mass media and public opinion*. Cambridge, England: Polity Press.

McCombs, M., Holbert, R. L., Kiousis, S., & Wanta, W. (2012). *The news and public opinion: Media effects on civic life*. Malden: Polity.

Morgan, M., Shanahan, J. & Signorielli, N. (2015). Yesterday's new cultivation, tomorrow. *Mass Communication & Society*, *18*(5), 674–699. https://doi.org/10.1080/15205436.2015.1072725

Mutz, D. (1998). *Impersonal influence. How perceptions of mass collectives influence political attitudes*. New York: Cambridge University Press.

Pierre, J. (2020). Nudges against pandemics: Sweden's COVID-19 containment strategy in perspective. *Policy and Society*, *39*(3), 478–493. https://doi.org/10.1080/14494035.2020.1783787

Potter, J. (2012). *Media effects*. Thousand Oaks: Sage.

Schmitt-Beck, R. (2003). Mass communication, personal communication and vote choice. The filter hypothesis of media influence in comparative perspective. *British Journal of Political Science*, *33*(2): 233–259.

Shehata, A., Andersson, D., Glogger, I., Hopmann, D-N., Andersen, K., Kruikemeier, S. & Johansson, J. (2021). Conceptualizing long-term media effects on societal beliefs. *Annals of the International Communication Association*, *45*(1), 75–93. https://doi.org/10.1080/23808985.2021.1921610

Shehata, A., & Strömbäck, J. (2014). Mediation of political realities: Media as crucial sources of information. In F. Esser & J. Strömbäck (Eds.), *Mediatization of politics* (pp. 93–113). London: Palgrave Macmillan.

Slater, M. (2015). Reinforcing spirals model: Conceptualizing the relationship between media content exposure and the development and maintenance of attitudes. *Media Psychology*, *18*(3), 370–395. https://doi.org/10.1080/15213269.2014.897236

Taber, C., & Lodge, M. (2006). Motivated skepticism in the evaluation of political beliefs. *American Journal of Political Science*, *50*(3), 755–769. https://doi.org/10.1111/j.1540-5907.2006.00214.x

Wilson, T. D., & Hodges, S. D. (1992). Attitudes as temporary constructions. In L. Martin & A. Tesser (Eds.), *The construction of social judgments* (Vol. 10, pp. 37–65). Hillsdale: Lawrence Erlbaum Associates

Zaller, J. (1992). *The nature and origins of mass opinion*. New York: Cambridge University Press.

INDEX

Note: **Bold** page numbers refer to tables; *italic* page numbers refer to figures and page numbers followed by "n" denote footnotes.

actor constellations, pandemic phases and changes in 111–115
"advocacy boomerang" 131
Afro-Brazilian activism 128
"aid campaign" 140, 141, 145n4, 147
Akser, M. 139
Albuquerque, A. 125
de Alemão, Complexo 131
ALP *see* Australian Labor Party (ALP)
alternative digital journalism 121; local 130–131; national 124–130; projects 132
alternative media outlet 123, 140, 144, 146, 148–150
Althaus, S. L. 2
Alvarez, Manny 92
Amat, F. 159
anti-abortion law 193
"anti-constitutional populist backsliding" 194
anti-government participants 199, 202, 203
Arceneaux, K. 6
Aronoff, Kate 120
Atlas, Scott 87
Atton, C. 121
Attuch, Leonardo 126
audience mobilization 89
Australian Broadcasting Corporation (ABC) 176

Australian Labor Party (ALP) 181
Australian political communications about COVID-19 177–178, 188
Australian political elites 177
authoritarianism 136, 146; competitive 137; military-style 125; networked 33; in Turkey 140
'authoritarianism 2.0' 33
'authoritarian participatory persuasion 2.0' 35, 41
autoregressive models 217
Azar, Alex 95

Bachmann, I. 10
Baker, W. D. 4
Bækgaard, M. 21
Bakker, B. N., 6
Baum, M. A. 4
Bennett, Lance 8
Bernays, Edward L. 89
Besley, T. 8
Biden, Joe 7, 85, 97
bipartisan political agreement 188
Birx, Deborah 95
black genocide 128, 129
"blind retrospection" 160
Blumler, J. G. 20
Bol, D. 159, 204
"bold populism" 145, 146, 149

Bolsonaro, Jair 5, 7, 115, 120–130, 132, 133
Bos, L. 176
Bracciale, R. 11, 141
Brasil 247 121, 124–128, 130, 132
BrasilWire 121, 125, 128–130, 132
Brazilian Black Movement 128
Brazilian coronavirus outbreak 132
Brazilian government's response to COVID-19 outbreak 120–121; Bolsonaro's COVID-19 denialism 122–123; counter-framing and networked power 123–124; local alternative digital journalism 130–131; national alternative digital journalism 124–130
Brazilian public health institutions 126
Brazilian social movements 128
Buhl, F. 104
Bush, George W. 3

Calderwood, Catherine 24
Caputo, Neil 88
Cardenal, A. S. 10
Carlson, Tucker 10, 84, 87, 88, 94
Casalino, Rocco 66
Castells, Manuel 124, 130
Cavuto, Neil 88, 92
CBS 92
"centralized personalization" 65, 77
Centre for Disease Control and Prevention (CDC) 36
"Chilean model" 49
Chilean society 61, 62
Chile, covid-19 in 48, 61–62; game changers in political communication 56–60; Lackluster governmental response 54–56; political context 49–50; public perceptions of government performance 50–52
'China model' 42
'Chinese internet' 34–35, 42
Chinese state propaganda machine 41
Chong, D. 124
Churchillian style of "Britishness" 29
civic-military dictatorship 49
"coercive capture and discipline" 139
'coevolution' of civil space 44
cognitive schemas 213
commentary-based journalism 147
commentary-oriented partisan journalism 139
commercial social media platforms 35
"communication fatigue" 76–77
communication strategies 65

community health justice 130–131
"competitive authoritarianism" 137
competitive authoritarian regimes 137, 139, 150
Complexo do Alemao group 130
concentrated visibility 105
conservative media consumption 179
Constitutional Media Authority 194
constitutional referendum 139
Conte, Giuseppe 11, 65–68, 71, 71n5, 72–77
corona-related news media 219
Coronavirus Act 2020 26
coronavirus beliefs 217, 219
coronavirus narrative 39, 41, 42, 44
"cosmology episodes" 103
counter-framing 123–124, 129, 130, 132, 133
COVID-safe policies: federal-state support for 188; measures, public satisfaction with 186–187
crisis coverage 102, 109, 114, 116, 117
crisis journalism 102–105
CrowdTangle 106, 107
Cruz, Ted 98
Cummings, Dominic 24, 25, 29
Cyberspace Administration of China (CAC) 35

Davis, Aeron 7, 20
Davis, Mike 129
Davis, S. 133
Daza, Paula 57
"decision-making" elite actors 115
Democratic Socialists of America (DSA) 128
De Vries, C. E. 6
digital China, coronavirus outbreak in 33; absent mainstream media and digital samizdat 36–39; advancing narrative dominance and digital exodus 41–43; control and resistance 34–36; framing critical events in digital age 43–44; White Paper 39–40
digital journalism projects 132
digital mutual aid 130–131
'digital samizdat' 36–39
"dominant regimes of codes" 124
Doria, João 125, 133
DPCMs 67, 68, 71, 73–76, 78
Dray, S. 8
Drosten, Christian 103, 110
Druckman, J. 124, 213

Duda, Andrzej 193, 196, 203
dynamic quarantines 55

Edelman, D. 176
Edinburgh briefings 18, 22, 27, 29
Editora 247 126
"elite abuse" 50
elite polarization 161
emergency aid program 60
Entman, R. 43, 123
epidemiological denialism 120
epistemological denialism 125
Erçetin, T. 139
Erdoğan, E. 139
Erdoğan, Recep Tayyip 9, 137–138, 140, 149
estallido social 49

fact-checking initiatives 59
Fang Fang Diary 34, 36, 38–41, 43, 44
Fauci, Anthony 86, 87, 95, 177
favela-based activist groups 131
Fethullah Gülen movement 139
"filtering function" 211
Forde, S. 121
Fox News 89, 90; and hydroxychloroquine, networked propaganda study of 91–93; and Trump 85–88, 93–97
"frame breakers" 103
"framing/counter-framing" coupling 123, 124
framing strategies 141
"fundraiser campaign" 145n4
"Funk Cabinet against COVID" 131

Gabinete de Crisis de Alemao 131
Gagliardi, J. 125
Garland, R. 7
general visibility 105
German election campaigns 105
Ghersetti, M. 174
GitHub 42
"Giuseppi" 72
government competence 25
government policy and communication strategy 6–8
government communication 11, 21, 48, 193, 197, 202, 204, 205; engagement with 198–201, national emergency 192; phases of 67–77; role in 54
'Great Firewall' 34
Green Party 111

Groeling, T. 4
'guerrilla ethnography' 36

Hahn, K.S. 176
Hallin, D. C. 139
Hancock, Matt 23
Hannity, Sean 84, 86, 87
Han, R. 40
Harder, R. A. 104
Hart, P. S. 193
Hawley, Josh 98
health crisis 1, 2–4, 9, 48, 60, 62, 131, 157, 159, 174, 183, 185, 187
Henry Ford Health System 95
"herd immunity" 84, 86, 87
Herrera, H. 6
Hilton, Steve 86
Hobolt, S. 6
Hodges, S. D. 214
"horse-race reporting" 102
Human Rights Watch 140
Hunt, Daniel 128
Hu, X. 41
Hu Xijin 40
hybrid media system 104

ideological belief gaps 221
ideological-discursive approach 137n1
İmamoğlu, Ekrem 138
Immanuel, Stella 83
independent organizations 84, 88
Independent Scotland 27–29
"individualization" 105
"infodemic" process 70
Ingraham, Laura 84, 94–97, **96–97**
in-group dynamics 161
initial belief formation in Sweden 209, 219–221
"institutional personalization" 65
interactive propaganda 83–84; differs from more conventional forms 88–89; Fox cued Trump using 93–97; networked propaganda study of Fox and hydroxychloroquine 91–93; preliminary model of 89–91; qualitative evidence of co-production between Fox and Trump 85–88
"inter-imperialist rivalry" 130
international health crisis 4
International Journal of Antimicrobial Agents 95
interpersonal conversation 210
Italian singularity 66
Iyengar, S. 176

Jackman, S. 176
Jiang, M. 44
Johnson, Boris 5, 7, 8, 11, 17–19, *19*, 20, 21, 23–27, 29, 30, 113, 192
Jones, Alan 177
journalistic professionalism 139

Kaczyński, Jarosław 194
Kahn, L. H. 3
Keck, M.E. 131
Kidawa-Błońska, Małgorzata 196
Knowles, S. 175
Kosicki, G. M. 44
Krippendorff, K. 145

Laboratory of Opinion Research (LORE) 213
Lackluster governmental response 54–56
Laschet, Armin 110
Latin American leftist social movements 121
Lauterbach, Karl 110
Law and Justice party 194, 195
Lawrence, R. G. 2
leave campaign 24
Leeper, T. 213
leftist Workers Party 133
left-right self-placement 165
left-wing coalition government 211
Leininger, A. 159
Levitsky, S. 137
Liberal National party 180
life-threatening event 6
Lilleker, D. 7
Lincoln, M. 56
Lippmann, W. 210
Li Wenliang 36–38, 42, 43
local alternative digital journalism 130–131

Mañalich, Jaime 55, 56–57
Mancini, P. 139
Mandietta, Luiz Henrique 133
Mazzoleni, G. 11, 141
media choice questions 178
media commercialization 139
media coverage 2, 7, 36, 106, 124, 139, 161, 210, 211, 214, 215, 221, 222; and (lack of) criticism 8–9; 'normalization' of 11; role of 4; state 37
media outlets 148; alternative 123, 140, 144, 146, 148–150; pro-government 149; Turkish mainstream 146

media polarization 160, 164–165, 168, *168,* 170, 171, 204
"media populism" 138
media system dependency theory 210
"mediated populism" 138
"mediatization of politics" 138
mediatization of politics *versus* politicization of media 138–139
media trust 168, 174, 182, 187, 188, 204; and partisan allegiance, relationship between 184; and political partisanship 175–177
media use and political selective exposure theory 176–177
Meloni, Giorgia 73
Merkel, Angela 5–7, 9, 110–113
Merkley, E. 159
Mier, Brian 128, 130
Mihelj, S. 10
Milanez, Felipe 128
#MilanoNonSiFerma (#MilanDoesNotStop) campaign 70
Millennium Institute for Foundational Research on Data (IMFD) 55
"moderate populism" 145
modus operandi 73
Monti, Mario 77
Morawiecki, Mateusz 198
Morrison, Scott 5–7, 177
Mourão, R. R. 176, 184
Mueller, J. E. 3, 159
multilevel mixed-effects linear regressions 165
multi-level triangulation approach 106
Murdoch, Rupert 87, 87n2
mutual aid projects 131

narrative contestation process 33, 44
narrative dominance and digital exodus 41–43
Nassif, Luis 129
national alternative digital journalism 124–130
National Electoral Commission (NEC) 196
national emergency government communication 192
national identity, visions of 27–29
nationalistic sentiment 35
national leadership, visions of: Britain as one nation 26–27; Johnson, Boris 23–25; Sturgeon, Nicola 25–26
"National Solidarity Campaign" 137, 138

Index **229**

"nation-ethnic group" 146
"natural disaster in slow-motion" 103
NBC 92, 95
NEC *see* National Electoral Commission (NEC)
net partisan skew (NPS) 164
Netto, Walter Braga 129
'networked authoritarianism' 33
networked propaganda study, of Fox and hydroxychloroquine 91–93
neutral health information 38
'New Era' governance 33
Newman, N. 8
news media 101; coronavirus 107–109; coverage of political actors in crisis 105–106; crisis journalism 102–104; method 106–107; new platforms and news bursts 104; pandemic phases and changes in actor constellations 111–115; visibility of political actors 109–111
"news story" approach 104
non-probability sampling 141
non-state actors 43
Nord, L. W. 103, 116
"normalization" of the crisis 114–117

Obama, Barack 42
O Globo 125, 126
Olsson, E.-K. 103
Oneal, J. R. 4
"one size fits it all" logic 116
ordered logistic regression of trust **51–52**
Oswaldo Cruz Foundation (FIOCRUZ) 127

Pan-American Health Organization 123
pandemic aid campaigns 147, 150
pandemic-related restrictions 62
Pan, Z. 44
Papo Reto, Coletivo 121–122, 130–132
Paris, Enrique 57
partisanship pattern 180
Patel, Priti 23
Personal Protective Equipment (PPE) 69
PHA *see* Public Health Authority (PHA)
Piñera, Sebastian 48–50, 54, 54n2, 56–57, 60–62
Pinochet, Augusto 49
Pirro, Jeanine 86, 87
PiS-led government 194
Poguntke, T. 66
Poland: in COVID-19 pandemic 192–193; engagement with government communication 198–201; methodology 196–197; polarization and use of public service media 201–204; political and media context 194–195; political polarization 205; 2020 Presidential Election 195–196
polarization: elite 161; level of 6, 8; media 160, 164–165, 168, *168,* 170, 171, 204; political (*see* political polarization); public opinion and level of 9–10; societal 196; and use of public service media 201–204
polarized media system 136–137, 144; mediatization of politics *versus* politicization of media 138–139; methodology, data collection, and analysis 141–146; results 146–150; of Turkey 139–141
"polarized pluralist model" 139
"polarized pluralist" societies 139
police violence 2
Polish democracy 203
Polish media and politics 194
political activism 89
political actors 105, 148, 149, 157; in crisis 105–106; visibility of 109–111
political actor/socio-political camp 146
political capital 18
political elite cue theory 176, 184
political identities 49
political leadership 9, 50, 66, 73, 77
political leanings of respondents 179
political parallelism 50, 139
political partisanship 175–177, 188
political party ideologies 150
political polarization 158, 160, 163, 168, *168,* 169–171, 187–188, 204–205; Australian and US news selectivity 179–181; crisis communication studies 174; data and methods 178–179; frequency of news use and media type 181; hypothesis 161; interaction effects of *169;* media trust and political partisanship 175–177; media use, partisanship and concern about catching COVID-19 185; partisan differences 183–185; public satisfaction with COVID-safe policy measures 186–187; trust in journalists and other sources during pandemic 181–183; US and Australian political communications about COVID-19 177–178
political rationalization 210

political selective exposure (PSE) theory 176, 184
"politicization of media" 139, 150
politics-media-public triangle 2
Polski, Bank 201
populism index score for different outlets 146, *147*
populism index variables 145
populist frames: explanations and examples of 141, **142–143**; utilization 148, 149
'positive energy' 35
Prawo i Sprawiedliwość (PiS) party 195
predominant-party system 137n2, 150
pre-pandemic 175–176
"presidentialization" 66
"press-party parallelism" 78, 137, 139, 140, 146, 150
"privatization" 105
pro-government news outlets 146, 148, 149
pro-government outlets 148–150
pro-government participants 203, 204
pro-Islamist AKP 137, 146
pro-Kurdish HDP 148
"Protezione Civile" 69
provisional coding exercise 22
PSB *see* public service broadcasters (PSB)
PSE theory *see* political selective exposure (PSE) theory
"pseudo-journalism" 102
public broadcaster TRT 140
public broadcasting channels 198
public broadcasting outlet TRT 148–150
public broadcasting service 165
Public Health Authority (PHA) 211, 212
public health campaigns 23
public health interventions 120, 130
public opinion 20, 35, 57, 66, 67, 160, 209, 210; most fundamental issues in 213; and level of polarization 9–10
public-owned news services 181
public perceptions of government performance 50–52
public satisfaction with COVID-safe policy measures 186–187
public service broadcasters (PSB) 194
public service media 202, 203
purposive sampling method 141

Quandt, Thorsten 9, 11
quota sampling 50n1, 197

racial marginalization 129
'radical discontinuities' 34
radical reprogramming 124
rally-around-the-flag effects 10, 18, 51, 72, 157, 192, 212; analytical strategy 165–166; controls 165; data and measurements 162; main dependent and independent variables 162–165; political and media polarization 160–162; political trust in times of COVID-19 158–160; results 166–169; theory 3–4
random measurement error 219
Raoult, Didier 94
Ratcliff, S. 176
"rational retrospective evaluations" 158
"reprogramming" 124
Republican People's Party (CHP) 137
Riegert, K. 103
Rigano, Gregory 94
right-wing citizens 215
right-wing ideology 219
right-wing media network 90
right-wing nationalist government 193
right-wing political leaning 217
right-wing populist party 194
right-wing respondents 57
Robert Koch Institute (RKI) 110
Roberts, John 95
Roberts, M. E. 40

Sadurski, Wojciech 194, 195
"safe return" 57, 58
"safe stadium" 57
Salvini, Matteo 69, 73
Santiago Navarro F. 129, 130
Santiago, Raul 131
Schaub, M. 159
Schifferes, S. 175
Schraff, D. 204
Scottish coronavirus media briefings 21–22
"Scottish government" 22
"Scottishness" 29
"self-fulfilling prophecies" 70
semi-authoritarian regime 150
"semi-consolidated democracy" 194
semi-structured interviews 197
Sevenans, J. 104
"sexiest premier in Europe" 72
Seymour-Ure, C. 139
"shambolic decision-making process" 28

Shehata, A. 11
Siches, Izkia 60
Siegel, Marc 86
Sikkink, K. 131
Smith, Shepard 88
"socialized medicine" 124
social media platforms 2, 33–35, 38, 44, 216
societal beliefs 222
societal polarization 196
socio-political camps 136, 143, 149
socio-racial disparities 129
sociotropic belief formation 209, 210, 215, 222
sociotropic coronavirus beliefs 213–215, **218**, 221
Soder, Markus 110–112
"soft populism" 145
Souza, J. 133
spaCy 107
Spahn, Jens 110–113
Spiegel, Der 9
'stability maintenance' 36
Starmer, Sir Keir 18, 19, 25, 29
state media 35–37, 39–42
statutory law-making abilities 20
Stay at Home campaign 21
'strategic communication box' 2
Straubhaar, J. 133
Streeck, Hendrik 110
Strömbäck, J. 103, 116
structural racism 129
Sturgeon, Nicola 11, 18–20, 23–29
Sweden 209; change and stability of sociotropic corona beliefs in 213–215; COVID-19 and the great uncertainty 211–213; factors influencing beliefs about coronavirus in 215–219; importance of initial belief formation 219–221; sociotropic belief formation 210–211
Swedish Health Authority (PHA) 221
Szumowski, Łukasz 198

TCM *see* traditional Chinese medicine (TCM)
Technical Scientific Committee 69
Thomson, Robert 87n2
traditional Chinese medicine (TCM) 41
traditional journalism 2
'traitorous intellectuals' 41

Tren Digital 50n1
"trial balloons" 66, 71
TRT *see* Turkish Radio and Television Corporation (TRT)
Trump, Donald 5, 7–10, 83–84, 86–90, 90n6, 91–98, 109–112, 115, 122, 123, 127, 175–178, 180, 183, 184, 187, 188; qualitative evidence of co-production between Fox and 85–88
Trzaskowski, Rafał 193, 196
Turkish mainstream media outlets 146
Turkish media landscape 139, 140
Turkish Radio and Television Corporation (TRT) 140, 141, 144, 145n3, 146, 147–150

UK's management of pandemic 17, 19; crisis in public communication 20–29; rally-around-the-flag effects 18
UK-wide fiscal stimulus package 28
ultra-nationalist MHP governmental coalition 146
"uncertainty-identity theory" 161
"uncertainty reduction theory" 161
"unemployment pandemic" 57
Unidades de Policias Pacificadoras (UPPs) 130
US political communications about COVID-19 177–178

Van Aelst, P. 104, 105
Vida, Samuel 128
voluntary social distancing 211

Wallace, Chris 88
Way, L. A. 137
Webb, P. 66
Weick, K. E. 103
weighted media ideology score 179
Westlund, O. 174
White Paper 39–40
wide-scale public health crises 123
Wilson, T. D. 214
Woodward, Bob 86
World Federation of Trade Unions 128
World Health Organization (WHO) 55, 70, 91
writing style of different outlets 147, *148*
"Wuhan of Europe" 73

Xi Jinping 33, 34, 37, 39, 44
Xinhua 40

Yang, G. 36
Yavaş, Mansur 138
YouGov online representative panels 178
Yuan Zeng 11
Yunkang Yang 8

Zaller, J. 176, 184
"zero-level populism" 145
Zhang Boli 41
Zingaretti, Nicola 70

Lightning Source UK Ltd.
Milton Keynes UK
UKHW020350050222
398191UK00012B/285